Gerda Walther
Toward an Ontology of Social Communities

Women Philosophers Heritage Collection

English Version and Introduction

Edited by
Ruth Edith Hagengruber

In Cooperation with
Antonio Calcagno, Priyanka Jha, Rodney Parker

Volume 3

Gerda Walther

Toward an Ontology of Social Communities

With an Appendix on the Phenomenology
of Social Communities

Edited, Translated, and with an Introduction by
Sebastian Luft and Rodney K.B. Parker

DE GRUYTER

This work has originally been published in the German language:

Walther, Gerda. 1922. *Ein Beitrag zur Ontologie der sozialen Gemeinschaften: Mit einem Anhang zur Phänomenologie der sozialen Gemeinschaften*. Halle a. d. Saale: Max Niemeyer Verlag.

Walther, Gerda. 1923. "Zur Ontologie der sozialen Gemeinschaften." *Jahrbuch für Philosophie und phänomenologische Forschung* 6: 1–158.

ISBN 978-3-11-076307-2
ISSN 2510-9243

Bibliographic information published by the Deutsche Nationalbibliothek
The Deutsche Nationalbibliothek lists this publication in the Deutsche Nationalbibliografie; detailed bibliographic data are available on the internet at http://dnb.dnb.de.

www.degruyterbrill.com
Questions about General Product Safety Regulation:
productsafety@degruyterbrill.com

Gerda Walther ca. 1918. Source: Bavarian State Library / Image collection.

Contents

Toward an Ontology of Social Communities.

With an Appendix on the Phenomenology of Social Communities

Translators' Introduction

The following text is the first full English translation of Gerda Walther's book *Zur Ontologie der Sozialen Gemeinschaften*, originally submitted as a dissertation at the University of Munich on 14 January 1921 and subsequently published in the Yearbook for Phenomenology and Phenomenological Philosophy (*Jahrbuch für Phänomenologie und phänomenologische Philosophie*), edited by Edmund Husserl, Alexander Pfänder, and Max Scheler, in 1923.[1] Squarely set in the early Phenomenological Movement from an author recognized as a student of (mainly) Pfänder's and Husserl's, this work marks a milestone by extending the scope of phenomenological analysis to—broadly speaking—the social, sociality as an indispensable dimension of the human being.

Oftentimes decried as a form of Neo-Cartesianism or even solipsism, phenomenology always had to confront this verdict. Indeed, the focus on first-person experience and description in—as Husserl himself oftentimes emphasized—the "first person singular" gave rise, early on, to the criticism that phenomenology was an essentially self-centered and even solipsistic enterprise. It was not until 1930 that Husserl himself aggressively countered this critique in the famous Fifth Cartesian Meditation, which broadened the scope of phenomenology to include the inter-subjective. But looking at Husserl's then-unpublished manuscripts, one can trace the focus on the intersubjective and social aspect of the human person back to lectures delivered already in 1910/1911, and the topic was also tackled in his earlier research manuscripts of this period. Edith Stein, who worked on editing Husserl's early manuscripts on these themes, published her famous treatise *On the Problem of Empathy*, which is essentially an interpretive summary of Husserl's theory of intersubjectivity, in 1917. However, it is not widely recognized that there were more members of the movement interested in the problem of the social, such as Alexander Pfänder, Max Scheler—and Gerda Walther. Thus, questions such as, 'what is the social nature of the human being?', 'how can I have experience of the other?', and similar questions, indeed have a long tradition in the Phenomenological Movement. Yet, these topics were not known to be at the forefront of attention, at least from the main members of the Phenomenological Movement. Thus, besides Stein's more famous text, Walther's dissertation must be seen as one of the earliest works in the Phenomenological Movement on the social aspect of the human being.

Who is Gerda Walther? What kind of a work are we dealing with here, and what is its special importance?

---

1 On the history of this Yearbook, see Schuhmann 1990.

In what follows, we intend to first (1.1) provide a short biographical sketch of Gerda Walther (1879–1977). Next (1.2), we will give an overview of the book's relevance by focusing on the reception of the work in the immediate aftermath of its publication. We will then focus on the work itself and single out a few remarkable methodological and philosophical-substantial claims Walther makes (2–3).

1 On the Author and the Work

1.1 Biographical Sketch

Gerda Walther's biography, up until 1922, can best be summarized in her own (abbreviated) words, as the appendix to her published dissertation testifies:

> I, Gerda Walther, was born on March 18, 1897, in the Nordrach Colony in the Baden region of the Black Forest as daughter of the late owner and head physician of the lung clinic on location, Dr. Otto Walther and his [...] wife Ragnhild Walther [...]. I was raised irreligiously and am a citizen of Baden.[2] I enjoyed private tutelage from 1904–1909 [...]. From fall 1909 until summer 1911 I attended, as an internal student, the higher school for girls [...] of Mrs. Dr. Himmer. [...] From spring 1912 until spring 1913 I visited my grandparents in Copenhagen. From Fall 1913 until Easter 1914 I attended [...] "private high school courses for girls" in Munich and graduated from high school in July 1915 at the Royal Real-Gymnasium in Munich. From Fall 1915 until summer 1917 I studied, at the University of Munich, theoretical and practical national economics, history of economy, civil law, philosophy and psychology. From summer 1917 until winter 1919, I studied philosophy, mathematics and civil law at the University of Freiburg i. Br.; from fall 1919 until winter 1920/21 back in Munich philosophy, sociology, economic history, and civil law. (see 185 for the full version)

As becomes clear in these self-confident and deftly written words, Walther came from an intellectual and international family, was widely educated and spoke several languages (besides German and Danish). Graduating from high school (*Gymnasium*) in those days was certainly no matter of course for a young woman, much less attending university (and studying more than just the typical discipline for women, such as home economics). Instead, she must be seen as a prodigy from early on and was especially taken under the wing of the Munich phenomenologist Alexander Pfänder, for whom she had great admiration (and for a while also a bit of a crush). Pfänder sent Walther, as a young graduate student, to Freiburg to study with the master, Husserl, before returning to Munich to finish her dissertation. She was an active member of the Phenomenological Movement at the time, shuttling

---

2 Later combined to the State of Baden-Württemberg after the War.

between the centers, Munich and Freiburg, and a peer to the generation of phenomenologists that includes Martin Heidegger, Edith Stein, and others.

As will be detailed later, though she makes a point about being raised irreli-
giously, she later had a profound conversion to Catholicism (alongside Edith
Stein, who was originally Jewish, and others). Walther also had a mystical side
to her, claiming clairvoyant abilities and witnessing paranormal phenomena.
This was more than a peculiar personal character trait, for it played a decisive
role in her life and was something she sought to understand intellectually. Indeed,
by the time she was finished with her dissertation, one can say that her interest in
mysticism had taken over her more narrowly philosophical interests, as witnessed
in her work *Phenomenology of Mysticism,* which was published in the same year as
her dissertation. One can say that this interest, while increasingly dominating her
life, was also the death nail for her academic career, being (as she was) publicly
mocked by her peers, such as none other than Heidegger, whom she acknowledges
several times in this work as a congenial interlocutor. Husserl also disapproved of
her later development and withdrew his support, despite having earlier facilitated
her attempt at Habilitation with Karl Jaspers in Heidelberg. Her mystical side
brought her into contact with the *Georgekreis,* the Circle around the poet Stefan
George, which further estranged her from the academic scene in Germany. Her
rather turbulent life in the later twenties and then the Third Reich is detailed
in her own autobiography *Vom anderen Ufer,*[3] which was published in 1960, at a
time when her life had moved into calmer territory. One gets the sense that her
life during the war was chaotic, though she was rather lucky in the end. She continued to live a modest life in a village close to the Starnberger See outside of Munich and died there, in a nursing home, in 1977.[4] After the war, she wrote very little
on the topic of phenomenological philosophy, though continued to publish prolif-
ically and carried on an abundant correspondence, the remainders of which are
now housed primarily in the *Staatsbibliothek* in Munich.

---

3 Literally, "from the other shore," which certainly and in first instance refers to her conversion
from aggressive atheism to devout Catholicism. It is perhaps no accident that the phrase was also,
certainly in the post-war period up until recently, a codeword for homosexuality. The George Circle, of which she was a part in this time, was not just a circle of male poets and artists, but also a
clandestine grouping of pederastic men, who believed in the supremacy of men over women and
tolerated women only to the extent that they would serve men and their spiritual development.
Given that Walther herself became entangled with one man of this group (Percy Gothein), who rejected her, causing a great emotional crisis in her life, the title of the book is perhaps not acciden-
tal. Walther is very clear-sighted in her later account of her life that such company was a terrible
decision.
4 See the recollection of López McAlister 1996, viii.

1.2 On the Work and Its Reception

Given the importance of Walther's dissertation, it is a scandal of philosophy that it went largely unnoticed for almost a century. Only in the past decade has the importance of Walther's contribution to social ontology started to attract widespread attention. But prior to this, it did not go *entirely* unnoticed. For one, the current attention to Walther's dissertation can be traced back to Hans Bernhard Schmid's published Wir-Intentionalität (Schmid 2005) which paid significant attention to Walther. In 2012, the journal *Symposium* presented a special issue dedicated to Edmund Husserl and the Göttingen Circle containing Antonio Calcagno's essay "Gerda Walther: On the Possibility of a Passive Sense of Community and the Inner Time Consciousness of Community" (Calcagno 2012). These reintroduced Walther to the German and English speaking worlds of contemporary phenomenologists respectively.[5] For another, Walther's dissertation received some press after it was published in Husserl's *Jahrbuch für Philosophie und phänomenologische Forschung* in 1923, and was cited in a handful of books and papers. In the following, we shall discuss some of these early receptions.

1.2.1 The Müller Review and the Thesis Exam

Worth noting and appearing before the others is Aloys Müller's brief review of the sixth volume of Husserl's *Jahrbuch* in the 1926 edition of *Kant-Studien*. In his review, Müller notes the following about Walther's contribution, titled *"Zur Ontologie der sozialen Gemeinschaften"* (1923b):

> After the obligatory discussions concerning the concept of phenomenology, Walther initially defines social community at the first level, i. e., on the level of knowledge, so to speak. As an essential characteristic that distinguishes community from society, she identifies 'inner unification'. This does not refer to a feeling or knowledge of understanding others, but rather a peculiar inner connection of the soul with an intentional object. The common life of the members is built upon this. More is required for the community at the 'adult level'. This includes the knowledge of the *community* as such and the unification with it as such. Both are to be sharply distinguished from the knowledge of the *other members* and joining with them. Does the community really have personhood? Walther shows that although it is a supra-personal, psychic, and intellectual unity, it lacks the essential feature of a person, the Ego-center of consciousness and will. The investigation touches on many sociological and cross-cultural psychological issues. (Müller 1926, 370; emphasis added; translations [here and in the following] ours)

---

5 Schmid and Calcagno were followed shortly after by Caminada 2014, Luft 2016, and León and Zahavi 2016. These five works are the foundation of how we discuss Walther's contributions to sociology, social psychology, and phenomenology of sociality today.

Not a particularly philosophically engaging review but positive, nonetheless. Sadly, this may well be the only review of Walther's dissertation, appearing some three years after its publication in the *Jahrbuch* in 1923. We find only a smattering of references to Walther's work on social ontology in writings by phenomenologists and sociologists during the years thereafter.[6]

Karl Mannheim's *Structures of Thinking*, written in 1922/24 but not published until 1980, references Walther's dissertation while discussing the "existential relation to the Other" (Mannheim 1982, 190 – 191).[7] Mannheim was known for his rich use of metaphor. Perhaps Aloys Fischer, a member of Theodor Lipps' *Psychologische Verein*, would have found Mannheim's writing more stylistically favorable than Walther's. Of her dissertation, Fischer wrote: "the language is unnecessarily artificial, and the use of imagery seems a bit overdone, leading to some misconceptions that could have been avoided without it." He continues: "However, the overall flow of the work, the way it tackles problems, and a bunch of results (that) are applicable beyond just the Husserl perspective, make the work seem pretty valuable." These (mainly) positive notes on Walther's *Ein Beitrag zur Ontologie der sozialen Gemeinschaften: Mit einem Anhang zur Phänomenologie der sozialen Gemeinschaften* (Walther 1922) are found in the unpublished written submissions related to her doctoral thesis examination (Walther 1921). Preceding the comments by Fischer are opinions by Walther's other committee members, Erich Becher and Alexander Pfänder. Like Fischer, Becher criticizes the use of "strange" symbolism and imagery in Walther's writing, which serve to confuse and detract from, rather than elucidate, what she is attempting to describe or argue, the reliance on "almost incomprehensible" Husserlian jargon, and the frequently awkward and cumbersome sentence structures. (The translators of the present volume can certainly sympathize with Becher.)

When submitted to the First Section of the Faculty of Philosophy at the Ludwig Maximilian University of Munich, Walther's dissertation bore the title "*Ein Beitrag zur Ontologie und Phänomenologie der sozialen Gemeinschaften* [A Contribution to

---

6 See Takata 1927, 293–295, 299–306 (an influential Japanese sociologist and economist); Gurwitsch 1977, 172–177 (his intended habilitation thesis, written circa 1931; an English translation was published as Gurwitsch 1979); and Otaka 1932, 143–145 (Husserl's "best Japanese student," who visited Freiburg between 1930 and 1932; an abridged English translation of this work appears in Robbins 2023). Slightly later, Alfred Schütz makes a scathingly critical remark about how Walther and Stein's "naive use of the eidetic method in analyzing the problems of social relations, of community, and of the state led them to the formulation of certain apodictic and purportedly aprioristic statements which have contributed very much to discredit phenomenology among the social scientists" (Schütz 1959, 89). This list is not intended to be exhaustive.
7 Walther is cited in the note to this paragraph.

the Ontology and Phenomenology of Social Communities]." Becher provides us with the reason for the subsequent title change when he writes: "Since the final phenomenological part is so short in relation to the ontological part, I would suggest characterizing this part separately as a conclusion or appendix, omitting the words "and phenomenology" from the title of the treatise. One could simply add on the title page: "With an appendix on the phenomenology of the social communities." Thus, we get the title as it appears on the first published version of 1922. Precisely why the title was shortened again for inclusion in the *Jahrbuch* (especially given that it is slightly misleading[8]) remains unclear. However, given that the most succinct title was the one Walther ultimately settled upon, we have followed suit for the English title.[9]

By far the most extensive discussion of Walther's dissertation is contained within Pfänder's commendatory notes on the work, dated 4 February 1921.[10] Pfänder's remarks are too lengthy to reproduce here in full, but the selections below serve as a fitting introduction to the work, highlighting the central insights of Walther's investigation into the peculiar type of social organism we call a community.

> Walther sees the *essential* feature of a community in the fact that its members are *internally united.* This inner unification of the members can arise through mere internal cohesion or through habitually developed actual agreements. Depending on the foundation of this unity, whether it is directly through the individuals or indirectly founded through extra-human objects, different social communities emerge (personal and purpose-driven communities). [...]

> The differences in source points of the unification give rise to the classification of social communities based on the depth of their rootedness in the members. A demand is formulated that the depth of unification in the subject requires the corresponding depth of unification in the object. This part has a somewhat mystical tone.

> The *unification* of the members must be *mutual.* The essential nature of certain communities gives rise to specific requirements for the *type* of mutual unity necessary for their full development. *The common life* of the members must then be built upon this mutual unity. The intentional object of this common life does not necessarily need to lie outside the community (reflexive and iterated communities). An in-depth analysis of community life ('we-experien-

---

8 See Section 2 of this Introduction, below.

9 The versions of Walther's dissertation published in 1922 and 1923 are identical save for the fact that Walther's Preface and *curriculum vitae* are omitted from the latter publication in Husserl's *Jahrbuch.* These two items have been included in the present edition, the former providing some insights into the development of Walther's thinking with respect to the relationship between the individual and the social organism.

10 Pfänder, too, points out that the use of Husserlian terminology might possibly (negatively) affect the "general comprehensibility" of Walther's writing.

ces') follows, distinguishing it from other experiences that can easily be confused with it (empathic, sympathetic, imitative, suggested experiences). Community experiences originate intrinsically in some members, while in others, they may arise only through empathy and communication. The 'we' in the individual member is not an independent being standing behind or above them, but it is truly present within and with the individual self. Each member of a community either lives as a part of a 'we' or only as 'itself.' The communal experience, taken as a whole, is an overall experience of a higher order, which, in a certain sense, is experienced as originating and self-created only by the community as a totality. [...]

Beyond knowing each other and mutual unity, in a fully developed community, the members must be in intentional *reciprocal interaction* with each other, with all members directing themselves mutually, directly or indirectly, *toward* each other, and some members directing themselves to each other or to the community of others.

[Walther] then specifies what must be added to the aforementioned if a community is to be not only 'in itself' but also 'for itself.' First, *knowledge of the community* itself must be present in the members, i.e., knowledge about this peculiar, super-individual entity with its own being, essence, life, and norms. Furthermore, *inner unification with the community* as such must come into play. From this unity, members (as social persons) then perform *special social acts* 'in the name of' and 'in the sense of' their community. [...] The experiences and acts 'in the sense of' the community can arise from the historically factual meaning or from the 'idea' of the community. Both can be *inauthentic* for both the private person and in relation to the community, meaning that the private person may not feel these social experiences and acts adequately as private individuals, or they may consider their own private experiences and acts as social and attribute them to the community's name or idea, even though they do not correspond to either the empirical essence or the idea of the respective community.

Now, if a community has reached self-awareness, the question arises whether it is then a distinct *person*. Although it has its own 'self,' and in some communities, even its own real basic essence, it always *lacks the essential willing and self-determining Ego-point*, which is essential for personhood. It also lacks its own communal body. It is always dependent on the will and self-determining I-points of its members and on their bodies. However, it exists in reality insofar as there is a social self in the members, from which they live in the sense, possibly in the name, of the community, insofar as community life is real, insofar as objective, physical, or mental entities have been created by the members *for* the community or in its name, and insofar as the community has real basic knowledge. [...]

[She] then presents the main aspects for the *phenomenological* constitution of the social community. To grasp a community, one must, without introducing arbitrary auxiliary constructions, seek to come through specific knowledge-attitudes to the social self and through this to the community itself by way of community experiences, community behavior, and community works, while simultaneously examining the authenticity and adequacy of community phenomena. The approach to grasping a community is somewhat different for a member of a community than for a non-member; for the former, there is an 'internal,' for the latter, an 'external' constitution, both of which are described in great detail. –

Walther masters the subject with full awareness of all relevant, difficult, and intricate problems. She demonstrates great, well-founded expertise and outstanding talent in this field. Her method of investigation is very solid and thorough. Despite all the suggestions she has received, she remains entirely independent in their utilization and adds much of her own. I consider the main results of her dissertation to be correct; in some details, I would differ, such as distinguishing truly inauthentic community experiences from mistaken ones. I would wish for some details to be more elaborated, especially the phenomenology of social communities. Overall, however, the work represents *a significant and essential contribution to the scientific foundation of sociology.*

As a doctoral dissertation, the work is *quite excellent* and highly recommended for approval.

Walther received her doctorate *summa cum laude* on 10 March 1921. Pfänder's influence on Walther's investigation of social communities is abundantly clear. She regularly draws from his two-part treatise *Zur Psychologie der Gesinnungen* (Pfänder 1913, Pfänder 1916) and his unpublished *Grundzüge der Psychologie des Menschen* (Pfänder 1915/1916). A careful examination of Walther's dissertation alongside these works would be of considerable value to scholars of early phenomenology, and to anyone wanting to contextualize her work on social ontology in order to engage in meaningful dialogue with it. While consulting Pfänder's *Nachlass* would be the ideal route for studying the version of his *Grundzüge der Psychologie des Menschen* that Walther references, those writings were reworked and ultimately published as *Die Seele des Menschen* in 1933 (Pfänder 1933).[11] As the reader will quickly note, Walther's dissertation is an amalgamation of her interests in sociology, politics, psychology, Marxist and Hegelian philosophy, and phenomenology. We even get hints of her emerging interest in mysticism. In addition to Pfänder, other major influences were Max Scheler, Max Weber, Edith Stein, and Georg Simmel. She draws extensively from these figures and others, but also moves beyond them to explore novel insights of her own. But the one name that appears more than any other in Walther's ontological and phenomenological investigation of social communities is that of Husserl.

---

11 In a short announcement for the book, Pfänder writes: "Not until the year 1913 did I succeed in forming a systematic whole out of what I had gradually attained, so that, in the summer of 1914, I could venture to present for the first time as a university lecture course the fundamental ideas of the present work under the title of 'Fundamentals of Human Psychology' (*Grundzüge der Psychologie des Menschen*). I published parts of it in the treatise 'Concerning the Psychology of Sentiments' ('*Zur Psychologie der Gesinnungen*') in the years 1913 and 1916, other parts under the title 'Fundamental Problems of Characterology' ('*Grundprobleme der Charakterologie*'). This psychology of man met with unexpectedly strong interest, but only at the beginning of the year 1930, when I believed I had reached the goal of my wishes, at least in its main outlines, could I take up my mind to give in to the urging of so many people to publish this psychology. Unfortunately, sickness delayed the completion of the work until the end of the year 1932" (Pfänder 1967, 84).

1.2.2 The Freiburg Circle around Husserl

We maintain that it is scandalous that, despite the early (mainly) positive commentary and engagement from the academic community, Walther's dissertation went almost unnoticed for upward of another sixty years, that is, until the commentary provided by Linda López McAlister (1996). It is only since then that Walther has become a canonical figure in the history of the phenomenological movement—as one of the three central women of the movement, alongside Edith Stein and Hedwig Conrad-Martius, and as one of the notable students to begin their training in phenomenology with Pfänder in Munich before moving to Freiburg to study the transcendental, post-*Ideas I*, phenomenology of Husserl directly (though she disapproved of the Master's transcendental turn).[12]

During her time in Freiburg, from the summer of 1917 to the summer of 1919, Walther not only witnessed the inaugural meeting of the *Freiburger phänomenologische Gesellschaft*—the "Freiburg Circle"—she presented the first paper for discussion. The story of the founding of the Freiburg Circle is one worth telling here for two reasons. First, there are some details that, to our knowledge, have not been discussed at length elsewhere, and second, it helps to situate Walther within Husserl's "school." Recall that Husserl moved to the University of Freiburg from Göttingen in the year 1916, with Freiburg being a "hotbed" of Neo-Kantianism well after Heinrich Rickert's departure in 1916 from Freiburg to Heidelberg; phenomenology, in other words, was something rather unknown. Husserl ensured that his philosophy would fall on fertile ground, but for that, he needed help.

In a letter to Adolf Grimme on 27 January 1920, Husserl writes: "For one year now I have had a lovely philosophical circle here, as lovely as it was on the best of times in Göttingen" (Husserl 1994b, 84). This philosophical circle seems to have originated out of Stein's "phenomenological kindergarten"—a seminar for beginners in phenomenology that she began offering unofficially sometime in the winter semester 1916/1917,[13] and that began officially in the summer of 1917 when it moved into a university lecture hall. At that time, the group consisted of "three females, two males, one Benedictine priest, and one Protestant pastor" – one of the three females was Gerda Walther (Stein 2014, 69; Walter 1960, 204–207). And at this

---

12 Walther began her academic studies at the Ludwig Maximilian University of Munich in the winter semester of 1915/1916. Her first courses with Pfänder were in the summer of 1916. Prior to meeting Pfänder, she had no knowledge of phenomenology or, for the most part, philosophy in general—her interests lay in politics and sociology.

13 In a letter to Roman Ingarden on 28 January 28, 1917, Stein writes: "With *Bärchen* ["little bear," she refers to Otto Gründler], I am presently reading Investigation VI. Miss Konig is also participating again, and also Dr. [Friedrich] Loofs intends to join us. Thus, in the absence of a philosophical society, at least there is a philosophical kindergarten" (Stein 2014, 34).

time, Stein's kindergarten was the only thing resembling a "school" of students in Freiburg studying phenomenology. Husserl's inner circle was small at this time – due primarily to the First World War; the only members of the now-dissolved Göttingen Circle that followed Husserl when he took up Rickert's former Chair were Stein and Roman Ingarden. With Ingarden having completed his dissertation, and Stein having decided to give up her position as Husserl's assistant and leave Freiburg, Husserl needed to cultivate a new group of students.

Walther recalls the circumstances surrounding the founding of the Freiburg Phenomenological Society as follows:

> One day Husserl had invited all of us to a lecture that he was supposed to give for the Freiburg Society for the Philosophy of Culture, which I believe was founded by his predecessor, Prof. Rickert. Soon afterwards he revealed to his female students, somewhat embarrassed, that he had only found out afterwards that women were not allowed to attend the events. He tried, in vain, to get an exception – it was in the statutes. Was that not grotesque? Edith Stein, for example, probably knew more about Husserl's philosophy than many of the "Lords of Creation [*Herren der Schöpfung*]" who were allowed to participate. Of course, the purpose [of the statute] was to prevent scholars from bringing their wives with them at a time when there were no female students. As a consolation, Husserl then gave us an entire lecture on the problem area of the evening [lecture], which was taken from the unpublished *Ideas II*: the "constitution" of cultural "objects" as a new, additional "layer" that builds upon material things, such as a book, which is built upon the paper of the pages and the black colored lines of the printed letters.
>
> In addition, it was decided by the docents and students to found a "Freiburg Phenomenological Society," to which women, of course, would be admitted. (Walther 1960, 213)

Husserl's lecture to the Freiburg Society of the Philosophy of Culture took place on 21 February 1919 (*Hua* Dok I, 232). If Walther's memory is correct here, then the first meeting of the Freiburg Circle would have taken place in the spring of 1919. To avoid any chance of women not being able to attend, the venue for their meetings would be Husserl's home, during the time previously allotted to Stein's "kindergarten."

It is not known who all attended the inaugural meeting of the Freiburg Circle. Martin Heidegger, who had recently returned from military service and became the new assistant of the Philosophy Department (chaired by Husserl between 1920–21), led the meeting, and at the urging of Karl Löwith, Walther presented a paper titled *"Zur Problematik von Husserls reinem Ich"* (Walther 1960, 213–14). This paper is referenced at numerous points throughout her dissertation. In a letter to Erich Pryzywara dated 4 January 1958, Walther recalls the content of her paper as follows:

[...] another problem arises, which I addressed in my inaugural lecture for the "Freiburg Phenomenological Society" back in 1918. It was titled "On the Problematic of Husserl's Pure Ego." (Unfortunately, I lost the only copy when I lent it to Dr. Robert Steiger in Heidelberg in 1923 (now chairman of the Philosophical Society Baden-Baden), who accidentally took it to Vienna and could no longer find it.) The question was: If this "pure ego" is absolutely *empty and devoid of content*, merely a seeing eye" and nothing else, as Husserl defined it in his *Ideas*, then *why* can it have *qualitatively different* experiences and phenomena, both noetically and noematically? ("If not the eye was like the sun...!") Husserl was inclined once again to find this question posed in terms of *human* psychology. Heidegger backed me then: It is an extremely important problem. My solution was: If the quality does not lie in the "ego," then it must lie in the noeses, in their *sources* (here one comes to Pfänder's "self" and "basic essence [*Grundwesen*]" in humans)—but does the "pure consciousness" have such a thing? (*Hua* R III; Ana 317 C II – Gerda Walther an Erich Przywara [04/01/1958], unpublished)[14]

According to Walther, the discussion period that followed was taken up entirely by an argument between Husserl, Heidegger, and possibly Edith Stein. Heidegger believed that Walther had struck on an important weakness in Husserl's position. The paper was well received and there were intentions to have an expanded version of Walther's lecture published in the *Jahrbuch*.[15]

Walther foreshadows what we can only assume was a subsequent meeting of the Freiburg Circle in a letter written to Pfänder on 20 June 1919. Again, the problems raised in her inaugural lecture seem to have been the intended theme of discussion:

You might be interested to hear that a great campaign begins here tomorrow—not against the French, but against the pure ego. Leading the charge is Dr. [Julius] Ebbinghaus (son of the psychologist), who, due only to unfavorable circumstances, has not yet established himself as a private lecturer here. His background is Fichte and Hegel, and he recently raised objections in the seminar, which boil down to the idea that an "empty, essenceless, point-like" pure ego cannot will. Now, Professor Husserl has set aside every Saturday from 11:15 to 1:00 for a day of discussion, informal, for anyone who has questions. I have now incited a kind of conspiracy that there should be a general attack against the pure ego. Dr. Ebbinghaus will start. Then Dr. Heidegger will assist, taking a mediating position, that is to say, he claims that the primary *Ur-ego* is the qualified "historical ego," from which the pure ego arises through the suppression of all historicity and quality, but which could only be the subject of objective-theoretical acts. I intend to jot down some arguments for and against as well, but I'm not sure if I'll manage to finish. Mr. [Karl] Löwith has certainly already noted down a lot but, as a beginner, he doesn't quite dare. Whether anyone else will join in, I don't know. You may wish us victory! (*Hua* R III; Ana 317 C II – Gerda Walther to Alexander Pfänder [20/06/1919], unpublished)

---

14 See Walther 1960, 213–14.
15 See Pfänder's letter to Husserl from 17 January 1920 (Husserl 1994a, 160) and Husserl's letter to Winthrop Bell from 11. VIII. 1920 (Husserl 1994b, 15).

Such attacks from his students did not draw the ire of Husserl. In fact, the Master (as his students called him) seems to have welcomed such exchanges, perhaps as a way to refine the presentation of his ideas.[16]

On the heels of her successful presentation and newfound place in Husserl's inner circle, Walther took on the task of compiling an extensive subject index for *Ideas I* over the summer of 1919. At the same time, she attended Husserl's lectures on *Natur und Geist* (Nature and Spirit), which she references a number of times in her dissertation.[17] By Walther's account, Heidegger and Husserl both seem to have given her feedback on the index, which went untouched for two years (Walther 1960, 214–16). It was then included as an appendix to the second edition of Husserl's *Ideas I*, and contains her provocative entry on "phenomenological idealism" (Walther 1923a, 23–24).[18] After witnessing how severe and exacting the Master could be with his closest students, Walther went back to Munich to complete her dissertation under Pfänder in time for the winter semester of 1919/1920. As Walther had already discussed the proposed topic of the dissertation with Pfänder, Husserl agreed that she should return to Munich to complete it (Walther 1960, 244). As fate would have it, this provided Walther the opportunity to attend what would be Weber's final courses, which no doubt shaped her work on social communities.

1.2.3 Walther's Fate After Her Dissertation
With Husserl's endorsement (Husserl 1994c, 201), Walther went to Heidelberg to begin her Habilitation in the fall of 1922. One gets the sense that, for the better part of a decade, Walther was regarded quite highly among her teachers and fellow students of phenomenology. This is evinced by Husserl's letter to Jaspers on 24 October 1922 endorsing her for Habilitation in Heidelberg. All this however, seems

---

16 For example, in a letter to Ingarden on 21 February 1917, Stein writes: "Recently, I presented to the Master, quite solemnly actually, my reservations about idealism. It was not at all an 'awkward situation' (as you feared). I was seated on one end of the dear old leather sofa and then we had two hours of heated debate, naturally without either side convincing the other. The Master said he is not at all opposed to changing his point of view if someone proves to him it is necessary. So far, I have not succeeded. In any case, he clearly understands that he has to fundamentally rethink this point even though temporarily he has put it off" (Stein 2014, 48).

17 These lectures are also mentioned in Walther's letter to Husserl dated 18 May 1920. This letter and Husserl draft response are both worth reading in the context of Walther's understanding of the Ego (see Husserl 1994a, 257–265).

18 When Walther arrived at the University of Heidelberg to pursue her Habilitation in the winter semester of 1922/23, Husserl's predecessor in Freiburg, Heinrich Rickert, joked that her index was "so good and detailed" that one could almost study it on its own to orient oneself in Husserl's phenomenology and thus "save oneself the trouble of having to read *Ideas*" (Walther 1960, 333).

to drastically change following the publication of *Zur Phänomenologie der Mystik* (Walther 1923c),[19] and her shift in interest toward parapsychology, which displeased even Pfänder. In his 1923 lecture course, "Ontology: The Hermeneutics of Facticity," Heidegger remarks witheringly:

> Phenomenological research, which was supposed to provide a basis for scientific work, has sunk to the level of wishy-washyness, thoughtlessness, and summariness, to the level of the philosophical noise of the day, to the level of a public scandal of philosophy. The industry surrounding schools and their students has blocked the avenues of access for actually taking up phenomenology and doing it. The George circle, Keyserling, anthroposophy, Steiner, etc. – everything absorbs phenomenology. How far it has gone is shown by a recent book, *Phenomenology of Mysticism*, which appeared with an authorized publisher and with the most official sponsorship. (Heidegger 1999, 58)

Following Heidegger's harsh comments, the publication of Walther's index of was cut from the third edition of *Ideas I* published in 1928 and replaced by one compiled by Husserl's loyal assistant Ludwig Landgrebe. Notably, Landgrebe removed Walther's bifurcation of passages "pro" and "contra" idealism in favor of a single entry.[20] When she inquired concerning the reason for this, Husserl responded quite coldly, in a letter dated 3 May 1932 addressed to "Fräulein" Walther, that: "The decisive reason for me not assigning you the task of improving the index when republishing *Ideas* was that I was completely certain that you were not capable of actually understanding my transcendental phenomenology" (Institut für Grenzgebiete der Psychologie und Psychohygiene Archives).[21] Walther believed it may well have been her 1927 essay discussing Husserl alongside Ludwig Klages (Walther 1928), a member of the *"George-Kreis,"* or her interest in parapsychology

---

19 An English translation of the Introduction and Chapter 1 of this work are published in Parker 2018b.
20 Walther was of the opinion, as many of the early phenomenologists in Munich and Göttingen, that Husserl's idealism (and move towards transcendental phenomenology) was an aberration. For this reason, Walther separated the entry in her index on "idealism" into two parts, pro and contra, compiling passages that speak to both readings. Since Husserl was firmly committed to the idealistic stance after 1913, it is understandable that the index did not find Husserl's blessing, and thus Walther's index was replaced in the new edition of 1928 with a simpler one by Landgrebe, causing a rift between Husserl and Walther, when she noticed this in 1932. This story has not systematically been reconstructed, but we refer the readers to her Index, published by Niemeyer in 1923. Also cf. the following sequence of correspondence (all published in Hua BW): Husserl to Landgrebe 04/26/32, Landgrebe to Husserl 04/28/32, Husserl to Landgrebe 05/01/32 and Landgrebe to Husserl 04/25/32. Thanks to Thomas Vongehr for helping us reconstruct this "affair."
21 A copy of this letter can be found in the Husserl Archives in Leuven.

that caused a rift between them (Walther 1960, 215–216). It is at this point around 1932 when Walther almost entirely vanishes from philosophical discussion.[22]

Leaving aside her interest in the paranormal, and without debating the extent to which her attempts at a serious, scientific, phenomenological investigation of religious and mystical experiences remained objective, it is unfortunate that Walther's contributions to sociology, social psychology, and phenomenology went unappreciated for so long. This is not to imply that her dissertation is without its faults. We hope that this edition will enable the meaningful critique and criticism it deserves, based on the merits of the analyses and arguments presented herein.

In the following, we shall present some basic tenets and claims of her work. These are selectively chosen, but represent, arguably, some of the core thoughts of her landmark study on a phenomenological social ontology. The following, thus, is not intended as a summary of the book, but highlights some crucial aspects of the work.

2 Walther's Methodological Approach: Ontology-*cum*-Phenomenology

To appreciate Walther's work as a phenomenologist, one needs to start with her methodological approach. What is the distinctive mark of a specifically *phenomenological* approach to the problem of the social? In the introductory sentence she lays out her distinctive method, as opposed to a social-ontological approach to the phenomenon in question:

> Ontology aims at investigating the ultimate meaning, or the essence of every objectivity in the broadest sense; whereas phenomenology investigates the manner of givenness, appearance and cognition of every objectivity in pure consciousness as necessarily predelineated by this essence. Phenomenology takes its departure from this "pure consciousness" and its "pure Ego," as the most original, phenomenological-epistemologically pure (thus, not metaphysically absolute) starting point for all knowing. [...] T]he Freiburg phenomenology starts out from the absolute evidence of the current lived-experience, of the 'cogito' as such in the broadest sense, as well as of its immediately given object in the flesh ('originarily'), in liv-

---

22 For more information regarding Walther's life, particularly her formative student years, we refer the reader to Parker's previous publications on Walther (Parker 2017; Parker 2018a; Parker 2024). Doubtless, there are other episodes worth exploring to be found in Walther's autobiography, *Zum anderen Ufer* (Walther 1960). One such story, as hinted at in note 3, is that of her relationship with Percy Gothein and the circle around the poet Stefan George.

ing-through this lived-experience and in the immediate, immanent reflection on it on the part of the "pure ego." (43/{1})

The label "Freiburg phenomenology" is a nod to Husserl, especially his methodological approach known esp. from *Ideas II:* phenomenological fields of experience provide guiding clues (*Leitfäden*) for ontology. Phenomenology starts out from the evidence of the ego cogito, its first-personal experience. She further defines phenomenology as having two tasks: First, phenomenology is an *eidetic science*, of essences as intuited by an experiencing subject:

> These essences and their essential traits, however, are indeed *intuited* in the best adequacy possible, in their (empirically-real, phantasized etc.) individual embodiments, once the researcher observes these in "eidetic abstraction," thus when he grasps them *as* embodiment of an essence and in view of it while disregarding everything unessential. (47/{6})

Secondly, phenomenology performs the *phenomenological reduction:*

> The phenomenologist may not in any way presuppose cognitions derived from any of these other attitudes [other than the attitude of reduction], although what ontologies also investigate as the whatness of an object, [...] the phenomenologist, too, investigates among other things in the *intentional analysis* as the *meant meaning,* as *intentional correlate* of a lived-experience. (49–50/{9})

So far, so (Husserl) orthodox. The only thing to be noted is her focus on the noetic-noematic character of lived-experience. A known rejector of transcendental idealism, one may note here Walther's focus on the reduction as the exclusion of ontological questions in favor of intentional analysis (thus, reduction mainly understood as epoché), rather than a way to approach consciousness as transcendental (as constitutive).

But moving further, she introduces a second line of phenomenological investigation, which is represented by Pfänder: Phenomenology can, to be sure, be the analysis of the noetic-noematic structure of experience (Husserl). But it can also go further and perform an analysis of the *origin* of this experience (Pfänder). It is here that she introduces a core term of her work, the "metaphysically-real essence" as the true "being" of the subject:

> A constitution of a very peculiar sort, which coincides neither with immanent perception nor with psychic apperception in inner perception, is now the constitution of the metaphysically-actual essence, the "*basic essence*" of a subject in the sense of Pfänder's Psychology (analogous, say, to the "spiritual person" in the sense of Scheler, the "Ego in itself" and the "intelligible character" in Kant). [... W]e can investigate the lived-experiences in their intentional meaning [...]. But we can, now, also investigate their *actual* "welling point" in the actual sub-

ject, or better, the "direction" in the self from which they stem. Now there are, here, especially distinguished lived-experiences—which may be quite rare—which we feel and experience as coming from the deepest layer of our self. [These are] lived-experiences which, whatever may have triggered them, seem to flow forth from our ultimate ontic ground, from a 'sphere' in us which, as it were, lies "behind" the layer of the self, from which ordinarily the lived-experiences of our psychic life come forth. [...] Through an analysis of the type in which *these* lived-experiences arise in the background, and especially through an observation of their noetic quality, their "light," their "warmth," their "coloration" [...,] the Ego grasps its own "spiritual person," its metaphysically-actual essence, its basic essence—as a primal phenomenon, radically irreducible in pure intuition. (55–56/{15–16})

Thus, though she clearly gestures towards Husserl's main methodological points, eidetics and reduction (though she downplays the transcendental aspect of world-constituting consciousness), her real interest, as can be seen in the further course of the book, lies in this Pfänderian line of research: the research into the spiritual, metaphysical origin of the real, the "spiritual person," which underlies, arguably, the surface layer of the Husserlian analyses.

Now focusing on her express interest prior to the Husserl-Pfänder distinction, the constitution of social communities (consisting of such spiritual persons), the two approaches (ontological and phenomenological) can be also construed as follows:

These two ways now *open for constitutive phenomenology of social communities* [... are]:
(1) The "external" constitution of social communities, that is, their constitution for the *external bystander,* thus for a conscious subject which stands opposed to a social community as a closed-off totality. We have to distinguish this from
(2) The "internal" constitution for the *member,* that is, for a conscious subject that finds itself connected to one and in one social community, that feels as a member of this social community. (56/{17})

The account of social communities can, thus, be (1) in the form of an *ontology* of social communities (viewed from outside); and (2) *phenomenology* of social communities (viewed from within, from the *individual* member's perspective). While she is clearly on the side of a phenomenological account, it cannot be said in the course of her work that she sticks to it alone; indeed, she pursues both directions concurrently. This raises the legitimate question (as already raised above by one of the readers on her committee, 6), why does she call her account *"ontology* of social communities"? Any answer would be mere speculation, but suffice it to say that it, as sole title of the book, is certainly misleading. Further, she clearly stands in the distinction, one could even call it tension, between Husserl and Pfänder, that is, between a transcendental and realistic phenomenological method. Given her own skepticism towards the Husserlian transcendental-constitutive approach while having to please the Master (who was one of the main editors of the Year-book), along with her real sympathy for Pfänder's realism, these facts might ex-plain the title choice, ultimately situating Walther closer to her real teacher.

Caminada's reading (2014, 197) is more conciliatory, when he writes: "Despite the rigid distinction between realistic [Munich] and Husserlian phenomenology, we can profit from her account only [!] if we understand it as mid-point between those of Pfänder and Husserl, i.e., in-between the analytic-realistic and the tran-scendental-constitutive approaches." Thus, if Caminada is right, one would have to read her account *both* as transcendental-constitutive: it is about the constitution of world-as-experienced and also the self-constitution of experiencing agent. But it would *also* be a realistic account with respect to social communities and individ-uals as "connected to and in" a social community as a real entity in the world; a "thing" that can be described from the outside. Walther clearly shifts back and forth between both. Her shuttling back and forth between both "registers" can, thus, be read as trying methodologically to pay tribute to both methods. Rather than critiquing her account for failing to come to a methodologically clarified po-sition, one can instead see this hybrid stance as a reason for, among other things, the richness of her account.

3 Some Basic and Original Ideas from Walther

Moving to the main part of her work, one can single out four aspects or focal points of her work that deserve, we believe, special attention. They shall be dis-cussed briefly in the following section.

3.1 The Very Notion of a Social Community

Let us begin with the very notion of a social community (*soziale Gemeinschaft*), which gives the title to the work. What is a social community? By way of example, an ant or bee community (or lower life forms) are not a *social* community; it must consist of a community of *humans:*

> We thus would have to conceive of a social community a connection of human beings amongst themselves, only of human beings with human beings, furthermore, on a higher level, perhaps a connection, a community of such communities with each other. (58/{20})

Apart from a conglomerate of humans with a certain connection, it can also per-tain to such communities (Husserl's "personalities of higher order") in potency.

Also, it cannot *include* other creatures, such as animals (pets) or deities as members, though they may be *contained* in the lifeworld of such communities, as parts but not members (an important distinction). Furthermore, external qualities, bodily traits (badges/clothing) equally might be a sign of a community, but they, too, do not suffice.

> Thus, there must obtain an entirely or partially identical psychic-spiritual life with, at least partially, identical intentional contents or at least intentional directions, in order for a social community to exist. (59/{20})

What is required, thus, is a core of identical spiritual life with a core of identical intentional content and in mental-intentional reciprocal effect (*Wechselwirkung*). What makes a *group* a *community*, thus, is the mental (spiritual, psychic, "inner") connection. Walther gives the example of a community of scholars, who are scattered across the world but in contact over common issue, mutually influencing each other.

> In order for them to be conjoined in a community, 'communalized,' the members of a social formation have to stand ... not only in any intentional reciprocal effecting in general, but they will also have to live ... the identical mental-spiritual life in relation to the same intention contents in the same sense and in the same manner. (62/{22})

Apart from the very timely nature of this example, radically exacerbated in the age of the internet (and perhaps not fully realized until now), we now have the core constituents of what counts as a social community: it has to consist of (1) human beings alone (pets don't partake in the spiritual aspect); (2) they partake of (or constitute) a core of identical spiritual life (noetically) with (3) a core of identical content (noematically). It is the same, identical life, but it is, as it were, "everybody's and nobody's"; there can be no single bearer, since it is social; and it is open for potentially all others (potentially everybody could become a member of this community of scholars devoted to a common theme).

Walther now further characterizes this "common intentional life-content":

> The common intention need not refer neither to an external actual object nor an external actual relation on the part of the members as content, it does not have to be a physical, physiological or psychic actual object. ... [T]he object of the common intention ... must have some relation to actuality, be it that it is an ideal demand, which is elevated to a guiding star by the communalized people through their actual behavior ..., be it that we are dealing with an actual working-out of a scientific system, the actual realization of an aesthetic ideal, etc. Such a relation of whichever form to actuality must, to be sure, obtain in the case of the common content of the communal life; yet this is not to say that the meant content ... would itself have to be at all times something actual. (63/{24})

Thus, this common content can be imagined ("pretend" reality, as in child's role-play). But it must be the identical (real *or* imagined) intentional content and its common meaning (as meant), possibly with a material addition, which, however, is not essential. Finally, it can be meant and contributed to differently. Her vivid example is "Germany's victory," which can be the content of the life of a simple woman knitting socks for soldiers and the Kaiser and the generals planning the next move on the battlefield. As she says:

> The unified nexus of meaning ... is like a pervasive Leitmotif, which runs through the mental-spiritual life within the community in all of its members, although all of them play it in different variations and with different instruments. (66/{28})

Thus, the communal life is primary and not the products as result, and does not have to be concurrent, but can be interrupted, as when a game of chess from afar is interrupted by other activities (vs. Wundt's account, cf. 67/{28–29}).

Thus reads her full definition of a social community:

> We found a given number of people who refer, in a certain stratum of their life, to the same intentional it object in the broadest sense. These people had to have a knowledge-of-one-another and in their relation to the identical intentional object. Based on this knowledge, they entered into direct or indirect reciprocal interaction with one another and from this reciprocal effecting arose a common life (perhaps with common products), which was motivated by that intention toward the identical object in the broadest sense immediately or mediately in a unified sense. (68/{29–30})

Community is thus contrasted with *sociality*: the latter has no genuine "reciprocal interaction" (*Wechselwirkung*), no "inner connectedness" (other than through "external" tradition or convention); there is no "feeling of belonging together." Thus, to summarize the main constituents of social community: it is a unified meaningful nexus (noetic); with identical intentional content (noematic); and it requires a reciprocal effecting, which is primarily pre-reflexive and pre-linguistic; thus, intersubjective here is defined as the reciprocity of subjects.

3.2 Inner Unification

The next systematic piece in conjunction with a social community is the dynamic of "inner unification." This analysis deepens the concept of "feeling of belonging together": what it is and how it comes about. Here is the definition:

> With inner unification, rather, we designate this peculiar inner-mental unifying-with an intentional object. (72/{34})

It is important to note that it is not cognitive or theoretical, but *felt*. Further, it is a unification of subject with an *object*.

> Caused by any some external object, in the subject there arises the feeling of unification and it now strives to unify itself with this object. (72/{34})

Thus, unification can occur "behind the Ego's back" or subconsciously, in which case it is "mere concrescence." It is important to note that this inner unification occurs first and foremost *habitually:*

> But it essentially distinguishes itself from [recollected unification] through its position toward the source of the lived-experiences. For it is not severed from it and cut off ultimately, as the dead, extinguished, recollected lived-experience, but it is still connected to it, has not yet severed the stream of live, and a new, noetic, mental(-spiritual) stream of life constantly flows towards it from that source, although it does not actualize itself now, ... such that it does not swing along in its present current lived-experiences. The ego is perhaps not aware of it, perhaps it even "thinks" it is extinguished. But this is not the case; it can, rather, arise *itself,* as the same, *identically* lived-experience from the background, from the self, nourished from the same sources as before, and grasp the ego (or be grasped by it) and actualize itself. It is the *same, identical* lived-experience, *not* a *new,* similar one.... It is, hence, the position vis-à-vis the welling point of lived-experience, which distinguishes the living, habitual from the dead, recollected lived-experience, while it shares with it the ego-distance, the pushing-back into the experiential background, into the self, on the part of the ego, which has turned away. ... These habitual unifications of all sorts are now even more important for the grounding of communities and communal life [than the current ones]. (79–84/{42–48})

An important trait of inner unification, thus, is that it is, with Husserl's terminology, a matter of *passive synthesis.*

Walther now offers an intentional analysis of this inner unification: Intentional acts of unification can be directed at other things (and cultural artifacts, also ideal ones), but also at other humans. But what is constitutive for inner unification is that this unification with objects occurs *together with* other human beings:

> Thus, not only the unification with other human beings, but also the unification with other random non-human objectivities can be grounding for a social community, but only *when* —and this the *conditio sine qua non*—this unification, in turn, becomes grounding for the unification *with other human beings.* (85/{49})

The constitution of a social community, thus, involves a unification with other things in conjunction with unification with other human beings. Now, two modes are possible here; a unification can be intentionally directed

(a) Directly at other human beings, with whom the subject then unifies to a community (or wether...);

(b) The subject unifies itself with certain non-human objectivities or spheres of objects and only on the basis of this unification feels unified with other human beings, 'who also' are combined with these objects or stand in any other positive ... relation to them. (85/{49})

What must occur, thus, is what one may call a "constitutive triangulation" of I – other – thing (in the broadest sense). The intentional distinctions here involve intentional hierarchies (sub-, equi-, super-ordination); "circumference" (directed at only sub-group of community); essential-factual/empirical. Finally, to repeat what has been said before, a unification must be spiritual, not physical.

The last piece of the account is the aspect of *reciprocation*, which was already identified above (under 3.1) as a constitutive element of communality. Only reciprocation creates unification with others is:

The last essential insight concerning the unification as a basis for the community: that the unification has also to be reciprocated, if a true communalization is to take place. For a grounding, for an innermost funding of a community what is needed is not just the unification of *one* subject with all others and a reciprocal interaction between them, but instead a unification of *every* subject with *all* others, a *general 'reciprocal unification,'* which is experienced by the standpoint of the individual subject as a reciprocal unification, respectively. ... All communalization presupposes precisely unification *and reciprocation* of the unification, *reciprocal* unification, all socialization presupposes some form of intentional relation of *response*, a reciprocal interaction. (97–98/{63–64})

Community, thus, depends on *responsivity/responsiveness*. Multiple iterations are possible, as she indicates in the Figure (117/{86}). One may be reminded here of later phenomenologists who emphasized this aspect, such as Lévinas and, to a greater extent, Waldenfels; they have their predecessor in Walther.[23]

---

23 See Emmanuel Lévinas' *Totality and Infinity: An Essay on Exteriority* (1961) and Bernhard Waldenfels' work *Antwortregister* (1994).

3.3 The Common Life and Its "Behavior"

How does the common life *live* concretely, how does it "behave"? Walther's guiding questions are here: (1) How does the common life of a community play itself out (focus on the internal working, not the intentional directedness)? (2) Is there necessarily always a common object? Let's begin with the second question. What kind of communities are those without such a common object ("external purpose")? Do they even exist? They do, and Walther calls these *reflective* communities, those which are turned back upon themselves:

> [H]ere..., the common life will be permeated and governed by a common meaning, and this meaning is here precisely the unification, here the community *itself*: the community and the life in therein here are ends in themselves. It is here the goal of this common life to "live out" the unification and the community of the members, to prove it, to deepen it, to unfold and to preserve it. Under certain circumstances, however, one cannot say ... that it would not have a common meaning, no guiding objectivity, but there is no external object or meaning here lying outside of the community and its members. (101/{67})

In this case, the community *itself* is the common object. Her example is the family nucleus, which, for instance, gathers together to decide what to do in a challenging situation (shall we stay or leave?). The reason for this gathering might, to be sure, be caused by external events, such as war, but if the family decides what to do with itself, its thinking is turned back upon itself. This form of reflexivity is to be distinguished from *iterative* communities, a community within the community, whose purpose is the furthering of the community itself, for instance political leadership of a party, or (her example) a "Society for the Preservation of the Danish Language," which can only exist within an existing linguistic-cultural community (Denmark). Thus, in both cases, the object is the community itself. Systematically, it is not her claim that there is a "nested" relation between reflexive communities, which are *then* turned outwards; rather, it is a possible mode of a community to turn back upon itself from time to time reflexively or to conceive of ways to enhance it iteratively.

Turning to the first question, how should one describe the "commonality" of the common life of such a community? Her main thesis is that the dominant constituent is not an *activity* (contra Weber), but "*it is first and foremost the habitual unification, which ... must found and fundamentally ground our entire communal life.*" (102/{69}) Habitual unification is an activity, to be sure, but an ongoing one, not a sudden one following from a decision; it takes place in passivity. But who is the *agent* of this habitual unification? Habituality is something that occurs passively, "in the dark background," and includes, indeed is constituted by, others. But who are they? It is here that Walther proposes one of her most original ideas:

These others are *"people who also…" (Menschen, die auch…)*; here is her description:

> This "also" can be determined in very different ways, depending on the type and intentional founding of the unification, as humans, who "also" value thusly, who "also" have such goals, "also" feel this way, will, think, etc., as the respective subject itself. Certainly this "also" does not always relate merely to some *external* goals, manners of behavior, lived-experiences, etc. Rather it can also pertain to the basic stances towards life as a whole, the entire cosmos, regardless of its differentiations and expression in individual lived-experiences, opinions, actions, and so on. … These "people, who also…" are always somehow present in the background of the subject, albeit ever so indeterminately. The subject is aware of them not only darkly, but is also unified with them, in *those* layers, which the meaning of the community demands. (103/{69 – 70})

As the "agent" of common life, these "people, who also…" are what underlie our individual stances, values, and thoughts (we value as they do, etc.). With the peculiar concept of "people, who also…," it is fair to suggest that Walther describes here what Heidegger in *Being and Time* of 1927 describes as *"das Man"* (the They), as the anonymous and hidden force that guides our existence in all aspects of life. Indeed, Heidegger is cited several times as reference and as a conversation partner (cf. 52 & 64/{12 & 25}), which gives a keen insight into the phenomenological scene and its discussions around this time and puts the singularity of Heidegger somewhat in perspective. This is not to say that Walther's analyses display the same sophistication as Heidegger's distinction between authentic and inauthentic existence and his entire analysis of facticity, but at least one can say that Heidegger's fascinating analyses of common life have a predecessor, at least in nucleus, in Walther, and arguably, both analyses are compatible with one another.

Now this common life does not "swallow up" the I, the I exists as an autonomous member of the community, yet anonymous others rather exist "in me," they are part of the anonymous background in me. This raises the question, how do *we* experience? What is the We? Is there such a thing as a We-experience, a communal experience? Walther's position here is clear: The We is not a separate entity removed or above the Egos, there is no such thing as a "communal Ego-center":

> The "we" is … not a bodiless subject of its own that would be grasped by the individuals in a special type of empathy and whose lived-experiences they now make into their own on the basis of this empathy…[24] (103/{70})

---

24 One could say, borrowing a phrase from Zahavi: "No plurality without subjectivity."

The We is experienced by individual Egos, but since it is *not* experienced through a form of empathy, it cannot be an entity of its own, a "higher I." The We may form a certain character, but it is not adequately described as an identity; rather such a We (a "personality of higher order," to use Husserl's vocabulary) is visible through its activities and behavior. A person has an identity, in other words, but a We cannot be said to have an identity in the same way as an individual. It makes no sense, in other words, to speak of identity of the community "fans of soccer club X," though there is such a thing as a communal experience when I am immersed in a chanting stadium with other members of the fan club.

And yet, is there such a thing as a "genuine" We-experience? Is there such an experience, where the individual experiences as part of a community? That indeed exists: We-experiences "enact and actualize themselves indeed in the *individual ego*, in the ego-center of the individual members" (104/{70}), but in this case, the "others, who also..." are *in me:*

> "My" lived-experiences, to the extent and *only* to the extent they are precisely communal lived-experiences, do not merely well up from myself, from my isolated self, my only-I-myself behind the ego-point; instead they well up at the same time from the other *in me*, from the we, the "people, who also," in whom I rest and with whom I am one. (104/{71})

"People who also" are thus part of the Ego, but not the current *individual* ego, but part of the background ("passivity"). Thus, my individual experience, which is mine alone, rests on a passive sediment of "others who also," who have contributed genetically to my current and actual self (including my values and opinions). We-experiences, thus, are communal, but not in a way that the individual dissolves in a sea of We-ness.

An important lesson to be drawn from this phenomenological description is the distinction between communal lived-experience and empathy; these are *sui generis* distinct forms of experience, which are systematically related but to be kept apart descriptively. Empathy is the experience of the other:

> In the case of empathy, I grasp through words, mimicry and other forms of expression the lived-experience of others, and yet I am immediately aware that *it is not I* who experiences these lived-experiences in an originary manner and in the flesh, that these lived-experiences belong to the other, that they arise from *his* self and are actualized in *his* ego-center and are given to me only through phenomena of expression. They stand opposed to me as non-originary lived-experiences, grasped by me, objectified, separated from my ego and are not mine. (106/{73})

Communal lived-experience, on the other hand, can be *incited* through empathy, but it is something altogether different; Walther continues:

> Now, suddenly, a strange "merging together" of my lived-experiences and his into my lived-experiences and his into mine takes place: We are all of a sudden "together," the intentional "wall" ... has been broken, it is as if what he experiences, *I myself* experience, from me, as if he, and I, in him, experience it. (If we experience *concurrently* originarily *exactly the same currently* as I, then we would have a "we-lived-experience" in the most intimate sense, this would be an especially distinguished special case of communal lived-experiences.) His lived-experiencing *now also belongs* "*to me*," although it is he who experiences, I am in it as well, almost as if I am also concurrently and originarily 'in it' in my own identical or similar lived-experience. ... This [is a] strange "belonging-to-me" of lived-experiences of another in the we-lived-experiences... (108/{75})

Communal lived-experiencing is thus also no *imitation (mimicry)* of the other(s). It is an experience *sui generis,* and not something of which everyone is capable of to the fullest extent.

The last question Walther discusses in this context is that of communal life and reciprocity. Is reciprocity still needed for a communalization? Ideally, the following is necessary:

> It is, to be sure, presupposed from the beginning that this reciprocal effecting is an intentional reciprocal effecting in the sense already discussed and it is 'equally intentional.' Likewise, this intentional and consensual reciprocal effecting in the broadest sense by no means has to be enacted by one or all subjects in question here, nor even intended. ... That a reciprocal interaction of *all* members of a community must necessarily obtain, in which they also directly or indirectly (through oral or written notifications, requests, commands, agreements, and so on and so forth) orient themselves *at* each other and are not just oriented *by* each other, does in no way seem necessarily to belong to *every* community 'as such.' But yet it seems to us that a fully developed community is hardly conceivable in which the members are not more or less, directly or indirectly, oriented *by* each other. (121–122/{90–92})

The methodological caveat to be considered here is that in empirical-factical communities, reciprocity is neither necessary nor always the case. It is an ideal to be aspired to, but rare and difficult to realize. One could call this the normative element in her account: reciprocity is a moral ought.

3.4 Social Acts

We now come to the last of the highlighted themes of Walther's texts: social acts. This discussion is continuous with her analysis of We-experiences. Her focus now is not on experiences, but acts stemming from a We. Her main definition goes two ways, centrifugally, centripetally, as it were:

> Following what we have just analyzed, we can now ... understand by "social acts" and "social self" all those acts, which *direct themselves at the social communities as such* (as well as other social formations), knowing, willing, position-taking, unifying, acting, and so on, as well as to the sphere in the self, from which these acts (and so on) come forth and in which they, once they have become habitual, reise in the subject. (103/{103})

Walther's guiding question asks, what kind of "intention" guides these acts? What motivates them? Here she distinguishes between acts "from oneself *or* "in the name of" the community. Both are *my* acts, acts of an individual self, but stem from different motives. Acts from myself are simply acts I do from my own motivation. More interesting are the former. Acts "in the name of" constitute what it means to be part of a community; this entails responsibilities:

> Now it is also possible that a subject lives in this manner *from the "spirit" of a community itself,* and here too by compulsion, with or without his will or also deliberately. (133/{103})

Social acts in the name of the community can be defined as acts by me, but for the sake of the community, and perhaps even against my will or (personal) conviction. This is not necessarily with negative connotation, but stems from a commitment to the community, which entails obligations (to "take one for the team," as one might say colloquially). To speak in Heidegger's terminology, it is what *one* does (goes to church on a Sunday although one would prefer to sleep in). These social acts "in the name of" are further defined as follows:

> All lived-experiences, activities, and so on, of this sort in the broadest sense are enacted, to be sure, by the respective subject itself, they actualize themselves in its ego-center, but [he] experiences and enacts them not as 'his own' lived-experiences, but precisely as lived-experiences "in the name," "in lieu of" the other.... With these lived-experiences "in the name of..." the experiencing subject can unify itself, and yet thereby they do not become its own lived-experiences in the strict sense, attributed *only to it itself,* but perhaps it takes a position (although it itself enacts them—and yet not) to them, assenting, negating, ... as to any other lived-experiences that another subject enacts. (134/{104–105})

Acts and experiences "in the name of," thus, enable unification with a community, even though there might be a personal reservation or even a moment of critique (one dislikes the national anthem, yet sings along at the appropriate moment). Yet, there can be an extreme form of disagreement, when there is a contradiction between personal belief and the communal will. This explains why some social acts can cause inner conflict between personal conviction and social commitment, as in, e. g., case of the judge who has to sentence a friend to jail. But what kind of conflict is this? In this example, social acts can conflict with personal beliefs, and yet:

Yet it would be quite erroneous to think that we are dealing here with *two spheres* in reality, strictly separated, as it were spatio-mechanically distinct and sides in the inner-mental self of the subjects experiencing as social and private persons... (135/{105})

Thus, there is a distinction between a real conflict and a rather artificial or arbitrary split; the latter can occur in "mere employees" (135/{106}); these are people who are acting in the name of, but otherwise do not (have to) care. The mere employee, say a server in a restaurant, may be friendly to a customer whom she is indifferent about; thus, there is a split but no conflict because the server knows it is her job to be friendly. Such a split, in other words, does not have to cause inner pain, as in the case of the judge, who is torn between his professional duty and personal sympathy.

A real conflict, indeed, arises when there is a real commitment on the part of the individual:

[I]n general, the communal "soul" (the "social self" in *this* sense) and the individual "soul" (the private or individual self) in the members as well as the lived-experiences arising from them, are so closely woven together and intertwined, that it is almost impossible for both the external observer as well as the experiencing subject itself to discern where one of them "begins" and the other ones "stops," which lived-experiences (and so on) have their origin in one, which in the other. This is, to be sure, the case to an exceptionally high degree in the communities founded in the spiritual or empirical personhood of the members. (Marriage, friendship, certain religious communities, etc.). (135/{106})[25]

Social acts, thus, where the personal and the communal interest are "in sync" as it were. Thus, in general, a full flourishing of a community can only take place when both unfold and fulfill each other.

Not only *can the community not fully unfold its essence, if it does not count the individual persons as among their members demanded by this essence,* but the same holds vice versa: *only when a personality finds or creates the community demanded by its basic essence, can it fully unfold.* (136/{107})

Thus, Walther's account of the individual and the community and their relation is not a romantic one of the individual's vanishing or dissolving in the community and the community being a higher self. In a more sober view characteristic of Walther, while the inner unification of individuals in the community is a clear ideal and even moral demand, such a unification must never lead one to abandon

---

[25] There is a special case, however, of the incarnation of the communal spirit in a leader who polarizes; someone, in other words, who pulls apart this very communality through radical claims or demands (cf. 139/{109–110}).

one's own stance. Her account focuses on the "dialectical" relation, as one might say, between both and a constant reflection that is demanded of the individual as member of one's communities. Her view of self and community is, thus, both realistic and enlightened, optimism checked by realism.

Much more could be said about Walther's highly original work, which was written—something that should be kept in mind—by someone who was 24 years old at that point in her life. The points highlighted above are merely those that stand out perhaps most prominently, but the work as a whole has a plethora of interesting details and observations in footnotes and side comments and ought to be appreciated in its entirety. Fortunately, some recent scholarship has begun to explore Walther's work, but more research has presumably been held back by the lack of translation into English. It is the translators' hope that an English rendering may now increase the reception of a hitherto underappreciated female philosopher and startingly original member of the Phenomenological Movement.

4 Acknowledgments

Section 1 of this introduction was written (mainly) by Rodney Parker; Sections 2 and 3 were written (mainly) by Sebastian Luft.

The translators would like to thank the following persons in particular: Sebastian Luft would like to thank Dan Zahavi for some suggestions to improve the translation. Furthermore, the Summer School of 2021 at the Center of Subjectivity Research under the guidance of Dan Zahavi in Copenhagen was an excellent sounding board to present some of the ideas of this introduction (Sections 2 and 3). Luft would also like to thank Thomas Vongehr (Leuven) for being an as-usual reliable source for historical information, which we were able to incorporate. Thanks as well to Julia Mühl-Sawatzki for creating the image from Walther's schematic drawing of we-experiences.

Rodney Parker would like to thank Ruth Hagengruber and the Center for the History of Women Philosophers and Scientists for enabling his research into Walther's unpublished papers, correspondence, and related historical documents. Thanks as well to Antonio Calcagno for his feedback on Section 1 of this Introduction, as well as his help with the final edit of the entire text. Special thanks must also be given to Thomas Vongehr for his invaluable assistance and mentorship in transcribing and editing the unpublished source materials used in this Introduction.

The translators would like to acknowledge the help of Christoph Schirmer from De Gruyter for helping us conceive this project and shepherd it through to production. We would like to thank, in addition, all the people from DeGruyter who were involved in the final typesetting, Inga Lassen, Anett Rehner. Finally, we would like to thank Celina Herbrechter, Eliana Kos, and Philipp Schlotjunker (all Paderborn University) for their help with proofreading the German and creating the name and subject indices.

Paderborn/London (Ont.), May 2024

References

Calcagno, Antonio. 2012. "Gerda Walther: On the Possibility of a Passive Sense of Community and the Inner Time Consciousness of Community." *Symposium* 16 (2): 89–105.

Caminada, Emanuele. 2014. "Joining the Background: Habitual Sentiments Behind We-intentionality." In *Institutions, Emotions, and Group Agents*, edited by Anita Konzelmann-Ziv and Hans Bernhard Schmid, 195–212. Dordrecht: Springer.

Gurwitsch, Aron. 1977. *Die mitmenschlichen Begegnungen in der Milieuwelt.* Berlin: Walter De Gruyter.

Gurwitsch, Aron. 1979. *Human Encounters in the Social World.* Pittsburgh: Duquesne University Press.

Husserl, Edmund. 1994a. *Briefwechsel II. Die Münchener Phänomenologen.* Vol. III/2 of *Husserliana* Dokumente. Dordrecht: Kluwer.

Husserl, Edmund. 1994b. *Briefwechsel III. Die Göttinger Schule.* Vol. III/3 of *Husserliana* Dokumente. Dordrecht: Kluwer.

Heidegger, Martin. 1999. *Ontology: The Hermeneutics of Facticity.* Bloomington: Indiana University Press.

Husserl, Edmund. 1994c. *Briefwechsel VI. Philosophenbriefe.* Vol. III/6 of *Husserliana* Dokumente. Dordrecht: Kluwer.

León, Felipe and Dan Zahavi. 2016. "Phenomenology of Experiential Sharing: The Contribution of Schutz and Walther." In *The Phenomenological Approach to Social Reality*, edited by Alessandro Salice and Hans Bernhard Schmid, 219–234. Dordrecht: Springer.

López McAlister, Linda. 1996. "Gerda Walther (1897–1977)." In *A History of Women Philosophers, Volume 4: Contemporary Women Philosophers, 1900–Today*, edited by Mary Ellen Waithe, 189–206. Dordrecht, Springer.

Luft, Sebastian. 2016. "Do We-Experiences Require an Intentional Object? On the Nature of Reflective Communities." In *Women Phenomenologists on Social Ontology*, edited by R. Hagengruber, S. Luft. Dordrecht: Springer.

Mannheim, Karl. 1980. *Strukturen des Denkens.* Frankfurt: Suhrkamp.

Mannheim, Karl. 1982. *Structures of Thinking.* Translated by Jeremy J. Shapiro and Shierry Webar Nicholsen. London: Routledge.

Müller, Aloys. 1926. "Jahrbuch für Philosophie und phänomenologische Forschung." Vol. 6. *Kant-Studien* 31: 370–371.

Otaka, Tomoo. 1932. *Grundlegung der Lehre vom sozialen Verband.* Vienna: Springer.

Parker, Rodney. 2017. "Gerda Walther and the Phenomenological Community." *Acta Mexicana de Fenomenología* 2: 45–68.

Parker, Rodney. 2018a. "Gerda Walther (1897–1977): A Sketch of a Life." In *Gerda Walther's Phenomenology of Sociality, Psychology, and Religion*, edited by Antonio Calcagno, 3–9. Cham: Springer.

Parker, Rodney. 2018b. "Phenomenology of Mysticism, Introduction and Chapter One." In *Gerda Walther's Phenomenology of Sociality, Psychology, and Religion*, edited by Antonio Calcagno, 115–133. Cham: Springer.

Parker, Rodney. 2024. "Gerda Walther (1897–1977)." In *The Oxford Handbook of Nineteenth-Century Women Philosophers in the German Tradition*, edited by Kristin Gjesdal and Dalia Nassar, 307–321. Oxford: Oxford University Press.

Pfänder, Alexander. 1913. "Zur Psychologie der Gesinnungen." *Jahrbuch für Philosophie und phänomenologische Forschung* 1 (1): 325–404.

Pfänder, Alexander. n.d. *Grundzüge der Psychologie des Menschen. Vorlesungsmanuskript WS 1915/16* (345 Bl.) Bayerische Staatsbibliothek, Pfänderiana C I 9.

Pfänder, Alexander. 1916. "Zur Psychologie der Gesinnungen, Zweiter Artikel." *Jahrbuch für Philosophie und phänomenologische Forschung* 3: 1–125.

Pfänder, Alexander. 1933. *Die Seele des Menschen: Versuch einer verstehenden Psychologie.* Halle (Saale): Niemeyer.

Pfänder, Alexander. 1967. *Phenomenology of Willing and Motivation, and Other Phaenomenologica.* Evanston: Northwestern University Press.

Robbins, Derek (ed.). 2023. *Tomoo Otaka: Foundation of a Theory of Social Association, 1932.* Oxford: Peter Lang.

Schmid, Hans Bernhard. 2005. *Wir-Intentionalität. Kritik des ontologischen Individualismus und Rekonstruktion der Gemeinschaft.* Freiburg im Breisgau: Karl Alber.

Schuhmann, Karl. 1977. *Husserl-Chronik. Denk- und Lebensweg Edmund Husserls.* Vol. I of *Husserliana Dokumente.* The Hague: Nijhoff.

Schuhmann, Karl. 1990. "Husserl's Yearbook." In *Philosophy and Phenomenological Research,* vol. L, 1–25.

Schütz, A. 1959. "Husserl's Importance for the Social Sciences." In *Edmund Husserl, 1859–1959,* edited by Jaques Taminiaux and Hermann Leo Van Breda, 86–98. Den Haag: Martinus Nijhoff.

Stein, Edith. 2014. *Letters to Roman Ingarden.* Washington D.C.: ICS Publications.

Takata, Yasuma. 1927. "Die Gemeinschaft als Typus." *Zeitschrift für die gesamte Staatswissenschaft* 83 (2): 291–316.

Walther, Gerda. 1921. *Promotionsakte.* Universitätsarchiv der Ludwig-Maximilians-Universität München, Bestand O-II-8p. [Unpublished]

Walther, Gerda. 1922. *Ein Beitrag zur Ontologie der sozialen Gemeinschaften: Mit einem Anhang zur Phänomenologie der sozialen Gemeinschaften.* Halle (Saale): Max Niemeyer.

Walther, Gerda. 1923a. *Ausführliches Sachregister zu Edmund Husserls "Ideen zu einer reinen Phänomenologie und phänomenologischen Philosophie" Bd. 1.* Halle (Saale): Max Niemeyer.

Walther, Gerda. 1923b. "Zur Ontologie der sozialen Gemeinschaften." *Jahrbuch für Philosophie und phänomenologische Forschung* 6: 1–158.

Walther, Gerda. 1923c. *Zur Phänomenologie der Mystik.* Halle (Saale): Max Niemeyer.

Walther, Gerda. 1928. "Ludwig Klages und sein Kampf gegen den 'Geist.'" *Philosophischer Anzeiger* 3(1): 48–90.

Walther, Gerda. 1960. *Zum anderen Ufer: Vom Marxismus und Atheismus zum Christentum.* Remagen: Otto Reichel.

Translators' Notes

1 Principles of translation

1.1 Fidelity and readability: a difficult synthesis

In this translation, we attempted to strike a balance between fidelity to the original German, while producing a readable and easily flowing English text. This is an ideal and it is always difficult to achieve. In the case of Walther, this ideal was even more difficult to attain, since her prose is full of run-on sentences, which are hard to follow even for the native speaker, and full of interjections in brackets or hyphens, which interrupt the flow of reading, even in the original. When possible, the translators tried to break up long sentences and render the interjections as relative clauses. In some cases, this simplification for the sake of translation was simply not possible, since the internal grammatical references would have been lost. Still, the run-on sentences, where the translators saw no good solution, are kept to an absolute minimum. In some cases, making a text easily readable, which is not easy to follow in the original, is simply an impossible ideal. Overall, the translators hope to have succeeded in producing a readable text that is perceived as faithful to the original and which will be met with approval.

1.2 Adherence to existing conventions

Every philosophical author, tradition or movement has, for better or worse, its own jargon, and this jargon extends, again for better or worse, to translations, which shape the scholarly debate. For instance, everyone who knows a bit about Kant's vocabulary, will note the notorious difference between knowledge and cognition (for which Kant uses, in both cases, the term *Erkenntnis*). The same goes for certain terms that have been used by the classics of the school in question—phenomenology—where the tradition of translating them is almost as old as the primary texts themselves. That is to say, there is a certain virtue ("principle of tenacity") in adhering to a certain convention of translation, which, while perhaps not always offering a perfect rendering, nevertheless points the reader to a certain tradition or practice of translating, which the learned reader will recognize and where it would cause more confusion or misunderstanding were one to deviate from it and reinvent the wheel. Examples of established translations within the phenomenological tradition, despite their likely difficulties, are "lifeworld" for *Lebenswelt* or "empathy" for *Einfühlung*. These terms, one can argue, are so established in the phenomenological literature that no special mention of them is necessary neither in the translation nor the glossary. Since Walther is close to Husserl (and the early phenomenologists, in general) in her terminology, we advise the reader to consult existing translations especially of Husserl's classic works, such as *Ideas* I, *Ideas* II, the *Crisis*, and others.[1] Although these translations might differ here or there, or the respective translators have made different decisions given the context in question, one should see such translation standards as a self-perfecting enterprise (albeit with an infinite limit) rather than as immanent competitions. Thus, for the reader not versed in the original German, it is always advisable to compare different translations. The principle in this translation was to stick as closely as possible to the established translations, so long as one is dealing with terms known from other authors. The glossary, thus, pertains mainly to terms germane to the content of her writings.

Furthermore, the translators kept the text readable and without interruptions for the reading eye, which means we attempted to keep footnotes explaining translations to an absolute minimum.

We refrained from "gendering" Walther's text. Mostly she uses examples in the masculine, which would also make sense given her historical setting (the army general as "he," for instance). It would have been too much of an intervention to change her practice.

2 Conventions for citations

Regarding Walther's copious citations, we attempted to track down all of them and give the references of current editions, so that readers may find them for themselves. Our principles here were:
- If the work cited by Walther is translated into English, we provided the citation of the translated work. The works cited are to be found in the bibliography.

---

1 *Ideas to a Pure Phenomenology and Phenomenological Philosophy,* Book I, has been translated first by W.R. Boyce Gibson (1931, already during Husserl's lifetime), then by Fred Kersten (1982) and, finally, by Daniel Dahlstrom (2014). *Ideas,* Book II (1989) was translated by Richard Rojceicz and the *Crisis* (1970) was translated by David Carr. Most of these standard translations have glossaries. Cf. especially the newer translation of *Ideas* I by Daniel Dahlstrom, which can be seenas a significant improvement over the first translations by Boyce Gibson and Kersten. See also the glossary in the translation of Luft and Naberhaus of Husserl's *First Philosophy* (2019).

- If the work cited by Walther is not translated, we attempted to track down the latest edition of the original author (oftentimes available now in critical works, such as those by by-now classics, such as Max Weber) and cite its pagination.
- If Walther cites a work not published at the time (such as, e.g., Pfänder's or Husserl's writings), but published now, we cited the published version (e.g., of the *Husserliana*) and attempted to point the reader to the correct passage, since Walther sometimes does not cite, but merely refers to a work. We tried to be as precise as possible in pointing the reader to the passage she might have had in mind.
- Some works Walther cites were not and are still not published (e.g., some of Pfänder's lecture courses). We also pointed this out where applicable and made a reference to the *Nachlass* locations (e.g., Staatsbibliothek, Munich) of these texts, where possible.
- We attempted to keep all additions and comments stemming from the translators, which are to be found only in the footnotes, to an absolute minimum and add information only when it is absolutely vital to understand what she writes. The translators also provided references and dates of birth of all people she mentions in passing and also added some biographical information of those, who were much-talked about in her time and who might no longer be easily recognizable today (e.g., the "celebrity" Lafcadio Hearn, cf. 143/{113}). All additions by the translators are in square brackets [ ].

3 Brief discussion of especially difficult words

Translators are not interpreters; thus their translations of especially difficult cases should not offer, or based on, an interpretation favored by them. Still, in some cases this neutrality is impossible. Thus, in the glossary, we consequently only list those terms, which are especially notorious or difficult, without offering a lengthy explanation, which would amount to an interpretation. A few special cases shall be mentioned, however:

- *Gemeinschaft* vs. *Gesellschaft:* Walther distinguishes between a "mere" *Gesellschaft* and a "real" *Gemeinschaft*, the latter being the object of her actual analyses. These terms were translated as "society" and "community," respectively (including their cognates in the form of adjectives).
- *Grundwesen/Wesensgrund* is probably the most notorious pair of terms. The terms designate Walther's notion for the basic "metaphysical" essence or ground of an individual human being's existence, hence it is mostly accompanied by the adjective "metaphysical." Since its usage is ubiquitous, it is oftentimes used (more or less) interchangeably. We rendered the term as "basic es-

sence" (for *Grundwesen*) and "essential basis" (for *Wesensgrund*); yet the reader should bear in mind that the terms are oftentimes synonymous, at least given the frequency of usage.

– *Real/wirklich:* we rendered *real* primarily as "actual" and *wirklich* as "real," since *real* is oftentimes used in the pair actual-potential known from Aristotle's distinction.

4 References

Husserl, Edmund. 1931. *Ideas to a Pure Phenomenology and Phenomenological Philosophy,* Book I.
    Translated by W. R. Boyce Gibson. London: George Allen & Unwin Ltd.
Husserl, Edmund. 1970. *Crisis of European Sciences and Transcendental Phenomenology.* Translated by
    David Carr. Evanston: Northwestern U Press.
Husserl, Edmund. 1982. *Ideas to a Pure Phenomenology and Phenomenological Philosophy,* Book I.
    Translated by Fred Kersten. In Husserliana *Collected Works.* Dordrecht: Springer.
Husserl, Edmund. 1989. *Ideas to a Pure Phenomenology and Phenomenological Philosophy,* Book II.
    Translated by Richard Rojceicz. Dordrecht: Springer.
Husserl, Edmund. 2014. *Ideas to a Pure Phenomenology and Phenomenological Philosophy,* Book I.
    Translated by Daniel Dahlstrom. Indianapolis/IN: Hackett.
Husserl, Edmund. 2019. *First Philosophy.* Translated by S. Luft and T. M. Naberhaus. Dordrecht:
    Springer.

Glossary

Aktualisierung	actualization
aktuell	current
Gegenständlichkeit	object/objectivity
Geist/geistig	spirit/spiritual
Gemeinschaft	community
Gemeinschaftserlebnis	communal lived-experience
Gemeinschaftsleben	communal life
Gesellschaft	society
Gesinnung	affect
Grund	ground/basis/foundation
Grundlage	basis
Grundwesen	basic essence (see also Wesensgrund)
Einheit	unity
Einigung	unification
einsichtig	reflective
erleben	to experience
Erlebnis	lived-experience
erlebnismäßig	experiential
fremd	foreign/other
Ichzentrum	Ego-center
Ich/Ego	Ego
"im Namen"	"in the name"
"im Geiste," "im Sinn"	"in the spirit"
Leib	lived-body
Leiblich	bodily
metaphysisch reales (Grund-)Wesen	metaphysically real (basic) essence
Mitglied	member
Moment	moment/element
Person	person/someone
Personalität	personhood/personality
Psyche/psychisch	Mind/mental
Quellpunkt	source/source-point
real	actual; real
Schicht	stratum/layer
Seele	mind/soul
Seelenleben	mental life
Sinn	significance; sense, meaning
Tiefe	profundity
Verbundenheit	connectedness
Vergegenwärtigung/vergegenwärtigen	presentification/to presentify
Vergemeinschaftung	communalization
Wechselwirkung	reciprocal interaction

Wesen	essence
Wesensgrund	essential basis (see also Grundwesen)
Wirklich	real
Wir-Erleben	we-experience
Zusammenwachsen (n.)	concrescence

―――

Toward an Ontology of Social Communities.

With an Appendix on the Phenomenology of Social Communities

Preface

{III} Even prior to my university studies, I was roused by the liveliest interest for the social problems of our time. The life of the individual in social communities, through them, for and against them, seemed to me to be one of the most important problems of human life as such. An elucidation of the relation of the individual to the community seemed ever more important for the solution of all other ethical and metaphysical problems of human life. I was first motivated to reflect on these questions through the doctrines and basic thoughts presented by the historical materialists such as Karl Marx and Friedrich Engels, as well as the main representatives of Marxism. Apart from the writings of Karl Marx, Karl Kautsky, August Bebel, and so on, the attempts of the Viennese Kantian and Marxist Dr. Max Adler to provide a deeper grounding and expansion of Marxism were especially important in allowing me to glean the breadth of these problems. In his writings (especially in "Marxist Problems" and in "Causality and Teleology in the Dispute over Science"), I encountered for the first time an attempt to clarify the meaning and essence of social communities (at the time, the writings of Georg Simmel and others were still unknown to me), and they made a profound impression on me. These problems were ever deepened in discussion with friends, and they came to a head especially in the question regarding the individual's freedom of the will, despite and within their social context, especially with regard to the extreme social determinism on the part of some Marxists. Already in my first semesters of studies, Prof. Alexander Pfänder's lecture course on the *Fundamentals of Human Psychology* and his *Introduction to Philosophy* shed some light onto this chaos of problems, at least to the extent that it related to the individual's mental life. Yet, even here, I did not find a conclusive solution to the problem of *social* determinism. Then, in the writings of Simmel and Georg Wilhelm Friedrich Hegel, as well as —albeit {IV} in a radically different sense—in the writings of the mystic Meister Eckhart and others, I found most valuable discussions and profound intuitions related to my questions. Only much later, after having already dug deep into these problems myself, did I encounter Max Scheler's inspired intuitions in this area, as well as some writings and lectures by Prof. Max Weber. But all of this did not seem to afford an ultimately satisfactory answer to my questions. In the meantime, I penetrated (under the guidance of Prof. Pfänder in Munich and Prof. Edmund Husserl in Freiburg, as well as of their students and followers) ever deeper into the meaning and the method of phenomenological research, and it appeared to me ever more indispensable as a first prerequisite for a solution to my problems that I clarify ontologically and phenomenologically, first and foremost, the essence of social communities "as such" and their "constitution."

The present work is an *attempt* at a meager contribution to the ontology and phenomenology of social communities. To be sure, one must dispense with the hopes of a somewhat exhaustive solution to all the relevant problems, given the necessarily limited scope of this work. For such an encompassing treatment, more elaborate research work over many years would be needed, whose results would certainly require many tomes. There can be no talk of this here. I merely wish to give some guidelines for the path that an ontology and phenomenology of social communities would have to take, as well the results that such investigations would presumably yield.

Before turning to my actual theme, for the sake of a better understanding of my procedure, I wish to first present a brief sketch of the task and method of ontology and phenomenology, as these have been conveyed to me in the lecture courses and seminars of their main founders, Profs. Husserl and Pfänder, as well as in private conversations with them. It is to them, as well as also to Mr. Private Docent Dr. Martin Heidegger in Freiburg, Ms. Dr. Edith Stein, Prof. Husserl's previous assistant, and the other pupils of Prof. Husserl with whom I collaborated, as well as the above-mentioned writers and scholars, to whom I here express my most profound gratitude.

1 Introduction: The Task and Method of Ontology and Phenomenology

{1} *Ontology* aims at investigating the ultimate meaning or essence[1] of every object in the broadest sense, whereas *phenomenology* investigates the manner of givenness, appearance, and cognition of every object in pure consciousness as necessarily pre-delineated by this essence. Phenomenology takes its departure from this "pure consciousness" and its "pure Ego," as the most originary, *phenomenological-epistemologically* pure (thus, not metaphysically absolute) starting point for all knowing.

What does this mean? Like Descartes and Augustine, Freiburg phenomenology[2] commences [its investigations] from the absolute evidence of actual lived-experience, of the "cogito," understood in its broadest sense, as well as of its immediately given object in the flesh ("originarily"), in living-through this lived-experience and in the immediate, immanent reflection on it on the part of the "pure Ego." In every lived-experience of this sort, of any type whatsoever, the experiencing Ego is immediately certain of the fact that it now experiences *in the way in which* it currently experiences, that it now has in view, in knowing, feeling, willing, valuing, whatever it may be, an object that is now meant and given in this and no other manner ("intended," "conscious");—an object that is meant precisely *as* this particular "something" in a particular lived-experience in the broadest sense. This intuitive or reflective {2} evidence of "living-through"[3] a lived-experience is one of phenomenology's points of departure. In "immanent reflection"[4]—that is, by a change in attitude or adjustment of the "Ego-gaze," looking back reflexively, observing and analyzing a conscious lived-experience that just arose, is passing by and has passed by (in immanent "retention" and "protention"[5])—every lived-experience is described, investigated, and ascertained in its *essential* content in all directions and in its typology. Phenomenology thus deals with the *essence* of the most varied lived-experiences and the objects intended and given in them in the broadest sense as *correlates of consciousness*. Phenomenology is *not* about, say, a description, as exact as possible, of single, individual lived-experiences and their givennesses in

---

1 Husserl 2001 and Husserl 2014, 11 ff., 18–19, 40–41, 280. See also below, 45/{3}, note 7. [Walther does not specify if she is referencing the 1901 or 1913 edition of the *Logical Investigations*.]

2 Not all phenomenologists concur here; see, e.g., Scheler 1917.

3 Ingarden 1921, 556–557, 562 ff.

4 Husserl 2014, 66–67, 78 ff., 139–140; Stein 1989, 28 ff.

5 Husserl 2014, 144.

any individual empirical subject[6] in all factual contingencies of its stream of experience. Let us attempt to better clarify this for ourselves!

Whatever we know, we know only through conscious lived-experiences, that is, through the fact that the gaze of our "pure Ego" directs itself to an object in the broadest sense, experiences it, grasps it, knows it, and so on. This is why the analysis of conscious lived-experiences, in which we experience objects, and of the manner in which we experience them in these experiences, must precede (according to the phenomenologists' view) all other sciences as well as all philosophy and epistemology, and so on, with respect to these objects. Now this analysis can take different directions, such that we have to distinguish in phenomenology, accordingly, different manners of investigation.

As we saw, we found at first an Ego, that is, a living and experiencing something having consciousness, directing itself in one, at first always presentative, ray of gazing, continually passing from one now into the next, at different external (transcendent), inner, ideal and formal objects, or that can at least do so in principle. In these rays of gazing, every object is meant as a *specific* something (this red here before me, say, as a "rose," not as an "apple"). The object is, thus, experienced in a certain intention, which has its very discrete, {3} sharply contoured, analyzable sense, distinguishable from other intentions and *their* sense. In these sense-clarifying (ontological) investigations we now investigate these different objective senses, that is, the unified What that consciousness "means" with a certain object, respectively, in perception (in the broadest sense of every originary givenness), representation, phantasy, recollection, and so on. This sense of the object, its whatness, the What as what it is meant to be, is now taken *within phenomenology* merely as counterpart, a correlate of a lived-experience, as its "meaning" or intention, *never,* however, as something existing in itself, something absolute. Phenomenology, thus, does not investigate how something is in and for itself, but instead in the manner in which it is meant by consciousness or in the manner in which it gives itself to it. Indeed, consciousness can thus ascertain that something is meant as being, as existing, as autonomous in being and existence and how it is meant and given. However, phenomenology can *never* say anything about whether the so-meant is also *real*—this is, rather, the task of epistemology and metaphysics. At best, the phenomenologist can only illuminate this much: in what types of conscious lived-experiences something will have to be given, in order for it to display itself as existing in any sense whatsoever—for instance, as being-actual—to consciousness, such that its intention toward its being can fulfill itself most evidently, adequately and originarily. Phenomenology thus does *not* investigate (actual) being

---

6 Husserl 2014, 96 ff.; Stein 1989, 37 ff.

and the actual and otherwise *existing* essence of the different objects,[7] insofar as
this essence and being of whichever sort may appear in phenomenology among
other objects as what is intended, as what is meant in certain lived-experiences
—precisely those that deal with these (e. g., in the positing of existence or of the
intuition and analyses of essences)—as its counterpart. The *region* of phenomenology {4} thus does not coincide with the sum of all essences of all conceivable objects; the latter is, rather, the region of the different *regional ontologies*. This, of
course, does not preclude that the intuition of essences plays a large role as *method*
in phenomenology, for phenomenology does not wish to deal with certain factici-
ties of consciousness and empirical-contingent individual lived-experiences, but
wishes to investigate their essence, essential differences, and structural intercon-
nections. *Thus, phenomenology is itself a science of essences,*[8] *which deals with
the essence of the object-constituting consciousness in the broadest sense.* (Thus,
not only does it deal with the consciousness "of" theoretical objects, but also
with the consciousness of aesthetic, ethical, practical, religious, and so on, objects.).
To this extent, it stands alongside other sciences of essences and different ontologies. But since phenomenology, on the other hand, investigates, among other
things, every grasping and givenness of essences, thus also essences of conscious
lived-experiences, it is superior to all other sciences of essences and ontologies,
also superior to itself as science of essences. This has to be rigorously kept in
mind in view of the constant confusion between phenomenology and ontology,[9]
of the phenomenological and the ontological-eidetic attitude and method, especially the confusion between the so-called phenomenological suspension or reduction
vis-à-vis the "eidetic" suspension or reduction practiced by the ontologies. The ontologies, to be sure, abstract from everything empirically-contingent, from all fac-
ticities, in order to bring to givenness pure essences, in order to grasp the pure

---

7 On essence, (apart from Husserl) Hering 2021. Then also Aristotle's *entelecheia, ousia, to ti en
einai* (*Metaphysics*, ch. 4 ff.). In his doctrine of the eidos and the eidetic reduction, Husserl connects
to Plato. Yet, the Husserlian essence is distinguished from Plato's ideas in that he does not ascribe
to it, as Plato, an actual existence, independent of its actual bearer and its being, even as he as-
cribes to it a separate manner of cognition and being. But just as little as Aristotle's entelechy,
the Husserlian essence is not *a priori* the essence in its *actual* embodiment (*Metaphysics*, ch. 6,
1031a–1031b). Husserl rather designates it as "ideal possibility" that can equally be grasped in
phantasy modifications.
8 Husserl 2014, 109 ff., 119 ff., 134 ff., 266.
9 A confusion to which also, e. g., Scheler succumbs in his article "On the Essence of Philosophy,"
(1917, 49 ff.) and *Formalism in Ethics and Non-Formal Ethics of Values* (1973a, 48 – 50), and also August Messer in his *Contemporary Philosophy* (1918, 104 ff.). [August Messer (1867–1937) was a professor of philosophy and psychology at the University of Gießen and a member of the Würzburg
School of psychology.]

"What" of the different objects without regard to their empirical embodiment. Yet, they do not grasp these essences merely as correlates of certain conscious lived-experiences, but precisely as pure essences in their own, genuine sense. They, too, thus reduce the individual givennesses, yet only to pure essences, but not to mere counterparts of lived-experiences purified of all empirical admixtures, in the way in which the *phenomenological* {5} reduction does it, in contradistinction to the ontological, *eidetic* reduction.[10]

After performing the eidetic reduction, the different formal and material ontologies now investigate the essences of all formal and material objects of any sort whatsoever in their different levels of generality and, thus, order themselves into investigations of regional,[11] general, specific, and "individual" essences.[12] Thus, for example, the ontology of living creature would have to investigate the whatness, the essence of living creature "as such," then of the different genera, species, types, and so on, of living creatures, all the way down to the essence of the most primitive essence of a particular individual living creature belonging only to it, if there is such a thing. Similarly with other ontologies, like, for instance, the ontology of social communities. The ontologies must bring all such essences to the most clear and distinct givenness possible, to bring to an essential intuition[13] all of them in their peculiarity and their essential constitution, according to their essential characteristics (in their *ontological* "constitution"). The ontologies must present, investigate, and analyze them.

Now there are different manners of proceeding in these different analyses of essences. Regarding the individual, but also some general essences, we are dealing with so-called primal phenomena, ultimate givennesses that can no longer be traced back to something else, further analyzed or defined by something else. One can only "have" them or "not have" them. Strictly speaking, one can also not explain them to others, although one can entice others {6} to perhaps also

---

10 Husserl 2014, 5, 13, 124 ff.
11 Husserl 2014, 31–32, 107, 129–130, 296–297, 305–306.
12 Strictly speaking, individual essences do not exist for Husserl, yet to us it appears necessary to expand the concept of eidos in this sense, following Pfänder. We understand this claim as maintaining that every eidos that can be embodied in only one exemplar, according to its own sense, as for instance in every spiritual person in Scheler's sense (1973a, 371 ff.), in every basic essence in Pfänder's sense, also the essence of "angel" or of a unique artistic creation (e.g., Beethoven's Ninth Symphony) would belong here. *Some* of these individual essences would perhaps coincide, in our view, with the eidos of the "*donnés immédiates*" of Henri Bergson (see Bergson 1999, 51, 53, 60–61). We cannot further develop this here. [The original French version of *Introduction à la Métaphysique* was published in the *Revue de métaphysique et de morale* (1903).]
13 Husserl 2014, 11 ff., 123 ff., 296–297. Also, Conrad-Martius 1916, 352 ff. Also, Scheler 1973a, 48 ff. (Also, Heiler 1921, 7.)

"have" them (to the extent that they are at all capable of this, which is in principle possible for every conscious subject as such, but not for every empirical subject), by demonstrating them to others. This demonstration can now consist in showing them the way, the attitude of consciousness, which leads to the intuiting and grasping of these ultimate givennesses. (This procedure has—in terms of content—a great similarity to the constitutive analyses of phenomenology to be discussed below, with the difference that it does not perform a reduction to mere contents of consciousness.) Secondly, one can identify an essence by comparing it with other, already known essences and by pointing out their similarities and differences in relation to each other in order to distinguish their characteristics. Thirdly, one can also explicate the sum total of the essential traits and elements of an essence (which can, of course, *never* be identical with it) and perhaps the essential ways of relation and the relations of these elements to each other and to other essences, in which one essence expresses itself, in which and through which it comes to appearance, comes to reveals itself. The essential elements and so on converge in this essence and have their meaningful unit in it. In and from these characteristics, the essence constitutes itself: it has its ontological constitution in them.

These essences and their essential traits, however, are indeed *intuited* as adequately as possible, in their (empirically-real, phantasized, and so on) individual embodiments, once the researcher observes these in "eidetic abstraction," thus when he grasps them *as* embodiment of an essence and in view of it while disregarding everything unessential. An essence of any type whatsoever (also the essence of ideal objects) can only come to be adequately given in the best possible manner when it is given as embodied in the flesh. Likewise, it can only partake of the actual existence in an *actual* embodiment, by entering, so to speak, into exemplary embodiments—and thereby into their actual existence in a sort of *methexis*,[14] without, of course, thereby leaving its ideal {7} sphere of being in any way. Thus, the embodiment is no mere "imitation" of the essence, the eidos (the "idea") in the Platonic sense, to which pertained merely a secondary being vis-à-vis the essence. Rather, the essence, the eidos, can be "valid" in an ideal sphere apart from the embodiment. Likewise, it can also be intended and conceived without such an embodiment by an actual consciousness; but never can it "exist" without

---

14 In *Ideas* I, in contrast to his lecture courses, Husserl does not make this distinction in the way we do here. In other phenomenologists it is in part quite common, albeit, depending on the case, oftentimes in different formulations. Here we owe—besides the work of Hering—special thanks to Prof. Pfänder in Munich and Prof. Paul F. Linke in Jena for valuable insights. We cannot, unfortunately, delve further into this here. [Paul F. Linke (1876–1955) was a former student of Theodor Lipps in Munich and Wilhelm Wundt in Leipzig. He has been called an "unorthodox" student of Husserl.]

this "embodiment" in an actual object or the phantasized formation of an actual subject. A "direct," so to speak, partaking in an *actual* being of such an essence only obtains in its actual embodiments in an actual object; it can obtain a derived, indirect partaking in addition in the phantasized formations and images that an actual, conscious subject forms for itself of its exemplars, or by such a subject intending it in any way whatsoever without mediation.

Whoever overlooks this and attributes to the *eidos*, the essence in *this* sense, the genuinely actual being, and only a derived being in relation to its embodiments, seems to us to commit a fateful confusion of the *eidos* with the metaphysically "actual" essence of an object. One may not succumb to fateful equivocations through identical or similar terms, which in each case do have a fundamentally different meaning. Thus, one can, for instance, also speak, of the metaphysically actual essence, of its embodiment in the "world" and of its being "beyond" the world after and possibly also before its embodiment. (Such as, for instance, in relation to Plotinus' divine emanation, or with respect to the spiritual "spark" from the divine primal being in Meister Eckhart, and others.) *This* essence is itself something actual, something metaphysically actual (accordingly also already in a certain sense individual, whereas the *eidos* is always a "general" object, even if it is to that extent "individual," as it can only embody itself in *one* exemplar—and perhaps essentially and necessarily so). For that same reason, the metaphysical essence may not always require an embodiment in order to be real—although it may require this for the sake of an unfolding and completion of its being—something that would be meaningless in the case of an *eidos*. Thus, both have to be sharply distinguished. Of course, one may say that every metaphysically actual essence has its *eidos*, but at the same time it seems impossible, in terms of essential necessity, that an eidos could ever have a metaphysically real essence. This also does not seem to be the case when the actual exemplars of the eidos might have such a metaphysically actual essence. {8} To be sure, this does not preclude, on the other hand, the fact that every object falls under some *eidos* and stands under eidetic-general essential laws and essential relations to other objects, and that, moreover, *these* essences and essential relations are cognized by actual subjects and can be made into rules and norms for their behavior in the broadest sense of the term—none of this precludes that this very fact may have an indirect significance for metaphysical problems. Yet, we cannot delve further into this here, since it would take us too far afield from our theme.

Now, to be sure, the ontologies deal only with the "general" essence, the eidos, of objects; they are concerned as little with the metaphysically actual essences of objects as with the other actual individual exemplars of an *eidos*. The ontologies investigate merely the *eidos*, even of the metaphysically actual essences, only insofar as they do so with respect to the *eidos* of other objects as well.

Phenomenology, as we already demonstrated, does *not* investigate these essences, although it may perhaps utilize them as "transcendental guiding clues."[15] That is, once the ontologies have analyzed and settled on the different essences in this manner, only then does the actual task of phenomenology begin. The ontologies, accordingly, *may* precede phenomenology, but by no means *have to.* (One can also reverse this relation, by starting out with specific sense-clarifying intentional phenomenological analyses.)

If, in ontology the experiencing Ego and its consciousness were entirely directed toward the objects and their essence, by living in them, seeking to grasp them and their meaning, then, in phenomenology, this "natural attitude"[16] is left behind entirely, turned into its opposite, turned on its head, so to speak. For now, the Ego —as *pure* subject of cognition, as the vantage point in every current lived-experience of the now, as the something that is directed at the most widely varied objects as knowing, feeling, willing, perceiving, and thus not the Ego as human, animal, or in any other way qualified and characterized subject[17]—this *pure Ego*[18] now observes its own respective lived-experiences, observes them themselves in {9} all their constitutive parts and seeks to investigate them and grasp them in their essence.

The phenomenologist places himself into this "zero point of cognition" and observes all objects in the broadest sense (thus also the psycho-spiritual ones, such as soul, personality, and so on)[19] merely now as meant, as intended objects of certain types of lived-experiences and continual series of lived-experiences, without any regard as to how they are or exist in themselves, in the external world or in any other ontic spheres. For their existence and ontic mode *external to consciousness,* and all that we know about them from research in the non-phenomenological attitude, now becomes radically bracketed, suspended in the so-called *phenomenological reduction.*[20] (This does not mean, to be sure, that existence is doubted or held to be false. All that happens is that it is "excluded," since it belongs to a different sphere, another "world" from that of consciousness.) The phenomenologist may not in any way presuppose cognitions derived from any of these other atti-

---

15 Husserl 2014, 296.
16 Husserl 2014, 3, 48 ff.
17 Husserl 2014, 90, 100, 154; Stein 1917, 4 – 5, 39 – 40.
18 Husserl 2014, 82, 105 – 106, 153 – 154, 158, 184; Stein 1989, 38 – 39; Natorp 1912, 3 – 4; and our (unpublished) lecture for the Freiburg Phenomenological Society, "On the Problematic of Husserl's Pure Ego." [This lecture is no longer extant. Walther lent a hand-written copy of it to an acquaintance, who lost the manuscript. See the Translators' Introduction, 11.]
19 Stein 1989, 42 – 43, 96 ff.
20 Husserl 2014, 4, 55, 57 ff., 91, 104, 107, 133, 196, 266; Stein 1989, 3 ff.

tudes, although what ontologies investigate as the whatness of an object, as we already saw, the phenomenologist also investigates, among other things, in *intentional analysis* as the *meaning meant*, as *intentional correlate* of a lived-experience.

If we now survey these objects and their senses from the standpoint of phenomenology, then we find that they, for the most part, do not give themselves in a single, isolated, static lived-experience. They are not given completely, adequately, clearly and in the flesh (originarily) in a *single Ego*-gaze, but rather every givenness in the moment also contains, besides what is originarily given, "empty components."[21] (Thus, for instance, the front side of a bodily object is given originarily and adequately, but not the back side: the latter is only "co"-meant in empty components.) The essence of every object—of any type whatsoever—now prescribes to consciousness, in which manner it can bring to fulfillment, as adequately and originarily as possible, its intention toward this object, the manner in which the empty components can be transformed, in continual syntheses of identification,[22] into originary givennesses. {10} Thereby consciousness "continually holds" the meant as "guiding idea," utilizes the meaning of the objects as a "transcendental clue." This constitution of objects, prescribed to consciousness through the meaning and essence of the object, in continuous series of lived-experiences (motivational complexes), connected through the same intentional meaning, this *"constitution"*[23] of the objects, prescribed through its essence, *in consciousness* (not to be mistaken with the *ontological constitution* of an object or of an essence in its essential traits and of the *actual constitution* of an actual individual object in its actual traits), this is now what *constitutive phenomenology* has to investigate for all basic types or regions of objects.

Besides phenomenology's intentional and constitutive analysis, we must briefly mention the differences between *noetic* and *noematic analysis*.[24] (To be sure, all these different types of analyses within phenomenology are intertwined with each other, interpenetrate, and mutually illuminate one another.) The noetic analysis deals with all that has to do with the Ego, that which is experienced in the lived-experience in the strict sense, thus, e.g., the Ego's turning-of-attention, but also intentionality, the "brightness," the "velocity of the flow," the "force," the characters of "vacillating" and so on of lived-experiences as such.[25] The noematic analysis, on the other hand, deals with the "objective" side of the lived-experiences, the

---

21 Husserl 2014, 123, 274–275; also, Schapp 1910.
22 Husserl 2014, 71–71, 75, 77–78, 148, 169–170, 180–, 194 ff., 248 ff., 267 ff., 288–289, 300 ff.
23 Husserl 2014, 91, 196 ff., 199, 269, 296 ff., 306 ff.
24 Husserl 2014, 172 ff., 198 ff., 254 ff.
25 Pfänder 1913, 38; 1916, 1 ff., 59 ff.; n.d.-b. [Concerning Pfänder's *Fundamentals of Human Psychology* (n.d.-b), see the Translators' Introduction, 8.]

objects, purely *as* meant, intended objects, taken as correlates of lived-experiences (the noemata),[26] in the manner in which they are precisely meant in a lived-experience, and as they are contained in it as what is originarily given with the empty components.

In the noetic analysis we have first the investigation of the lived-experiences as such, in the way in which they are vividly enacted and lived through by the Ego as individual acts[27] in their succession {11}, perhaps also as *continua* or *syntheses* of lived-experiences. Let us call this the *current noetic analysis,* which thus investigates the individual lived-experiences, the moment that the pure Ego lives in them, gazes through them, where they, thus, enter the Ego, where they are "actualized" through it.

From this we distinguish the *noetic background analysis* of lived-experiences, which continues through the lived-experiences, but which does not continue toward their *objective* background of "indeterminate co-givennesses"[28] "*a fronte,*" but which aims at the *conscious background*[29] "*a tergo,*" from which the lived-experiences emerge as impulses, before they enter the Ego. This object of noetic analysis, which thus aims at the background, the "subconscious" (in *this* sense), in which the pure Ego is "mentally" embedded in the manner of lived-experiencing, we now call *background reflection or reflection on being-embedded.*

Let us get clearer on the meaning of the method that we wish to apply, especially in our further proceedings, besides the noematic-intentional analyses.

In *pure* consciousness, as already shown, we always encounter the *pure Ego,* which gazes and experiences, actualizes lived-experiences (in the sense of Husserl), and besides this a stream of consciousness, in which this pure Ego lives. Now this stream of consciousness consists in being (1) alongside the current lived-experiences, in which the Ego currently lives, and (2) in past lived-experiences of the pure Ego that were current previously. In the second case, we mean lived-experiences in which the Ego once currently lived and in which it now no longer lives, but which can, in recollection, once again come to be given perhaps *as objects* (which then, thus, constitute themselves as such), or which perhaps still live on, having a lingering effect on what is now experienced. Furthermore, we have in this lived-experi-

---

26 Husserl 2014, 175 ff., 194–195, 198.
27 "Acts" we take here in Husserl's sense as *Ego*-lived-experiences in the pregnant sense (Husserl 2014, 61–62, 63 ff., 153–154), not in the sense of Scheler, for whom "acts" are apparently only lived-experiences of the "spiritual person," of the basic creature. (Scheler 1973b, 26 ff.; Stein 1989, 30.)
28 Husserl 2014, 60, 162; Leyendecker 1913, 23 ff.
29 Husserl 2014, 81, 154; and our lecture ["On the Problematic of Husserl's Pure Ego"], cited above.

ence the current *impulses*[30] of lived-experiences "in the now," which still linger in the Ego, while it currently is directed toward one (or several) definite other lived-experience, without, however, its "gaze" going through these impulses. (As when one, say, concentrates on one's thoughts, but simultaneously "hears a noise," without attending to it.)

Of course, one has to be careful in assuming that the pure Ego could, in a given moment, only ever live in *one* current lived-experience. {12} This is, rather, only the case in the most intensive concentration, a case which probably occurs much more rarely in the total course of a stream of consciousness, than many epistemologists (and psychologists) seem to assume. Instead, the Ego commonly lives in a complex of lived-experiences that are most intricately interwoven,[31] in which only through reflection and theoretical analysis after the fact is it able to distinguish different individual experiences and to separate them from one another. In themselves, however, they form an unseparated unity whose parts the experiencing Ego, for the most part, does not differentiate between, although they are not always— apart from this unity of being experienced concurrently—united in their intentions by an inner complex of meaning. (As when a facial perception and a sensation of touch are united for the sake of the perception of one and the same object. Moreover, an involuntarily inner melody and the concurrent view of a landscape also form such a unity.) The stream of lived-experiences is thus not only a chain of *discrete* current lived-experiences arising from one another and passing from one to the other, which are moreover surrounded by a halo of non-current impulses. Rather, more adequately, it is a stream of such complexes of lived-experiences, whose individual elements (which, in the course of their being lived through in experience are not differentiated and distinguished) permeate one another continuously, shift, and follow one another. The concentration by which the Ego lives in such a total complex of current lived-experiences, as well as in individual elements of it, is hereby, to be sure, entirely different both in terms of the concurrent or subsequent total complexes as well as the concurrent or subsequent individual elements of one (or several) complexes. Also, it is extremely difficult, if not impossible, to distinguish those lived-experiences in which the Ego lives in only very weak concentration (which are, to this extent, almost not actualized at all) from the completely non-current impulses in the "background." It is nearly impossible to draw a clear boundary here. We thus have, besides the current lived-experiences, always non-current ones, but also current impulses of lived-experiences that

---

30 Husserl 2014, 162, 244.

31 Here we thank Mr. Private Docent Dr. Martin Heidegger in Freiburg for valuable insights in this matter.

pass over into current lived-experiences when they enter into the Ego (by living in them and gazing through them), or yet, which again are submerged without having been actualized. Every current lived-experience is surrounded by such a "halo" of non-current impulses, of which the pure Ego is more or less aware, which more or less accompany its total lived-experiencing {13}, although it does not actually and currently live in them. Only in the case of the most intensive concentration will one find no such impulses at all. This is the meaning of the "pure Ego" in its stream of current lived-experiences, with its background of non-current impulses of lived-experiences, as we find them within the phenomenological sphere of *pure* consciousness.

If we drop the phenomenological reduction, we can now also speak, in an entirely different, albeit related sense, of an Ego and its background in the concrete-*psychological* attitude. Again, an Ego is given to us here, however as an actual (non-spatial, to be sure) "point" in a *real* subject, thus not only as an abstract-formal element of gazing and actualizing of concrete, *pure* lived-experiences, as it is presented to us in Husserl's pure Ego in *pure* consciousness. This Ego is, to use an expression from Pfänder, the "culmination," in a certain sense the "experiencing kernel"; or also, among other things, the "element supplied with consciousness" of the actual mental subject.[32] In every actual conscious subject is enacted, doubtlessly, and only in it, also the actualizing and the gazing characterizing the *pure Ego*, but it is not identical with it. It is, also and especially, the power center of the will and the self in the *human* subject that can follow its strivings and impulses, but can also resist or take them up willingly, which can decide, and so on. This Ego-"point," this *concrete Ego*, has, speaking *ontologically* and *concretely,* a pure Ego in itself; on the other hand, however, it constitutes itself—viewed *phenomenologically-epistemologically*—also again in the pure Ego. We thus wish to distinguish rigorously between the *pure Ego* and the *actual Ego*, or the concrete Ego-point,[33] of a real subject.

---

32 Pfänder 1916, 67 ff.; Heiler 1921, 73.

33 Of course, we can speak here of an Ego-point only metaphorically. In no way do we want to claim that this Ego is somehow spatially located at a certain place in the brain or would at all times have to be: we leave all these and other views completely unsettled. Just as little are we claiming that we are dealing here with an element that is completely severed from the rest of mental life, only externally bound to it. If we want to avoid stating completely misleading views, everyone must, rather, absolutely attempt to seek what is meant here in himself—otherwise we cannot avoid the strangest errors. We must, however, make use of such images and delineations in order to bring into relief the distinct element of a unity that is, in reality, unified. That the latter is thereby in a certain sense "brutalized," is the collateral damage of all scientific research, which is unavoidable. It can only be diffused if everyone, instead of remaining with theoretical concepts and definitions, returns back to irrational reality and grasps it in its complete undivided fullness (albeit

{14} Now the *actual Ego*, too, is embedded in a background, but this background has a different meaning from that of the *pure* Ego. The latter was *formally* determined through the element of non-actuality of its experienced impulses. The former is, like its Ego, something *concretely real*, the "self," in which the concrete Ego is concretely embedded, and in a part of which lie perhaps all so-called "mental dispositions" and so on, in which the past, the habitual and others, and also the future, potential lived-experiences are "inscribed." This self is something mentally real, in which the Ego-point lies and from which the experienced impulses immediately enter into the concrete Ego (although nothing is here yet said about its source; see below[34]). It neither coincides with the real lived-body (and its givenness), nor is it the sum of the objects given to an Ego in the *now* and the lived-experiences in which they are meant, together with a representation of the objects previously had or also of those that are phantasized now or earlier, and so on (and perhaps future ones). The self is not characterized in this sense objectively-noematically, although we may count among this the noemata of all these past, habitual, potential and non-current lived-experiences as something intended, as the "meaning" of the lived-experience (to be sure, not the transcendent meant). This self, which is embedded in the concrete Ego, is now *its* background of lived-experience, which constitutes itself once again in a peculiar manner in pure consciousness and *its* pure Ego, that is, in *inner perception*[35] (distinguished from immanent perception) in the sense of Husserl. Now it seems to us that this *actual* background of the *concrete Ego* constitutes itself for the *pure Ego* through the analysis of the background of the pure Ego, especially through an investigation {15} of the manner in which its *impulses* of lived-experiences arise in it, and furthermore through comparing the types of lived-experiences in which impulses arise amongst them, back into the most distant past.[36] Certain rules for the emergence and expiration of certain types of impulses and their connections, as well as for certain types of impulses, complexes of impulses and their syntheses that are especially frequent, can be gleaned through comparisons and analyses, thus also with respect to a certain individual subject (this would then yield the empirical character of the respective subject, which constitutes itself, say, as a subject in which certain lived-experiences of a certain type obtain especially frequently (for instance, emotions or

---

not necessarily un-*differentiated*), without letting himself be confused by distinctions that scientific thinking can and must make in its work—but also without overlooking and dismissing their cognitive value in the joy of undivided seeing. Whoever is not able to do justice to both manners of consideration and to their respective values in their respective spheres—we cannot help.

34 [See below, 55/{15}.]

35 Stein 1989, 29 ff.

36 See our previously mentioned lecture ["On the Problematic of Husserl's Pure Ego"].

intellectual impulses) or connections of the latter, or also through the fact that its lived-experiences direct themselves preferably toward certain objects or object regions, and so on). All of this constitutes itself on the basis of an analysis of the impulses of lived-experiences as they arise (and arose) empirically-"historically" in a subject's past and present, and through comparing and combining these lived-experiences. All of this constitutes itself on the basis of an entirely peculiar attitude, in which the pure Ego observes its present and past lived-experiences and impulses in "mental apperception,"[37] with an intention toward its own *empirical* character, as it reveals itself in these lived-experiences.

Now a constitution of a very peculiar sort, which coincides neither with immanent perception nor with mental apperception in inner perception, is the constitution of the metaphysically-real essence, the *"basic essence"* of a subject in the sense of Pfänder's [*Fundamentals of Human*] *Psychology* (analogous, say, to the "spiritual person" in the sense of Scheler,[38] the "Ego in itself" and the "intelligible character" in Kant[39]). As we already saw, we can investigate the lived-experiences in their intentional meaning, their noematic object, their noetic quality, or also in their connection with other lived-experiences. We can, furthermore, observe them in their modifications of actuality, or also in their manner of arising in the background. But we can, now, also investigate their *actual* "source" in the actual subject, or better, the "direction" in the self from which they stem. Now there are, here, especially unique lived-experiences—which, to be sure, may be quite rare {16}—which we feel and experience as coming from the deepest layer of our self. These are lived-experiences which, whatever may have triggered them, seem to flow forth from our ultimate ontic ground, from a "sphere" in us which, so to speak, lies "behind" the layer of the self, from which ordinarily the lived-experiences of our mental life come forth (see below, Section 2.3.6 on "The Differences in the Sources of Unification").[40] There are different layers of the actual background of our self, from which lived-experiences can spring forth (a precise "analyses of sources" of the types in which these impulses arise in the self, of the "whence", so to speak, from where they come, would further illuminate this, but we cannot delve into this here.) Now it seems to us that we here can grasp a layer, a "direction of origin" in the subject, in which the lived-experiences break through as a new creation from the ultimate, deepest ground of the subject.[41] (This layer, too, is differentiated within itself, depending on whether we are dealing with emotions, deepest decisions,

---

37 Husserl 2014, 99–100; Stein 1917, 29–30, 39–40.
38 Scheler 1973a, 371 ff., 382 ff.; Stein 1917, 96 ff.
39 [Kant 1998.]
40 [See below, 91/{55}.]
41 Pfänder 1916, 73; Stein 1989, 96 ff.; Scheler 1973a, 332, 336 ff., 386–387.

and so on, or highest insights, perhaps divinations,[42] as they lie at the bottom of all ultimate, deepest, absolute insights and intuitions, thus not mere "ideas.") Through an analysis of the manner in which *these* lived-experiences arise in the background, and especially through an observation of their noetic quality, their "light," their "warmth," their "coloration" (thus in the immanent perception of such an "act" in the sense of Scheler), the Ego grasps its own "spiritual person," its metaphysically-real essence, its basic essence—as a primal phenomenon, radically irreducible in pure intuition—or through a convergence of *these* lived-experiences as elements of this essence with this essence. In like manner, it grasps, through an empathetic immersion into such lived-experiences of others, *their* basic essence in the highest adequacy and originariness possible.

In conjunction with this, we can distinguish, phenomenologically, in the constitution of all *psycho-spiritual* objects between the *inner constitution* that takes place in the immanent and the inner noetic reflection or in the analysis of the source, and the *external constitution,* which is based on the immediate or foundational givenness of perceived, phantasized, and so on, hyletic data of affection.[43]

{17} Two ways now open themselves up for the constitutive phenomenology of social communities (which, to be sure, do not entirely coincide with the above distinction between internal and external constitution):

1. The "external" constitution of social communities, that is, their constitution for the *external bystander,* thus for a conscious subject that stands over against a social community as a closed-off totality. We have to distinguish this from:
2. The "internal" constitution for the *member,* that is, for a conscious subject that finds itself connected to one and in one social community, that feels itself as being a member of this social community.

We would have to presuppose for these constitutive analyses of social communities, to be sure, a completely worked-out ontology and phenomenology of human personhood,[44] a phenomenological analysis of empathy as the cognition

---

42 Stein 1989, 107.

43 Husserl 2014, 63, 72–73, 165 ff., 194 ff., 197–198, 267.

44 Here, we build almost exclusively on Pfänder's *Fundamentals of Human Psychology* (n.d.-b), which is unfortunately as of yet unpublished; also, in some respects on Scheler's analyses and the thoughts of Stein, which are closely connected to the former. We could, however, not take into consideration Edith Stein's [*Philosophy of Psychology and the Humanities,* Second Treatise:] "Individual and Community" (Stein 2000), in Husserl's *Yearbook,* vol. V (1921). [Volume V of the *Yearbook* was not printed until 1922. From this note it is clear Walther knew Stein's *Philosophy of Psychology and the Humanities* was forthcoming.]

of other subjects,[45] and an ontology and phenomenology of "society," which is, in a certain sense, the basis of communities.[46]

However, we can presuppose these investigations only in very imperfect form and it would be impossible in the framework of the current work to supply them all ourselves. We nonetheless want to attempt to provide at least some pointers and prospects toward the ontology and phenomenology of social communities.

We begin with the ontology of social communities—what we are mostly interested in here—in which we want to attempt to work out the essence of "social community as such" as well as the essence of individual types of communities.

---

45 Stein 1989; likewise, Scheler's "Appendix" to his *Phenomenology and Theory of Feelings of Sympathy* (1913) contains, in our opinion, valuable additions to the work of Stein—despite his negative criticism of her views. [Scheler does not criticize Stein directly in this work, though she is mentioned in the second (1923) edition of the book, with the slightly altered title *The Nature of Sympathy*. There is no English translation of Scheler's 1913 text, and because of the extensive changes Scheler made to the text for the 1923 edition, which serves as the basis for Peter Heath's English translation of *The Nature of Sympathy* (2008), we have not provided updated pagination for references to *Phenomenology and Theory of Feelings of Sympathy*.]

46 Parts of such analyses can be found most notably in Husserl's (unpublished) lecture course *Nature and Spirit* [Husserl 2002]; also in Scheler 1973a, 563 ff.; in Reinach 2012; in the works of Georg Simmel, as well as in Weber's lecture courses and his *Collected Essays on the Sociology of Religion* I (1920). Also, Weber 1981. [Husserl gave several lecture courses under the title *Nature and Spirit* with significantly different content. Walther is referring to the lecture course she attended in the Summer Semester of 1919 that bore this title, which is now published in *Hua Mat* IV (2002). Content-wise, this text largely paraphrases analyses familiar from *Ideas* II (1989). Husserl also delivered a lecture with the title "Nature and Spirit" to the Freiburg Society for Cultural Studies while Walther was his student that is essentially a summary of the 1919 lecture course. This lecture is published in *Hua* XXV (1987). See the Translators' Introduction, 10. Walther's reference to Weber here simply says "Sociology of Religion." Based on other references found in the text, it seems she is referring to the first volume of Weber's *Collected Essays on the Sociology of Religion* as we have indicated here. This should not be confused with the chapter in *Economy and Society* (1922) titled "Sociology of Religion," an expanded version of which is translated into English as *The Sociology of Religion* (1993).]

2 Ontological Delimitation of the Essence of Social Community on the First Level of the Social Community "In Itself"

2.1 The Meaning of the Concept "Social Community" and the Preliminary Definition of its Essential Traits.

{18} We wish to deal with communities, more precisely *social* communities. What kind of communities are these? There are all kinds of communities, thus—first and foremost—of connections of objects into a unity encompassing the individual parts, which are, however, contained in it. One could speak, say, of a community of carbon or hydrogen atoms in a benzene ring and other communities of this sort. But commonly one speaks of communities only in the case of connections of living creatures. But is this already a *social* community? Besides humans, the category of living creatures includes plants and animals, and all kinds of phantasy creatures would also fall under this concept. Is thus a community of plants, such as the ball-shaped volvox algae, a *social* community? Or is an ant or bee colony, a pack of predatorial animals or the famous symbiosis between the hermit crab with the sea anemone a social community? We may perhaps call these formations communities in a certain sense, but never *social* communities. Also, a community of angels, fairies, dwarfs, mermaids or centaurs, and so on, would not be a *social* community.

Rather, a social community seems always to have to count *human beings* among its members. But would *all* of their members have to be human beings, or just one or several of them? A community between God and human beings, angels and human beings, fairies, and so on, and human beings, also a friendship between a human being with his dog or his horse would doubtlessly be some type of community—but would it count as a *social* community? Surely not! We would thus have to conceive of a social community as a connection of *human beings amongst themselves, only* of human beings with human beings, furthermore, on a higher level, perhaps a connection, a community of such communities with each other. But what is a community? What must obtain such that human beings form precisely a *community?*

Already the word "community" points to something *communal,* we will thus have to pay special attention, in investigating the essence of {19} the social community, to what this commonly shared thing might be. One could think, at first, that such a community existed precisely when one can find the same distinguishing external trait among different human beings. And indeed, we notice this quite frequently among the members of social formations that we call communities. We thus find in many associations that their members wear a badge of this association. The members of a tribe and similar formations often wear the same traditional dress, the members of a guild have the same animal insignia as a tattoo, the members of one family have the same name. Indeed, one could thus be led to believe that a certain communal external trait would be essential for a community. But if we look more closely, we see that this claim cannot be upheld. There are communities without such an external trait that would be common to all members—for instance, the closest friendship ties oftentimes bear no external trait —although, undeniably, oftentimes such a *symbol* or *sign* may be a trait of such an affiliation. But then the community, not that trait, is what is primary. It is thus certainly no essential or necessary constitutive element of a community "as such."

Now, one could think such a purely external, common trait would surely not suffice to ground a community. Rather, we would have to assume common bodily traits, for instance a similar facial form, similar build, and so on. Certainly, there may be such commonalities in many communities among their members, especially in the case of family relatives, racial communities and the like. But, on the other hand, there are indeed many humans who have these and other similarities and parallels without thereby forming a community. Likewise, in many communities, their members by no means display any similarities of this kind. Thus, the same bodily features also do not constitute the community "as such," although they may be, perhaps necessarily, found in the members of certain types of communities.

But if it is not the body, perhaps it is the *corporeal life*, which must, among the members of the community, under all circumstance run its course identically or similarly, be it the life in its entire course or just during a stretch of it. But, also, human beings, who have the same corporeal life, {20} by no means always appear to form a community, while, vice versa, human beings with very different corporeal life (handicapped and healthy people) are frequently united in a community. Thus, corporeal life, even it if is the same, does not suffice for the grounding of the community "as such."

Thus, it seems there must obtain an entirely or partially identical *mental-spiritual life* with, at least partially, *the same intentional contents* or at least intentional directions, in order for a social community to exist. This is undoubtedly an essential definition of a social community; but is it also sufficient?

Let us assume a man in China, a man in Argentina and a man in Norway have all three devoted their lives to the solution of one and the same scientific problem, and they have also used the same methods and tools. The course of their mental-spiritual lives would thus have, to be sure, largely the same intentional contents and would be carried out in the same manner. Nonetheless, so long as they do not know of each other, they will not form a community.

"So long as they do not know of each other," we said, so perhaps we only have to add the *knowing-of-each-other* to the sameness of the mental-spiritual life and its intentional contents, as a whole or in part, in order for a social community to obtain? At first glance it could seem that this would be the case. Nonetheless, we believe, this would still not suffice. Undoubtedly, it is absolutely necessary that the members of a community know-of-each-other in order for such a formation to obtain. But let us assume, each of the three men knew of the others strictly intellectually—they know that they are investigating the same problem in the same manner as he himself. Would then already a community be given? Surely not!

But what if, once they were to come into contact with one another, if they were to exchange the results of their research and compare them, in order to come to a solution to the problem "communally," in short, if to the knowing-of-each-other a *reciprocal interaction* was added. Would not here a community be given?

Indeed, many sociologists have seen the essence of a *society* in such a reciprocal interaction of its members and have attempted to derive, from these forms of reciprocal interaction, social types. In this way especially {21} Simmel,[1] Weber[2]—in a part of his *Categories*—and partly also Husserl.[3] Yet, is such a mere reciprocal interaction sufficient for the existence of a community?

Of course, we must ask what type of reciprocal interaction this is—physical, physiological, mental, conscious-intentional—or something else? A purely physical reciprocal interaction obtains, say, when two fishermen's boats crash into one another in impenetrable fog—and both boats sink and both fishermen drown. That such a purely mechanical-physical reciprocal interaction has little to do with a communalization of both fishermen—although they lead somewhat the same life with somewhat the same life-contents—is clear. It is similar in the case of a purely physiological reciprocal interaction. Let us take two students who study the same subject—say, medicine—but who, living in different countries, not knowing each other in the least, meet each other on vacation in the same train compartment. They do not talk to each other but see perhaps in their dress and the books they read, that the other also studies medicine; they thus know of their partially

---

1 Especially Simmel 2009.

2 Weber defines "social action" as all action that is oriented to the behavior of other subjects—and indeed also without relating to the same contents, as their behaving. Weber 1981, 159 ff. This identical content through "agreement" is also not relevant to him (cf. 162 ff.), something that seems essential to us.

3 In his (unpublished) lecture course on *Nature and Spirit* [Husserl 2002].

identical life-contents. Let one of them have a common cold, the other typhoid: the student with typhoid infects the one with the common cold and vice versa, without knowing this either now or later. After riding together for a short distance their paths part ways and they never hear from each other again. Here, too, there is certainly no community between the two, despite the purely physiological reciprocal interaction in their mutual infection.

Since the community is a psycho-spiritual being, we must therefore exclude from the beginning all purely physical, chemical, physiological, and so on, types of reciprocal interaction, unless they are a necessary accompanying phenomenon of intentional lived-experiences or determine the triggering of certain lived-experiences of this sort. (But even then, the intentional lived-experiences triggered by them would be what is most relevant.) A reciprocal interaction of human beings, no matter {22} what type it may be, which is not a reciprocal interaction of mind to mind, of mental life to mental life, of consciousness to consciousness, from spirit to spirit (or mediated), we shall not consider. It can, thus, only be an *intentional reciprocal interaction* (not to be mistaken with an intended-deliberate reciprocal interaction) or at least a mental reciprocal interaction with intentional components.

What do we mean by this? We wish to conceive this in the broadest sense, in that the mental-spiritual being and behavior, in the broadest sense, of a (human) subject through some kind of intentional lived-experiences, in the broadest sense, of another human subject has some kind of influence on *its* mental-spiritual being and behavior and that the being and behavior of this second subject (in itself and from the very beginning, or also only on the basis of a peculiar influence through the first subject) also, in turn, somehow influences the mental-spiritual being and behavior of the second subject through its intentional lived-experiences.

But does this kind of intentional reciprocal interaction between the mental lives of two or more human beings, in conjunction with the other elements we have already mentioned above, suffice for the constitution and existence of a community? Two human beings who mutually scold and slap each other in the face, also, to be sure, stand, among other things, in the relation of an intentional reciprocal interaction and exhibit, in part, the same contents and expressive forms of their mental life. Yet, one cannot claim that they form a community, even if one might say they are, following Simmel, *socializing* in the broadest sense.[4] A *communalization*, however, is not the case here despite the presence of an intentional reciprocal interaction along with the two other elements. What is missing here?

---

4 [Simmel 2009, 26–27.]

Above, we spoke of the mental life of communalized people having to run its course, entirely or in part, in the same or a similar manner, and would have to have the same or similar intentional contents in order for a community to obtain. What about this now? In order for them to be interconnected in a community, "communalized," the members of a social formation have to stand, as is apparent, not only in any intentional reciprocal interaction in general, but they will also have to live, in reciprocal interaction with one another, the identical mental-spiritual life in relation to the same intention contents *in the same sense* and in the same manner.[5]

{23} Besides the reciprocal interaction, they would, with regard to the same *intentional* contents, have to live the same mental-spiritual life. Is this correct? Do we have in the case of every community, besides the members' knowing of each other and their reciprocal interaction, also the same conscious contents, to which they all intentionally relate in exactly *the same manner?* In many communities, this is undoubtedly the case, for instance, in communities of students and in all communities where the same goal is striven for without any division of labor. But such communities are only a certain sub-type of community "as such." We would thus mistake the definition of a specific essence of a community with that of its general essence were we to consider this definition as salient for the essence of a community "as such." It seems that this definition is too narrow. For as soon as in the reciprocal interaction of the members of a community a division of labor ensues, they do indeed intentionally relate to something common, but by no means in the same manner. Nor do their mental-spiritual lived-experiences run their course in exactly the same manner. We can already see this within the family—in which, as is known, historically the first division of labor began. Certainly, already in the most primitive family husband and wife are communalized and their lives relate to the same goal: the sustenance of life for themselves and their kin. But they do not relate to it in the same manner. The wife serves this purpose say through farming, the making of baskets and mats and cooking food, while the husband pursues the same purpose through hunting, fending off enemies, and so on. We will, therefore, have to dismiss the same intentional and perhaps also other identical life-contents, and the partially identical mental and spiritual life, as essential constituents for a community!? But, on the other hand, we saw earlier that the mere knowing-of-each-other and the reciprocal interaction of individuals may very well suffice for socialization in the broadest sense, but not for communalization. We saw, rather, that for the latter a reciprocal interaction must obtain in relation to the same content in the same sense. How can we escape this dilem-

---

5 Reinach 2012, 19 ff.

ma? We seem to have arrived at a dead end—or have we perhaps merely left out of consideration some equivocations, which, if we made some distinctions here, would resolve these contradictions? Let us once again carefully investigate our concepts!

It seemed to us that part of communalization would be a "communal" (identical), mental-spiritual life with the same intentional {24} life-contents among the members of the community, and where the members know of each other and stand in an intentional reciprocal interaction. On the other hand, we saw that, especially in the case of a division of labor, in the broadest sense, the lives of the members in the community run their course in quite different manners.

Let us first investigate more precisely what this means: the members would have to have some intentional life-content in common. Does this mean that a certain *actual* object belonged to them communally, say a house or the like, to which they could all relate in their consciousness? Of course, these communalized people *may* have such a common possession, it actually *is* possible that the community rests on the intention toward a common possession or some other actual relation they have in common (as, for instance, a common heritage or a common relation of bondage, and so on), but this *need not* be the case. Such an actual relation, of whichever type whatsoever, to any actual objects may indeed be lacking, without for that reason there no longer being a community. The common intention need not refer either to an external *actual* object or to an external *actual* relation on the part of the members as content, it need not refer to a physical, physiological or mental, actual object. But this is not to say that the content of a communal intention could or even would have to be, as such, entirely severed from all past, present, and future actuality. Since the communities we are dealing with here are *social* communities, thus communities of *actual* human beings, such a complete severance of this content from all relations to actuality in a meaningful community is, to be sure, necessarily impossible. Of course, the object of the common intention does not have to be actual, but it must have some relation to actuality, be it that it is an ideal demand, which is elevated by the communalized people to a guide star for their *actual* behavior (perhaps only within the community), be it that we are dealing with an *actual* working-out of a scientific system, the actual realization of an aesthetic ideal, and so on. Regardless of its form, such a relation to actuality must, to be sure, obtain in the case of the common content of the communal life; yet this is not to say that the meant content, the object of the common intention, would itself have to be at all times something actual. Let us elucidate this with an example.

{25} Let us assume a group of children playing who imagine a jolly fairy and build a temple for her, in which they worship her in a well-organized game. They would form a "community of servants of this fairy." Here, the intentional object of this community life (thus the life "in the service of the fairy") is indeed no actual object and is also not meant as such, because the children know, at bottom, full well that their fairy does not exist in actuality—they are only pretending. The only thing actual here is the children's behavior "in the service of the fairy." None-theless, here the children can be communalized "in the service of the fairy," even though they do not stand in an actual relation to it. It would certainly be a com-munity of a very peculiar sort, but a community nonetheless. Let us inquire what lies at the foundation of this community.

We have here, first and foremost, a common *intentional relation to a certain object*,[6] which is present in all members, in this case, the fairy. The meant object of this relation is the same and also every member assumes that it is the same that the others, too, mean, although it need not be actual.[7] The only thing actual here are the children's intentional lived-experiences, in which they "mean" the fairy, and the (actual) children's behavior which emanates from these actual lived-expe-riences and their intention. But for that reason, the intended object itself (the fairy) is not itself actual, nor does this object (the fairy) stand for that reason in yet another actual relation to the children—except for being-meant in an actual lived-experience. We have here, thus, neither an actual object nor an actual rela-tion (except for the intentional one) of actual objects to the members.

But the content of this identical intention is the same, namely the one and the same fairy. On the other hand, this does not mean that the intention toward this identical object has to be exactly the same in the different members, thus in the manner in which they intend it (mean, think, imagine, and so on). The noema (the representation, significance, sense) through which the *identically* intended ob-ject, thus the common "content" of the members' mental life, is meant, by no means needs to be the same or even identical for all. Only the object {26} itself, at which the noema aims, must be the same, even if it is—within certain limits, see below[8]—meant differently. Only in an ideal case would the noema be com-pletely identical in all members, but this is not required for a communalization. Rather, to return to our example above, the emphasis of feeling or the clarity of the image in the phantasy of the fairy can be radically different in the different children. What is necessary for the community is, thus, on the "objective" side, in the broadest sense, merely the same intention toward the same object in the broadest sense, whereby nothing yet is said about the manner of representation and being of this object. (It can be an actual, non-actual or fictitious formation

---

6 Aristotle, *NE*, bk. IX, ch. 6.
7 We thank Mr. Private Docent Dr. Martin Heidegger for important suggestions.
8 [See below, 65/{26–27}.]

of whichever form.) The intended lived-experiences as well as their subjects are, of course, actual. To this *may* (though not necessarily) be added the same actual relation (besides the actual intention) to this object (say, a common possession, common heritage, and so on) or to a symbol of this object (an idol, a tattoo of the animal insignia, and so on). *At all times,* however, only an (actual) *intentional* relation to the object must obtain, the other actual relation may be added to it, but not necessarily so. Likewise, the noema, in which this object is meant, can vary.

What is now the case with the "the same" mental life of the members? It must undoubtedly be the case that to the extent—and only to this extent—that the communalization reaches into the entire mental life of the individual, that it must be dominated by a more or less current or habitual, direct or indirect intentional relation to this same intended object, and indeed this intentional relation, in the broadest sense of the life of that object—and in spite of all differences in the manners in which it is represented, and so on—, must have the same meaning. (This is not to say that this object—say, in the sense of Heinrich Rickert's philosophy of values—must necessarily be a "value" from the start.[9]) We must, of necessity, express ourselves a bit vaguely, since every narrower definition of what is meant with this "same sense" can easily become too narrow, such that it would only hold for a certain type of community, not for the community "as such."

Perhaps one could elucidate the situation by showing that it must be possible to unite all the mental-spiritual expressions of life on the part of the members such that, *to the extent* that they are motivated through the common intentional object, they do not contradict each other or cancel each other out or neutralize each other. Where this nonetheless seems to be the case within {27} a community, we are dealing either not with a true community or we have "deformities" and "illnesses" of the communal life, which will have to vanish lest they lead to the dissolution of the community. This mental-spiritual life of the different members must rather—albeit, perhaps, in the highest sense mediated—allow itself to be united to a unified whole, to the same complex of meaning.[10]

Let us make this clear to ourselves with an example! Let us take, on the one hand, an entirely uneducated elderly woman living on a farm, who has never traveled outside her remote village. This woman now hears that Germany is at war and that it will have to win the war—all of a sudden, she knits socks for the soldiers in order to contribute *in her way* to "Germany's victory." Thus, Germany's victory is

---

9 [Walther is almost certainly referring here to Rickert's "On the System of Values" (1913), alongside Weber's "Categories of Interpretive Sociology" (1981). Walther studied under Rickert while attempting Habilitation in Heidelberg.]

10 [The term "complex of meaning [*Sinnzusammenhang*]" that Walther uses here is almost certainly borrowed from Weber.]

in this case the intentional object at which her actions are directed. On the other hand, let us take the German Kaiser as commander-in-chief of the army of the *Reich*, and his activities for the sake of a victorious outcome of the German army. Of course, here there is a nearly unbridgeable difference between the vision that the Kaiser has of Germany's victory—and his activities for this purpose—and that of the elderly woman regarding Germany's victory and her contribution to it. Nonetheless, both the Kaiser and the elderly woman refer intentionally to the same object—Germany's victory—and their activity motivated by the latter can, despite all differences, be united to *a common*, unified total action with a unified motivational complex, albeit mediated through many mediate members. (A similar example also obtains in the case of the different partial actions on the part of individual workers for the sake of the production of a pin, as we have it in Adam Smith's classical example for the division of labor in manufacturing.)[11]

Vice versa in the example above, the opposing generals might have a representation of the German army and its victory that comes much closer to that of the *Kaiser* than to that of the elderly woman. Nonetheless, between them and the *Kaiser* there is no unification, since the entirety of the generals' actions and endeavors intend, with respect to that same intentional object (Germany's victory), to foil everything the *Kaiser* undertakes. Their actions thus form no unified complex of meaning in the *same direction* {28} with his. Hence, the significance of the unified complex of meaning, which must obtain in the members of the community with respect to the same intentional object in their communal life and acting, has been clarified: it is like a pervasive leitmotif, which runs through the mental-spiritual life within the community in all of its members, although all of them play it in different variations and with different instruments. Everybody must play, in his own manner, such that he ultimately does not disrupt, despite all deviations, the entire piece with its total harmony, but instead lets it arise together with the other players and thereby realizes it.

From the life of the community's members thus arise, in some circumstances, certain communal formations and products, which, depending on the type of community and their members, are different: so, for example, economic, cultural, artistic, legal, ethical, religious (and so on) products, which refer back, according to their essence, as "works" in the broadest sense, to "achievements" on the part of individuals and communities as their origin.[12] Now, one could think that such

---

11 [Smith 1776, vol. I, bk I, ch. 1.]
12 We take these concepts from Edmund Husserl's (unpublished) lecture course *Nature and Spirit* [Husserl 2002].

products also necessarily belonged to the essential constituents of the community. And, indeed, many scholars have taken these products of the communal life as their point of departure in the sociological and historical investigation and research into these communities, especially Wilhelm Wundt, who especially investigates language, morality, religion, and so on, in their development in his *Social Psychology*.[13] All of these are, to be sure, very important phenomena of communal life, both as products and externalizations of its spirit, as well as in their being related back to the unfolding and development of communal life. However, in our opinion one must be cautious in the investigation of these products of communal life not to ultimately lose sight of the latter and the communities, and to take these products for the only actuality in these communities.[14] Rather, it seems to us that the communal life itself is what is primary and most important, and we {29} also do not think that community only obtains when such objective formations as communal products have come forth from the communal life of the members. (It is something entirely different, of course, when past communities and their life can only be *disclosed* from their products. See below.)[15]

Contrary to this foregoing claim, other scholars think such a community consists only in *actual* reciprocal interaction and the *actual* communal life of its members. Here, again, there is Wundt, who argues, in accordance with his social theory of actuality, that the actual essence of the "social organism" consists in the "actuality of its existence," the common traits of the members consist, "merely in its enactment." "All social formations" are "no dormant being, but processes, activities, and they only possess reality in this manner."[16] (The norm and the product of these activities are, however, morality, religion, law, and so on.)

Were one to think that the communities were fully constituted, when a given number of people stand in reciprocal interaction, knowing of each other and leading, thereby, an identical mental-spiritual life with a common unity of significance as "leitmotif," then such an interpretation does indeed suggest itself. But let us

---

13 [Wundt 1900–1920. Wundt uses the term *Völkerpsychologie* throughout his research to refer to cultural and social psychology. Translating this term as "folk psychology" is quite misleading, as the English term "folk" suggests something quite different from the German "*Volk*."]

14 This is a mistake that Wundt does not commit to this extreme degree; a mistake, however, which still haunts, for instance, many theories concerning national economy. It is Marx's immortal achievement (and that of the Marxists), to have pointed this out again and again in all emphasis. Marx 2024, the section on the "The Fetish Character of Commodities"; Hilferding 1904, sec. I and II; Adler 1904, 369. [Walther does not specify if she is referencing the 1867 edition or the second revised edition of 1872 of the *Capital*. The updated reference to the English translation is a translation of the 1872 edition.]

15 [See below, 156–157/{127–128}.]

16 See, among other passages, Wundt 1900–1920, 19 ff.

scrutinize once again our results up to now! What exactly was it that we have identified as essential, ontological constituents of the community "as such"? Have we
even found what is really the essential element for the community as such?
Were the traits we found sufficient or only necessary for the constitution of the
community?

We found a given number of people who refer, in a certain layer of their life,
to the *same intentional* object in the broadest sense. These people had to have
knowledge-of-one-another and in their relation to the identical intentional object.
Based on this knowledge, they entered into *direct or indirect reciprocal interaction
with one another* and from this reciprocal interaction arose a *common life*[17] (perhaps with common products), which was motived *by that intention* {30} *toward the
same object in the broadest sense, immediately or mediately, in a unified sense.*

Now, does all of this suffice for the constitution of a community? It is certainly
necessary—but does not all of this already obtain in the sphere of society? Is there
not an essential difference between community and society? And if it exists, in
what does it consist? Have we already laid bare the most intrinsic character
trait of community, the essential trait that must obtain everywhere a community
exists, something that is to be found everywhere, in *every* community, and *only* in
it?

2.2 The Distinction between Community and Society

Above, we spoke continually of the "same" intentional object and a common mental-spiritual life of humans standing in reciprocal interaction, also of a *communal*
intentional object and a *communal* mental-spiritual life. But have we thereby not
already included in our definition what we first wanted to search for? Have we not
presupposed what we wanted to elucidate?

Does a community already obtain in every instance where people know of
each other, refer to each other in reciprocal interaction, where they follow each
other in their mental life and their actions, thereby referring themselves to the
same intentional object in the broadest sense? Certainly, we will not find a community where all of this was lacking—but are there not formations similar to communities where all of this obtains that are, nonetheless, not communities?

---

17 The social life characterized by these three determinants is roughly identical with what Weber
calls "communal action" (Weber 1981, 166 ff). [The term *Gemeinschaftshandeln* in Weber is translated as "social action." We have opted not to follow this convention in order to retain the distinction between community (*Gemeinschaft*) and society (*Gesellschaft*).]

Let us take, as an example, a number of randomly collected workers, Slovaks, Poles, Italians, and so on, who work on a construction site. They do not understand their respective languages, do not know each other, have never had any dealings with each other in the past—all they want is to make a living and have been accidentally hired by the same contractor. Now they have to erect a wall. Some bring the bricks, others pass them to the others and finally pass them on to the bricklayers, who butter them with mortar and lay them upon one another. The work must be done in a certain rhythm in order not to be held up—everybody has to {31} recognize the other, and take and pass on the bricks at the same pace in order not to interrupt the continuity of the work. Perhaps the workers also cook and live together, so long as they are employed at the site. Now, do they form a community? Seen from the outside, it might well seem so. Indeed, we have here a number of people who know of each other and recognize each other in their behavior in reciprocal interaction. Here would obtain what, for instance, Weber calls "communal action." Moreover, they refer, in one stratum of their mental life, in a meaningful unity, to the same intentional object: the bricks, the wall, the entire construction site. This partially results in a similarly characterizable mental-spiritual life, which is guided by a meaningful unity, which in turn is guided by the same intentional object (the construction site and making one's living by working on the site). All of this obtains, and the workers know of this. Now, do we have a community here?

We assumed that the workers do not know of each other any further; we added that they belonged to different nations with different languages. Now let us further add that they beheld each other in a suspicious or even inimical manner, as competitors for the wage, as members of foreign nations. Can we, in this case, speak of a community, despite all conscious external reciprocal interaction and same sense of purpose in their behavior? In our opinion, one can only speak here of a *social* connection, of a certain type. But how can we advance here, how do we get from such a formation to a community, both of which seem deceptively similar?

We could, following in the footsteps of Weber,[18] believe that we can find the primal-original essential trait of the community in the relatedness of human beings to each other, in reciprocal interaction. What if, for instance, this reciprocal

---

18 Weber 1981. In this article, Weber is, to be sure, not interested in the essence of the community; to this extent our analyses are *no* critique and polemic against Weber. We are merely attempting to apply his method and criteria for distinction to *our* problems, and *here* they appear to be most valuable and fruitful, but not sufficient. But we are also quite cognizant of the fact that Weber himself investigated—and *wanted* to investigate—different problems and also different aspects and ontic spheres of social problems than we do.

interaction was regulated through {32} "agreement," through tradition, morality, or any other fixed rule—a law in the broadest sense. Would we not then have a community before us? Are things perhaps such that, in the case of social formations that are not communities, the relations of the members are looser, the "probabilities" (to speak with Weber[19]) fewer, that all members direct their actions in accordance with the others, than is the case in communities? Would the difference between communities and other similar social formations, accordingly, lay in the fact that the "probabilities" for a *harmonious* reciprocal interaction, for a regulation of one's behavior in accordance with the others' as much as possible, are the greatest in communities? In a community with a "communal spirit" (we shall see later what this is), the orientation of members to one another and their reciprocal interaction will surely be greater, their connectedness firmer, than in a mere society. But does the essential constituent of a community lie herein? Is it this harmony and the greatest possible probability for the constitution of a reciprocal interaction as such, corresponding to the meaning of the combination, that alone characterizes the essence of the community or are all of these merely *results* and *concomitant effects* of that which makes a community a community, what distinguishes it from other social formations? To apply some of Weber's categories, would, say, a society become a community by clearly regulating the relation and the members' reciprocal interaction through tradition, morality, agreement, convention, statutes fixed in writing or finally—as ultimate ideal—through upholding and enacting this fixed statute by members explicitly ordered to do so?[20] Surely not!

Let us take our earlier example of the workers on a construction site. Let us assume a working order were stipulated that regulated exactly at which pace, rhythm, in which order, and so on, the different tasks were to be carried out, when mid-day break, its beginning and end, occurred, and so on. All of this would be stipulated in a work order fixed in writing, and there existed for the sake of the enactment of this work order an army of foremen, managers, supervisors, and so on—but {33} apart from that everything was as before; the workers would not understand each other, would not know each other, each stands in opposition to each other as competitors, inimically or at least indifferently—could one then speak of a community? In our opinion, no! Now, some may think all that is needed would be that they all internally "align" themselves with the others and treat them as equals. But even if everyone treated everyone else equally, without suspending the wanton hostility or at least indifference with respect to each

---

19 [The word Walther uses here in scare quotes is *Chancen* (Weber 1981, 159 ff.).]
20 Thus, in an "institution" in Weber's sense (1981, 173 ff.).

other, even then no community would exist, in our opinion. But if, now, instead of inner alienation and indifference, even hostility, we added an *inner connectedness,* of whichever sort whatsoever—it can be as loose as possible, having a minimal extension, pertaining only to the common life of the construction site, and having only the duration of the same—to all these other determinants, do we then see a community before us?

It seems to us that here—and *only* here—do we have a true community. Only through its inner connectedness, that feeling of belonging together—no matter how loose or limited it is—does a social formation turn into a community. All social structures in Weber's sense, including associations, institutions, and so on, we would subsume, contrary to him, under the broader concept *societal formations,*[21] as long as this trait is lacking. (These too contain, to be sure, the most diverse subdivisions and variations.) We here stand on the ground of those scholars (as, for instance, Ferdinand Tönnies[22] and Franklin Henry Giddings,[23] to name only two), who see the essential trait of a community in "that *feeling of belonging together,"* that *inner unification.* All social formations that display such an inner unification of their members, and *only* those, are, in our opinion, communities, and only in these cases can one, strictly speaking (as we believe), speak of *communal* lived-experiences, activities, goals, strivings, willings, aspirations, and so on (vis-à-vis *the same* or *similar* lived-experiences, activities, and so on, which may only obtain perhaps in the case of social connections), but for that reason not *all social* connections[24] display such a feeling of belonging together, such an inner connectedness. For that reason, we naturally also do not believe {34} that one should reduce the *entirety* of sociology to these, as Giddings, for instance, attempts. We believe, rather, that this is the most essential point *only* for a sociology, and for an ontology and phenomenology, of *communities,* albeit not the only one, but *not* for other social formations, thus not for all types of socialization in the broadest sense.

2.3 Inner Unification as Essential Constituent of the Community

What kind of phenomenon are we dealing with in the case of inner unification? Above, we spoke of a "feeling of belonging together." What did we mean with this concept? We said it is a feeling, hence it is not an act of cognition or a judg-

---

21 [*gesellschaftliche Gebilde.*]
22 Tönnies 2002. As an aside, we do not follow all of Tönnies' further conclusions.
23 Giddings 1896.
24 [*soziale Verbindungen.*]

ment, as if, say, every member of the community (inwardly or outwardly-express-ly) ascertained or stated that he now viewed these other members as belonging to himself, that he takes himself to be connected to them in the totality of his being, or connected only in part, only in regard to a certain aspect, of his spiritual-mental life. We find nothing of this sort of cognizing or ascertaining in the case of inner unification, even though it may be added to the latter and built upon it. We also mean nothing of the sort of some vague awareness of the other members, no mat-ter how vague, an awareness in the background of our mental life, thus without any concentrated, attentive, intentional observing of the others. We mean none of this with unification, for otherwise it would not distinguish itself significantly from the knowing-of-each-other on the part of the members. With inner unifica-tion, rather, we designate this peculiar inner-mental unifying-with an intentional object, as Pfänder shows in *On the Psychology of the Affects* and his—unfortunate-ly hitherto unpublished—*Fundamentals of Human Psychology.* Let us remind our-selves what is asserted there!

Caused by some external object, there arises in the subject the feeling of uni-fication, and it now strives to unify itself with this object. How does this come to pass? All of a sudden, a warm, affirmative mental wave of greater or lesser power, more or less suddenly and forcefully or calmly and mildly, flows through the entire subject, or a part of it, or only a very "thin" sphere of it. This feeling seems to en-velop the entire mental life and its respective complex of lived-experiences with a warm light {35} and now also penetrates from the background of consciousness into the sphere of the awakened foreground of consciousness with its wakefully perceiving and all-experiencing Ego-moment. It seems to immerse it entirely, to stream through it toward its object. It is as if this wave carried the entire subject with its perceiving Ego, now fully immersed by it mentally, toward its object of uni-fication. It stops in front it, so to speak, and now sends rays of warmth and light back into the object, without hereby dispersing into its own closed-off unity. Or it pours itself, so to speak, into its object, in order to dissolve its own form in full abandon to this object. Perhaps this wave also flows around its object, or attempts to dissolve it within itself, so to speak; be it, to merge into a new unity with it, or to merely draw the other into itself, without surrendering its own form. The changes of the contour of the subject itself and its object of unification, while it is carried over to it in this wave of emotions, are quite different.[25] At one point it seems as if this wave stood against its objects as an equally strong, equally forceful, equally warm and equivalent wave; at another point it is as if a high tidal wave crashed over it, yet at other times it merely stirs up, pulling strongly or hugging mildly

---

25 Pfänder 1913, 56 ff.

at it from beneath. Thus, depending on all this, the subject in this unification feels either equal, superior, or inferior, while it is being carried over to it with its Ego by this wave of emotions, driving the wave, until it comes to rest in it, connected with it, or at least radiates out to it.

This unification is, at first, a current lived-experience, an act radiating out from the Ego-"point" in which it now lives. The Ego-"point" extends here to its object of unification and unites with it into a more or less powerful, warm and intense emotional "stream," which, arising in the background, enters into the Ego or is freely taken up by it, and now carries it over intentionally to the object of unification. The Ego now resides mentally in this object in continual calmness so long as the unification endures.

As shown, we are dealing here at first with a current unification; but before we move on, we must hence investigate whether the elements of unification listed above pertain to all cases, thus even when they are not current.

{36} According to Pfänder, the subject of unification extends its Ego inwardly-intentionally toward its object of unification. This extending-toward, however, will only obtain in the case of a *current* unification; it will most likely be lacking in the case of an un- or subconscious concrescence with the object of unification. Here it appears that the entire process of unification takes place "behind the back" of the Ego, it is as if the object and subject of unification came into that relation of mental residing-within-one-another without any additional action of the Ego, without its current lived-experiencing and knowing. This residing-within-one-another has to be characterized here, to be sure, in accordance with one of the modifications mentioned above (in relation to the proper order and the preservation of the inner-mental contours). (Perhaps it is characteristic of certain childish or subhuman (animal) unifications that they never get beyond this stage that is prior to the actual Ego-activity. It does indeed seem to belong necessarily to the fully unfolded unification of *persons* that it finds its fulfillment, or at least its acceptance, in a *current* unification of Egos—even if it has previously come forth from such a unification and sinks back into a similar stage after the return to habitual unification.) We must distinguish several elements here.

2.3.1 Mere Concrescence

This mere concrescence occurs without any additional activity, influence, and position-taking on the part of the Ego. It takes place in the "subconscious," in the background. The Ego of the respective person "knows" nothing of this, it is completely in the dark and in no way experiences it, because it takes place entirely "behind the back" of the Ego.

(One could ask how one could then know of such a unification at all. In our opinion, the latter constitutes itself for consciousness only in the moment when it arises in a current lived-experience of such a unification, perhaps through it being threatened. Here, the unification, which now actualizes itself, is not characterized as something that only now, in the moment of becoming-conscious, comes about, as a sort of novel creation, but it appears as a strengthening or a sanctioning of a unification that already exists—unknown and unconscious. Only in this moment of the already having-been-present, this concrescence constitutes itself directly for the experiencing subject, it can recover it indirectly retrospectively {37} in certain cases from those manners of behavior, which have come forth from it as communal lived-experiencing (see below).[26] (In these manners of behavior, it was already able—already prior to coming to the consciousness of the experiencing subject itself—to constitute itself to *other* subjects in an empathizing grasping of these manners of behavior.) One may not, by the way, mistake this feeling of the already "having-been-present" with the feeling of "already-having-known-one-another," of having "belonged-together before their acquaintance (or unification)," which accompanies some unifications. Here we are talking about a consciousness, according to which the intention toward this unification with the other (or others) has already, perhaps, a *potential* a disposition in the subject, while the characteristic of the already-present in the case above concerns indeed a *factually existing unification*, not a *potential unification* or an unfulfilled intention toward unification, albeit not yet actualized or known.)

This unconscious unification is to be distinguished sharply from a current unification that has become *habitual.* For the latter at one point was current, has already gone through the Ego, has been experienced and enacted by it. In this form of unification, there is always, in principle, the possibility (although it may not be able to come about factually for various empirical reasons) that the Ego presentifies in its current activity, through recollection, a prior point in time, while something of this sort is, precisely for essential reasons, excluded in the case of unconscious concrescence.

Likewise, of course, one should not mistake this unconscious concrescence with, say, a unification in which the freely functioning Ego-"point" merely lets itself be pulled passively into a unification by one's own or someone else's tendency toward unification, and then resides in it without taking any position to it from its own initiative.[27] Such a unity would also be a current lived-experience, which en-

---

26 [See below, Section 2.4.3.]
27 Pfänder 1916, 73–74.

acts itself in and through the Ego (albeit not necessarily *known* reflexively[28]), while the mere subconscious concrescence is precisely characterized by the lack of this element.

Thus, it seems that one cannot speak, in the case of this unification, of a conscious extending-out and a conscious equi-, super-, or subordination *of* the Ego {38} (although the subject may reside unconsciously in super-, sub-, or equi-ordination with respect to the object of unification), while the other modifications of the unification undoubtedly also obtain in unification.[29] We shall, however, not investigate this mere concrescence more closely (perhaps this is the type of unification Scheler has in mind as basis for his "life-community"[30]). We will also pass over the genetic question of whether such a unification is the necessary presupposition for every other unification and communalization.[31] One would have to negate it outright in the a priori-eidetic register, we believe, although empirically such a relation of priority may frequently factually and historically exist.[32]

We can count, at any rate, this unconscious, subconscious concrescence as part of unification in the broadest sense; it is then, so to speak, the germinating cell, although not yet the necessary starting point, for all other cases of unification and community. In it, the Ego, as we saw, plays absolutely no role, neither actively nor passively. One can only speak of a unification in the stricter sense where such a current lived-experience of the Ego obtains, which then, however, can pass over into a habitual lived-experience.

One can only speak of a unification in the strictest sense, however, where we are dealing with a *freely enacted* unification of the free Ego-point—it is, from both sides, the only unification of *persons* worthy of the name. In the case of a unification of persons with non-personal objects in the broadest sense, it would have to obtain at least on the part of the person.

---

28 Geiger 1921, 29 ff., 41 ff., 44 ff., 83 ff., 94 ff., 105 ff., 120 ff.
29 [Referring *"ihr"* to *"Einigung."*]
30 [Scheler 1973a, 526 ff.]
31 This is a view, which, e.g., Scheler seems to favor, at least with respect to formations, which he calls "society." Scheler 1973a, 530–531.
32 For example, Simmel 1890; as well as any random investigation of the primal history of the most primitive human unions. It is pretty much proven historically that it is always the human being living in a society or community in some form (perhaps unconsciously) that stands at the beginning of history, not the isolated individual.

2.3.2 Habitual Unification

In the case of the current unification, we find a constant onlooking of the Ego toward its intentional object of unification, accompanied by a stream of emotions continually issuing forth from the inner center of emotions and by a constant mental-intentional giving-of-oneself-into (of letting-of-oneself-be-taken-in by) of the subject into {39} the object of unification. It is a constant extending-of-oneself, or, better, a constant being-extended-into, stemming from the Ego of the subject to its object of unification, combined with a residing in it—a pulling-toward-itself or taking-into-itself of the latter respectively, if we are dealing with a modification thereof.

Now, what is going on in the case of habitual unification? Indeed, what is a habitual unification? To approach the essence of habitual unification, it is perhaps best to investigate what happens once habitual unification ceases.

What goes on in this case? To begin with, with the ceasing of the current unification, unification in general may cease: in this case, the subject with its Ego-"point" no longer extends out to the object of unification, it tears itself away, so to speak, more or less forcefully from it and its Ego moves on to other objects. It no longer looks toward the object of unification, and that stream of unification, which, so to speak, flooded out from the center of emotions in one's own self over to the object of unification, dries up—or suddenly it stops of its own accord, it no longer streams, nourished by the center of emotions, from the Ego to its object—and the Ego now pursues other experiential stimuli, directing itself at its own objects.

But what if, despite the ceasing of the *current* unification, the unification itself does not cease—what is the case then? Now the subject with its Ego-"point" indeed recoils—more or less vigorously—it no longer extends over to the object of unification, no longer looks to it—yet the "fabric" of unification is thereby not torn apart. Something very peculiar takes place here! It is as if the stream of unification streamed back into the center of emotions, as if it were now, however, soaked through by something in its object (something intentionally real, of course, but not physically and so on), and this something is now taken up as well into the mental subject, "behind" the Ego-point, into the source of this lived-experience in the self. The striving for unity arose, as a stirring, from the center of emotions in the self, "behind" the Ego-"point," with an intention toward a more or less determined object (or it was called forth from such a "dispositional stimulus"). It entered into the Ego-"point," was actualized {40} by it, radiated and streamed out from it toward its object, found in it its intentional fulfillment, resided in it and was, so to speak, permeated by it up to its fulfillment, was soaked through by it, so to speak, in a way that can no longer be described, which can only be experienced.

Now it ceases. In the meantime, while it lasted, the lived-experience has filled itself up intentionally with its object, has already pulled it mentally-spiritually-intentionally into the Ego, and now—and this is the crucial point!—it does not once again push it out of itself and also does not let it stand out there, outside of its innermental being. Rather, the lived-experience returns back into the self, sinks behind the Ego-point in the self. Yet, it does not return from whence it came. Something essential has changed in the meantime, for now it has fulfilled itself intentionally and, thus, *thusly* it now returns, intentionally permeated by its object. Now it carries, so to speak, a mental-(spiritual) something of the object with it (intentionally) and tucks it away in the self, deep down, behind the consciousness of the foreground and the Ego-"point." This Ego-"point" above it in the foreground of consciousness has, in the meantime, turned toward lived-experiences with other objects, but the previous lived-experience still radiates into these lived-experiences, it resonates, so to speak, through the entire stream of lived-experiences, although it is no longer contained as current lived-experience in it, and the Ego is also no longer aware of it. Nonetheless, this lived-experience reverberates throughout the entire mental life, like a note from an organ, imprints it with a particular coloration and in all lived-experiences, which somehow belong to it, softly rings out. And even if it no longer lingers in this manner, but has sunken, as if into the complete oblivion of sleep, into the deepest grounds of the "self" from which lived-experiences spring, it is not thereby gone for good. Instead, it can be awakened by some external event, or it can suddenly arise again by way of a power that is still within it, it rises up from its resting place of slumber in the depths of the self and seizes, as a background stimulus, the Ego once more, in order to once again fill up the foreground of consciousness.

The noetic (in terms of the lived-experience) range of a habitual unification as such (of course, also of any other random habitual lived-experience) would then determine itself according to the range of the lived-experiences, in which it once again echoes in this manner. But its duration would be measured according to the temporally extended part of the experiential stream, in which it can still resound, without requiring a new actualization. (This *noetic* circumference of lived-experiences, in which this habitual unification echoes, or resounds, may {41}, of course, not be mistaken with the *noematic*-intentional range of the unification, which is measured according to the objects or the domain of objects, which, besides the actual intentional object of unification, are indirectly included in it, because they stand in an arbitrary or meaningful complex with it. (See the intentional analysis below.) On the other hand, there is also perhaps a certain connection between these two ranges, insofar as the habitual lived-experiences also might resonate or echo more easily in those lived-experiences, whose intentional object is arbitrarily or meaningfully, directly or indirectly, connected with the former's intentional object.)

Yet, we must still distinguish several other essential points. We said that the lived-experience of unification takes its object into itself, into the self, mentally-intentionally, into the background of lived-experiences behind the Ego-"point." The same thing occurs, in a certain sense, also in the case of a current lived-experience, which does not pass over into a habitual one. Such a lived-experience, too, leaves behind its "traces" in the self, such that it can be reproduced together with its object as noema (thus as *object* of a different lived-experience). If the Ego, in the attitude of recollection, delves into the background of its live-experiencing, it finds there an "afterimage" of a once-lived experiential situation within a unity of what was previously *experienced* and what was previous *experiencing*, in which, only through a change of attitude, noesis and noema—experiencing and object of experience of the earlier lived-experience—can be distinguished. The earlier lived-experience, however, is strangely modified, it is "gone for good," "forever passed," it stands over against the Ego as an intentional inner object, although other, perhaps similar lived-experiences, can also break through by the recollection of it. (So, for instance, the recollection of a previous joy can incite a new joy about the same object.) What is the difference here? How is a habitual unification distinguished (a habitual lived-experience in general) from a recollected image of an earlier current lived-experience, and how, once again, is it different from the connecting of a new lived-experience similar to the earlier one from the repeated actualization of a habitual lived-experience?[33]

In the case of a recollection of an earlier lived-experience, the Ego turns its gaze toward the background of consciousness, it delves into its own self and reclaims from this what has been experienced earlier and the afterimage of the {42} earlier lived-experience, or these present themselves on their own before it. *Both—noesis and noema, lived-experiencing and what is experienced—*are here the *object* of the recollecting lived-experience. Thus, the recollected lived-experience is encapsulated within itself and has come to an end, it is "neutralized," dead, it has no more mental vital power within itself, which, streaming from a deeper source, could seize the Ego, such that it now could again live in it. If the Ego lives in it again, then only to the extent that it is able to experience, on the basis of a new lived-experience, an object standing over against it as *noema*, as *object* of a lived-experience, but not in the way in which it lives through a current lived-experience as *noesis*, as lived-experiencing, in which it now "stands" in a lived-experience, as streaming through it. And if a new, similar lived-experience

---

33 Geiger 1921, 116 ff.

attaches itself to that recollected one, then this occurs as a *new, never as of yet existing* stimulus breaking through from one of the sources of lived-experience in the self. It enters into the Ego and now directs itself perhaps at the same object, just as the recollected lived-experience—yet *this latter one itself* nonetheless remains irremediably dead and cut off from the living, pulsating stream of lived-experiences and its sources, it can no longer flow in this noetic-experiential stream. At best a new lived-experience coming from these sources directs itself at it as intentional object. It is ultimately past, deceased, only the recollected lived-experience and perhaps the new lived-experience, called forth by its similar, "same"—but *never* identical—object, is alive. Only it springs forth from the source of lived-experience, and only in it the Ego noetically lives. The recollected lived-experience, however, is *ultimately noetically cut off both from the experiencing Ego as well as from the source of lived-experience and the stream of lived-experiences*. It can never again enter *noetically* into them. It can only be grasped objectively-*noematically*-intentionally as something standing over against the Ego.

Things are quite different in the case of a habitual lived-experience. It has also, like the recollected lived-experience, receded into the background, into the self. The *Ego-point* no longer lives in it, no longer looks through it,³⁴ it has turned away from it and turned to other experiential stimuli and its object, in which it now currently lives. The habitual lived-experience thus shares this Ego-distance and Ego- proximity with the recollected lived-experience. But it essentially distinguishes itself from it through its position toward the source of the lived-experience. For it is not severed from it and ultimately cut off, {43} as the dead, extinguished, recollected lived-experience, but is still connected to it, has not yet severed itself from the stream of life. A new, noetic, mental(-spiritual) stream of life constantly flows toward it from that source, although it does not actualize itself now, although it is not lived through by the Ego and the latter is perhaps completely cut off from it, such that it does not resonate in its present current lived-experiences. The Ego is perhaps not aware of it, perhaps it even "thinks" it is extinguished. But this is not the case. It can, rather, arise *itself,* as the same *identical* lived-experience, from the background, from the self, nourished from the same sources as before, and seize the Ego (or can be seized by it) and actualize itself. It is the *same, identical* lived-experience, *not* a *new,* similar one, which might have rekindled itself from its dead recollected image. It is, hence, the position vis-à-vis the source of lived-experience that distinguishes the living, habitual from the dead, recollected lived-experience,

---

34 Husserl 2014, 60 ff., 63 ff., 82, 105, 111, 161 ff., 257.

while it shares with it the Ego-distance, the pushing-back into the experiential background, on the part of the Ego, into the self.[35]

In this way, the current unification that has become habitual is distinguished from the recollected unification by virtue of the position vis-à-vis the *source* of lived-experience—here the center of emotions—while it shares with it the same position vis-à-vis the Ego-point—the latter of which has, indeed, previously lived actively in the recollected as well as the habitual lived-experience. But the essential difference is that in the case of the habitual lived-experience, it can once again live through the *same, identical* lived-experience, while this is essentially impossible once and for all in the case of the extinguished, recollected lived-experience. On the other hand, the current unification, having become habitual, is distinguished from a mere concrescence through the position vis-à-vis the Ego, while it has the same position vis-à-vis the source of lived-experience. Neither have severed the stream of life from the source of lived-experience, but are constantly nourished by it, and both—the habitual as well as the unconscious lived-experience—"lie" in the background of consciousness, while the Ego, living in other lived-experiences, is directed at its objects. Both can {44} also shake up the entire mental stream of life "subterraneously." (The same holds for potential lived-experiences.) The current unification having become habitual and the unconscious concrescence are distinguished from this through the fact that this concrescence has taken place, so to speak, "behind the back" of the Ego and can only be perhaps actualized, lived through, and assented to only in the future, whereas the current unification having become habitual has already (once or several times) been grasped by the Ego, has been lived through and has only again receded into the background after this actualization.

Apart from a *current* unification that has become habitual, one can also speak of a *habitual unconscious* past concrescence (or of a "subconscious" habitual "lived-experience").[36] For the "mere concrescence" can, indeed also, if it has never crossed the threshold of the background of consciousness, immediately die off

---

35 If therefore—this is the necessary consequence—the *pure* consciousness only has one stream of consciousness and one pure Ego (the Introduction above), but no *concrete* background (no self), and no concrete sources of lived-experience, then it can also have no habitual lived-experiences as such in its immanence, but at best re-actualized, habitual lived-experiences. The non-actual, habitual lived-experiences can at best constitute themselves as intentional objects in it.

36 We owe valuable insights to a discussion concerning the habitual mental life (in connection with our discussion above) in the "Munich Philosophical Association." We especially owe deep gratitude to the explanations given there by Prof. August Gallinger. [August Gallinger (1871–1959) was a student of Theodor Lipps, a member of the Munich Circle (as Walther indicates here), and professor of philosophy in Munich from 1918–1935, when he was dismissed due to his Jewish heritage.]

again after it has arisen, as a flame in the center of a crater, which burns weakly and immediately turns to ashes, without ever having glowed brightly. Likewise, it can remain in constant connection with the sources of lived-experience and, nourished by them, "glow further subterraneously" as a *habitual, subconscious*—thus never hitherto actualized—*"lived-experience,"* until it is perhaps actualized at a later point. Such a subconscious habitual "lived-experience" can, in its way, color the total stream of lived-experiences, which flows along in the clear foreground of consciousness through the Ego (perhaps in dreams and the like), by continually shaking it up like a distant, subterraneous quake.

2.3.3 The Distinction between Unification, Love, and Habit

In the previous sections, we took our point of departure from Pfänder's analysis of current, positive affects, seeking to supplement them with an investigation of subconscious and habitual unification. We must get clear on whether every unification already entails such a positive affect (love, friendship, fondness) {45} or whether "affects" necessarily contain a unification, but not that, vice versa, every unification is already such a positive affect.

That every positive affect—be it current, subconscious, or habitual—already contains an element of unification and must necessarily do so, is surely convincing without further question. But is every unification also already a current, subconscious, or habitual affect of this sort?

We may well speak of an inner unification of a mental subject in those cases where the latter feels an object, in the broadest sense, as belonging to it internally, as intertwined with it—be it in the most peripheral or deepest inner strata. We are thus talking about a *feeling* of being intertwined—in some way—of belonging together, of being taken in or, in the case of a habitual unification, of being taken into a specific sphere of the inner mental-spiritual total being of the subject. We are thus dealing with a *feeling* of belonging-to-oneself of the object in some way on the part of a subject, not, say, with the explicit assertion that the subject views, or would wish to view, this or that object as belonging to it. Such an assertion may accompany the feeling of unification, certainly at times it can bring it about, but it is in no way identical with it, since the feeling of unification can fail to appear or disappear despite such a rational assessment or intention.

Such a unification obtains, for instance, when one enters a room and immediately feels "at home" in it, be it only for the duration of the visit in this room or also—as a habitual unification—when one is not even in the room and also does not think of it. Indeed, the intended duration of a unification has nothing to do with the actual spatio-temporal being-together of subject and object of unification. The unification can end even though such a being-together still obtains, but it can also continue when this has been annulled, perhaps is no longer possible. (So, for instance, some people are unified for the rest of their lives with their parental home and all its rooms, although it may have been destroyed a long time ago.) Despite the unification with the room, one will rarely speak in such and similar cases of love (in the broadest sense) for the object of unification. One could surmise that love {46}, in the broadest sense, could only pertain to other human beings, or at least to creatures with lived-bodies, mind, and spirit. But since one can, on the other hand, very well speak of a love (in the broadest sense) of an idea, an artwork, a landscape, and so on, and can do so legitimately (this is, of course, a special kind of love), the difference between unification and love not only lies in the difference between its objects. But what then is lacking in the case of mere unification in contrast to love in the broadest sense?

In the case of mere unification, we obviously do not find that wave of feeling we spoke of initially, which carries the subject with its Ego-point over to the object of unification and establishes a living connection between them. Of course, the unification *can* be established by the wave streaming forth from the sources of emotion of the subject, but this is, obviously, not necessarily the case. In our example above of the unification with the room, and in numerous other cases, there is obviously no such wave of emotions, although the feeling (however different) of "belonging-to-the-innermost-realm-of-the-subject" obtains here as well. What distinguishes first and foremost unification "as such" from its special case of unification, that of love in the broadest sense (as positive sentiment of whichever form) represents, is primarily the fact that this wave of emotions and its source are not part of it.

But what is it that now makes the difference—that *current* wave of emotions which breaks forth from the sources of emotion, in which the Ego *extends itself* to the object of unification, or the participation of that layer in the subject in which the wave arises? Some psychologists maintain that it is first and foremost that *current wave* of emotions (apart from some other elements, such as an affirmative valuing of the subject of unification, which we cannot discuss here), which makes the difference. But then, accordingly, a habitual unification, which has arisen from such a connection of the subject with its object of unification through that wave of emotions, could no longer be called love, but would be nothing more than a habitual unification. That would mean, likewise, a subconscious current or habitual concrescence and past concrescence would never be love. Yet both appear wrong to us. Both unifications, the current one that has become habitual as well as the subconscious one, it seems to us, insofar as, and only insofar as, that emotional sphere in the subject in its deeper or peripheral layers participates in it (see below, the "analysis of sources of unification"),[37] that they are indeed {47} love in the broadest sense, albeit with a certain modification in each case. This is the case if the subject of unification is currently unified with its object in a current emotional wave coming from *this sphere,* or if it is a current wave, coming from this source and taken into *this sphere* and remains lastingly connected to it or, finally, it has concresced through a subconscious unification "behind the Ego's back" with *this sphere.* We are dealing at all times in such cases, we believe, with a unification of love and affection in contradistinction to other forms of unification, simply if this sphere of the subject is part of it. Likewise, however, a unification, of whichever type whatsoever, is in our opinion a unification, but not love or positive affection, so long as this sphere of emotions does not enter into this unification in any form, be it now a current unification (as in the case when one unifies, upon entering a room, immediately with it), be it a habitual one, and so long as it is a unification with the participation of the Ego in the foreground of consciousness, or a mere concrescence.

Although those sources of emotion are not participants in the subject in the case of those unifications that cannot be counted among the affective unifications, we are dealing in this case with a sort of feeling, with a taking-in of the object into the subject and an inner feeling-of-both-being-unified. In this way, we also distinguish the unification in the broadest sense from other forms of lived-experience, in which various objects are combined with the subject, for instance, through habits, or also through any fleeting or lasting (habitual), rational or volitional or other intentional relations between object and subject. What is lacking in all these relations is the feeling of inner "belonging-to-one-another," which characterizes the relation of subject to the object in the case of unification. Also, in the *habituation* to an object, this difference seems to obtain, although here it is especially difficult to discern it, because in many cases a unification is added to the habituation. Nonetheless, there is undoubtedly such a thing as habituation without unification. For instance, it may come to pass that one may be forced to rent a room with the most hideous furniture and to live in it for an extended period of time. In the beginning, one is constantly annoyed with one's surrounding, but finally one "habituates" oneself to it, although one finds it as hideous as on the first day and separates oneself from it and distances oneself from it inwardly just as much as before. What habituation is, is hereby, of course, not yet clarified (the solution to this question does not belong {48} in this context), but, in any case, it is obvious that it can be combined both with an inner separation, or also inner indifference, as well as with

---

37 [Here Walther is referring to 2.3.6, "The Differences in the Sources of Unification."]

inner unification. In any case, habituation is different than unification—and this is all that counts here.

All these types of habitual unifications are now even more important for the grounding of communities and communal life than the unique, current unifications that are immediately extinguished. The significance of the latter lies especially in [the fact that] that the unification—be it one that has become habitual or an actualization of a mere concrescence—has to be brought to the members' consciousness, in order to transmit to them, among other things, a knowing of the community itself that is built upon this unification.

Above we have investigated which of the stipulated modifications and elements of current unification also pertained to habitual, potential, and unconscious unifications. The element of extending-itself, the observing of the Ego, seems, as already indicated, to come into question only for current unification. Contrary to this, the four modifications of resting-within-oneself—the rank ordering, as well as depth, impact, distance, and so on, of unification—only seem to occur in these aberrations, but not the velocity of the streaming and the like in the case of the emotional wave of affective unifications.

The unification that was current and the subconscious habitual one have, according to their essence, a certain intentional tendency toward a certain type of object, although we are not dealing here with a fully conscious intention of the Ego's gaze. The investigation of the intentional direction and tendency of unification is of utmost importance for an understanding of the grounding of the community in the phenomenon of unification. Therefore, we shall now turn, following these general considerations, to a special analysis of unification with respect to its intentionality.

2.3.4 The Intentional Analysis of Unification

As we already indicated, inner unification can direct itself not only at other human beings, but also to all kinds of {49} objects in the broadest sense: to objects of nature (plants, animals, landscapes, stones, and so on), artifacts (pieces of music, paintings, statues, buildings, literary works of all types, and so on), scientific formations (scientific systems, methods, certain branches of science, and so on), religious formations (creeds, "holy scriptures," rituals, and so on), technical formations (bridges, machines, and so on), ideal formations (geometric figures and mathematical formulas, syllogisms, and so on), social formations (certain constitutions, economic systems, certain communities, and so on), supra-human persons, fictitious objects, and so on. Intentional analysis shows that inner unification can be directed at all these different objects and types of objects.[38] Thus, not only can the unification with other human beings ground a social community, but also the unification with other random non-human objects, but only *when*—and this the *conditio sine qua non*—this unification, in turn, becomes the grounds for the unification *with other human beings*. The unification with non-human objects *alone* never suffices for the grounding of a community, as is always possible in the case of unification with other human beings. For the purpose of grounding a community, a unification with other human beings must always be built on the former. In the case of unifications grounding communities, we must distinguish most essentially, whether they orient themselves:

a) directly at other human beings, with whom the subject then unifies into a community; or whether

b) the subject unifies itself with certain non-human objects or spheres of objects and only on the basis of this unification feels unified with other human beings, "who also" are combined with these objects or stand in some other positive ("benefiting" in the broadest sense) relation to them.

This distinction gives us a supreme, most fundamental classification of communities from the standpoint of the intention toward unification. This certainly does not rule out that empirically-factually these different intentions toward unity constantly cross with and mix with one another. {50} Thus, one can, say, unite oneself with another human being, because he has, for me, a very sympathetic personality, but one can also unite oneself with him because he has the same views and goals as oneself—or for both reasons combined. However, one of these intentions is demanded in every instance of community due to the essence of community. In the first case, we shall speak of purely *personal communities*, in the second case of *objective communities*[39] (purposive communities in the broadest sense). A transition between the two types is formed, first, in those cases where one unites with others based on their and one's own unification with another person or a majority of them. (This obtains especially in the case of a following that a leader of any sort enjoys, an allegiance, insofar as it pertains to the personality of the leader as

---

38 In all essential components, we are here sticking to the analyses of Pfänder n.d.-b and 1913. We ask that the reader keep this in mind throughout so that we do not have to refer to them every time. From us stem merely the above analysis of habitual unification and parts of the analysis of the sources of unification (insofar as we do not explicitly refer to other researchers, such as Geiger, Stein and Scheler), and the special application of these analyses to the social sphere along with all consequences arising from this for the social sphere.

39 [*Gegenständliche Gemeinschaften*; cf. 112/{81}, where Walther uses the term *objektive Gemeinschaft*, which we also translate as "objective community."]

such—thus the unification no longer somehow refers back to his position toward certain objects. Also, especially in the case of a "fealty"[40] toward some warlord, or in the case of apostles or followers of a savior, prophet, sage, and so on.) Second, something similar obtains in the case of religious community "in God," which rests on the unification of the members *with* the personality of God. Third, an intimate relation of both forms above obtains where the position toward certain objects or regions thereof and the unification with them reaches into the deepest personal layers of the respective persons, where it must spring from their deepest personal layers, indeed, where it can only ever be enacted by personalities of a certain type. (As is the case in certain religious communities or communities based on other worldviews, especially in times where the belonging to such communities demands the courage of commitment, will to self-sacrifice, and the like, because it harbors dangers for the respective members *as members* (persecution of Christians, the Inquisition, laws against socialists, and so on).) Here, the unification with the respective object seems to be necessarily bound to a personal unification with certain parts of the persons of the members, but here too the unification with the object is what is primary, although in fact the two are barely distinguishable.

Let us make these distinctions clear with an example: Let us say that a person is completely unified with his God, He resides in the ultimate roots of his being and he derives the entire meaning and purpose of his life only from His hand. In mystical isolation {51} he does not care about other humans and their relation to God, because his own fulfillment by God entirely suffices for him. Here, he is thus devoted entirely to his extra-human object of unification and is not unified, on the basis of his relation to the latter, with other human beings.

But it can also be otherwise: That person could, on the basis of his unification with God, feel connected with all other humans who also love God, but he only loves them as "God's children," as humans, "who also" love God, *"who also"* are fulfilled by him, not as these particular empirical or spiritual persons, but precisely and exclusively on the basis of their relation to God. This is the first and last presupposition and the condition of his relation to them. This is the pure "community *in* God," unadulterated by other elements.

It is yet another case, when a person in his love of God also loves all other people who love God, who live in Him and He in them, but does not *only* love them *because* of their love of God. Instead, he loves them equally also as "they themselves," as these particular, individual creatures. In their devotion to God and

---

40 ["*Mannentreue*" is the term Walther uses here, which denotes the concept of fealty between knights in Middle High German literature, where the root "treue" is spelled "triuwe." See, for instance, the *Nibelungenlied.*]

their love and reverence for God, this person sees perhaps the most intimate, most individual basic essences of the others shining forth in their beauty, as in no other expression of God, and, on the other hand, by seeing God's essence shimmering through in the basic essences of the others, their own basic essence also appears to them with a purity never before seen. Then he must also love their basic essence for its own sake, as it is in and for itself, not only as something through which God can appear or that relates lovingly to God as he himself relates to Him "as well." And yet he loves these others in turn also precisely because they love God in their own way, and because they constitute precisely this "transparency"[41] for him, as determined through their innermost, most individual essence.

Finally, it is once again different when a person loves the others entirely *for the sake of themselves*, because they are as they are, and loves absolutely no one else—neither as basic essence, spiritual person, nor as mental-bodily, empirical creatures.

Thus, we derive important distinctions for the intentional grounding of a community depending on which types of objects {52} the unification that grounds the community is intentionally directed toward, and depending on how the unification with the other members is dependent upon their unification with some other object or their relationship to it.

But it is not only the objective direction of the unifying intention that is essential for an understanding of and the distinction between the communities rooted in this intention; also, the different manners *in which* the unification intentionally directs itself at its object is of importance. We already saw above, in line with Pfänder's *On the Psychology of the Affects* and his unpublished *Fundamentals of Human Psychology*, that the subject's rank ordering with respect to its object of unification can be quite different, that it can relate to it (according to the internal sense of unification itself, not necessarily willingly or explicitly) in the form of super-, sub-, or equi-ordination. We must now distinguish sharply three directions of this relation of order, which can vary in conjunction with or independently of one another, namely, we must distinguish the super-, sub- or equi-ordination of the unification with respect to:

1. the object of the community, the guiding idea of the communal life in the sense above, on which it is founded, from which it derives its sense and purpose, its norms;
2. the other members as individuals and in their totality. Here too, to be sure, we have to make further distinctions depending on which position these members have within the community, thus depending on whether:

---

41 Heiler 1921, 44 ff.

    a.   we are dealing with members as such, purely as members in general, or as members with a special characteristic;

    b.   as functionaries of the community[42] in different social positions, or finally;

    c.   as heads, leaders or rulers of the community;

3.   From this we have to distinguish, once again, the super, sub-, or equi-ordination of the members in their unification with the community itself as such (see below, on "The Community 'In and for Itself' on the Second Level"). This ordering is typically different in different communities according to their essence, likewise, as conditioned in part through the individual essence of the members or individual member groups, but also through their social position within {53} the community. (Thus, in the feudal state, royalty and clergy will have united themselves quite differently with the state than, say, the average citizens, again differently with the caste of farmers. Likewise, things are different in the case of the proletariat on the one hand and the bourgeoisie on the other vis-à-vis the capitalist state.) There may also be typical differences with respect to certain tribes, peoples, and races. (One should merely note how differently, say, the Americans and the British unify themselves with their states, compared with the Germans and the French, or how different the unification within the family is in Jews, Russians, Chinese, Americans, Germans, and so on and so forth.)

But unification shows its differences in all its forms according to super-, equi-, and sub-ordination; also, the *intentional range* of the unification is of a different sort depending on the different types of communities, as also in the different members and member groups within one and the same community. Thus, especially in larger communities, one part of it can feel unified with all members "as such" as sum total as well as with an individual in the same manner, even if the community is not already anchored in the empirical-factual or spiritual personhood of all members *as* individuals. Other communities, on the other hand, can only unite themselves with those members who are known to them factually and personally in full concretion, or at least by name, or through narratives of others, while all other members whom they do not know closely or distantly, directly or indirectly, have vanished into a foggy distance, such that they do not know what to make of them, that they—inwardly—cannot really get close to them in unification. (In this context, one may think of Simmel's analyses concerning the meaning of the num-

---

42 ['Organe der Gemeinschaften'; see below, 148–152/{119–122}.]

ber of the members[43] and their spatial relationship[44] to one another concerning the type and construction of the community.)

Likewise, as Pfänder emphasizes repeatedly, it is extremely important to note whether the unification—with other members, with the guiding idea of the community, and with the community itself—relates to its *empirically-factual being* or to its general, specific, individual, or its metaphysically-real *essence.* {54} (Among the members, one will further have to distinguish whether or not the unification pertains to their empirical-factual being or their ontological or their metaphysical essence as human being and as individual, and so on, or to their empirical-factual being or their essence "as members," thus as the *type of person* that the empirical being or the sense and the ontological essence of the community demands and presupposes.)

Finally, according to Pfänder, there is an intentional difference in the unification pertaining to its *temporal terminability,* the duration of the unification, that is, whether the unification, according to its *intended, immanent sense* (not, thus, according to its *factual* course) is *meant* and desired as *timeless-eternal,* or whether one enters into it only for this earthly life, or for a more or less determined period of time. (One may think here of the hero in Søren Kierkegaard's *Seducer's Diary,*[45] who, on principle, did not want to unite himself for longer than at most half a year with any female creature.) Finally, the unification in its three directions can be meant "apodictically" or "hypothetically," or better: with or without reservation. (We distinguish this from provisional unification, which can be both hypothetical as well as apodictic.)

2.3.5 The Noetic Differences in Unification

Likewise, in terms of the noetic, that is, purely according to the inner type of lived-experiences themselves, to the extent that they are not determined through the intentional direction toward their objects and the noematic differences, thus the manner in which the object of the lived-experience is given—several distinct characteristic differences obtain. These—insofar as they are embodied most adequately in all members, or their majority, or the "ideal member" as it is demanded by the essence of the community—can be typical for the whole community, be it regard-

---

43 Simmel 2009, 53 ff.
44 Simmel 2009, 565.
45 [Referring to the chapter "The Seducer's Diary" in Kierkegaard's *Either/Or* (1987, 301–445). The first standalone German translation of *The Seducer's Diary* by Max Dauthendey was published in 1903.]

ing their relation to its guiding object or be it in its inner structure, as it is determined through the relation of the members to each other and to the community.

Such a characteristic trait obtains, say, in the *real, understood in its fullest sense, peripheral or lower and higher sense*[46] of the unification, both in the current as well as in the {55} habitual sense (for the subconscious, mere concrescence of such differences do not seem to obtain). (For instance, the Frenchmen's unification with their *"patrie"* and its *"gloire"* seems easily to revert to something super-real, in contradistinction to the fully real-sober relation of the Englishmen to their "country," which, for that reason, in no way has to be less dear and less tenacious.)

Likewise, the *impact*[47] of unifications can be quite different (one may compare, say, Norwegians or perhaps Germans with Danes, Italians, and Frenchmen).

Likewise, the *warmth*[48] or coldness of unifications is different (Italians versus Englishmen).

The differently unified people and their communities also distinguish themselves through the intimacy of the unification.

Following Pfänder, we see, moreover, that the unification with objects, especially with other persons, always takes place in a certain *inner-mental distance* —it is as if there was a certain, inner-mental gap (of course not spatial) between the subject and object of affection, a distance that does not just obtain between the Ego-points, but, so to speak, between the collective persons as unity of Ego-point, self, and basic essence. It is a difference that also does not coincide with the above modifications of super-, equi- or sub-ordination—likewise not with the types of residing-within-each-other and the preservation of contours (also the "taking in" of the object of affection into the subject of affection, its being embraced by the latter, always has a greater or smaller distance, although it may be quite intimate despite this distance. Only in the case of a unification without contours this distance seems to approach zero). This distance seems to touch both the noetic as well as the noematic and intentional side of the unification, as also its embeddedness into the total subject and its stream of lived-experiences.

---

46 Pfänder 1916, 1ff.
47 Pfänder 1916, 61.
48 Pfänder 1913, 38; 1916, 59.

2.3.6 The Differences in the Sources of Unification

In the Introduction and in our investigation of "Habitual Unification,"[49] we already hinted, following Pfänder's *Psychology of the Affects* and his (unpublished) *Fundamentals of Human Psychology*, that we should picture the mental subject as {56} a trinity of experiencing Ego-center (in the foreground of consciousness), self, and basic essence. The Ego-point is surrounded by the self in which it is embedded, as an inner-mental formation of its own type, from which the different movements of lived-experiences issue forth, before the conscious Ego-center takes them fully up into itself, in either full concentration, or more or less diffusely and "scattered."

We shall once again explicitly warn of picturing this distinction of Ego-center, self, and basic essence as a combination of independent parts, similar to material forces, and the same with respect to the intimate combination of these three elements like a spatial relation of inter-nesting, similar to the internal combination of the figures of a Russian doll. All these images and metaphors are, to repeat, nothing more than that. If one wishes to penetrate more deeply, in order to understand the meaning of our explications, then no definitions and allegories of any sort could ever displace this intuition in the flesh, no more than definitions, measurements of vibrations in the aether, and comparisons with other objects of the same sort could stand in for the intuitive givenness in the flesh of blue and green for an observer who has never seen them. The same obtains here as well. Everybody should attempt to picture what is meant here through immersion into his own inwardness. Then he will not be tempted to misinterpret the three elements (Ego-center, self, and basic essence) in some spatial-static sense. What is most likely —to use yet another metaphor—is that it will seem to this observer as if he were placed on the inside of a spiritual-mental light. In its midst, there glows and shines the flame, which is the source of light, in and on a material body— just like the physical light on a wick, oil, gas mantle, coil, or whatever it may be. This flame now represents the conscious Ego-center: just as it sends out rays of light from itself, onto its surroundings—but also back to itself—in the same manner, the Ego-center means, intuits and grasps (and so on), in its myriad current lived-experiences in spiritual-mental intentions, and they too are able to—just as the flame's light illuminates itself and its rays—grasp the Ego-center itself and its myriad lived-experiences. And just as light may shine more intensely first in this and then in another direction, as it is turned away more or less in another direction, likewise, the conscious Ego enters more and less with its attention

---

49 [See Section 2.3.2 above, 76/{38}. This is the first instance in the text where Walther uses the term *"Ichzentrum."*]

into its different rays of {57} lived-experiences. But the flame has its power to shine —that is, the force that it transforms into light—not just from itself. It is also first being transmitted to it—as, say, the electric current of an electric light bulb—from a source of this force. Even if the luminance as such, the capacity to shine—as in the case of the Ego the being-conscious, the capacity to intend (of knowing-of, "meaning")—pertains to it and only it, nonetheless it receives energies, which it then transforms into this luminance. And it receives these powers, respectively, from very different sides, from different power sources. (As in the case of an electric light bulb, which receives the electric current from different wires coming from a dynamo or several of them.) Accordingly, the lived-experiences arise for the Ego-center also through different "layers," which we can compare with the wires. These can be charged to a greater or lesser extent with energy, with "potential" light. Things are very similar in the case of the self, which we can compare to the network of wires charged with energy. The ultimate source (or sources) of power for the light, the dynamo (or dynamos), are comparable to the source-"points" of the lived-experiences "beyond" the self, albeit most intimately combined with it. But this ultimate, deepest, most essential spiritual-mental power source of an Ego-center and of its self, its innermost "dynamo" (metaphorically speaking) is its basic essence. (Whether there are other sources of power, so to speak, inessential secondary sources, secondary "dynamos," we cannot investigate here.) Through this basic essence, the entire elasticity and qualitative type of its essence is determined, just like lamps, which differ essentially depending on whether their luminosity comes from electric energy from a dynamo, or gas, oil, or simply the wick in the wax of a candle (and so on). Only in the case of the psycho-spiritual subject, do the flame (Ego-center), wires and such (self), and power source (basic essence) seem to be contained in the most immediate, most intimate connection in the *unity* of a spiritual-psycho-physical creature. And, unlike all physical lights, it seems to be able to illuminate its own rays and to take a part of them back into itself, like burnt "waste," as recollected "matter," and seems to illuminate them anew. Likewise, the Ego-center—in contradistinction to all purely material systems of illumination—is capable of turning voluntarily toward its self and its basic essence, and of absorbing the flow of energy, now here, now there, or keeping it at bay.

{58} Depending on the inner-mental "direction" from which lived-experiences emerge from the self, one can now distinguish different "spheres" within it that seem to coincide in part with different loci in the lived-body, in part not—and this is extremely important as well. Thus, for instance, the direction from which an auditory lived-experience arises is given differently than that direction from which a visual perception, a sensation of touch (and so on) "comes."[50] The conscious Ego-center seems to reside at yet another position in the self, if it thinks hard about something without thereby looking at a certain intuitive givenness of whichever sort, although it may "co-mean" it. Here it is, so to speak, "curled up within itself," as if pulled away from all other parts of the self in its own inner being, although *realiter* it does not at all seem to be severed and cut off from it. Rather, the thoughts seem to "arise from" immediately "behind" and in it. Ideas, recollections, and other thoughts that seem to stream toward the Ego, seem, however, not to arise from it in this manner when it is "curled up within itself." They seem to emerge from a dark layer that cannot be characterized in greater detail, even further "behind" the Ego, so to speak. It is different, however, when the Ego experiences ultimate, absolute, completely indisputable insights and intuitions. (There are, to be sure, also non-evident lived-experiences that could be called "intuitions" in the broadest sense, but we are not talking about these at present.) These can be scientific insights or also ethical or artistic insights or intuitions in the metaphorical sense—if only they are absolutely and completely clear and indisputable. These seem to issue forth from a sphere "above" the Ego (not spatially, of course!). It is in these lived-experiences, as if "above" it and yet within its spiritual-mental total being "a light goes off," which now shines clearly and certainly into it, "illuminates" it, such that it now sees and knows absolutely evidently what currently occupies it. (To illustrate this, one should repeatedly recall such lived-experiences of one's own.) We shall call this the *spiritual* (indeed, *non-intellectual!*) sphere in the self. Its rays can illuminate all kinds of questions of theoretical, ethical, practical, aesthetical, thus not only scientific, nature. Not all true judgments and correct cognitions of the Ego issue forth {59} from it, although they all, more or less, seem to have arisen from the "direction" of this "light" on the way to it.

Things are different once again with respect to the already mentioned emotional source "point"[51] of the human self in the subject. We must investigate it especially, in order to distinguish the unifications—especially, to be sure, the unifications of love and affection—in its different layers of depth. This point seems to lay "beneath" the Ego and emotions seem to flow "from below, from the heart" (but surely *not*, say, as a *bodily-organic* stream) "up" into the Ego, so to speak. Here, too, there seems to be an ultimate, deepest "point" from which evidently only the ultimate, deepest emotions can stream forth, as for instance the deepest (mental-spiritual) love for another person (the bodily-vital love issues forth, to be

---

50 On this, see, apart from Pfänder n.d.-b, also Conrad-Martius 1916, 532 ff.
51 See, Pfänder 1913, 39; 1916, 51 ff., 73 ff.

sure, from a different sphere) or the love for a highest ideal, of which sort whatsoever, and so on. And likewise, the deepest ethical impulses of the "do this!" or "do not do this!" seem to arise from that sphere, although they require the clarifying light of spirit (in the sense above) to be *understood* as absolutely valid (for *this* specific individual as such, or for all individuals of this type, this species, or this genus) and binding. Now, all emotions of this sort seem to arise from the "direction" toward this this ultimate nucleus, on the way to it, although by far not all issue forth from it and its ultimate depth.

Now if the Ego-center receives its lived-experiences both from that spiritual sphere and that deepest layer from which its deepest emotions issue forth, or when it resides in both, is being illuminated by it, without currently living in a current individual act of cognition or emotion breaking forth from these spheres, directed at a particular object (in the broadest sense), then we can say: it resides in its *basic essence*,[52] it is, so to speak, "immersed" in it (as a nucleus in its protoplasm —only that, metaphysically {60} speaking, the protoplasm would rather correspond to the self, the nucleus to the basic essence, the chromosomes to the Ego), it lives from out of its spiritual person. The lived-experiences issuing forth from one of these two spheres, but especially those lived-experiences issuing forth from the unity of the two, we shall call "lived-experiences of the basic essence."

Now if, instead of residing in its basic essence and lingering therein, the Ego now, living forth from its basic essence, turns again to other objects and reflexively even further back, moving deeper inside, until it arrives, so to speak, at its own innermost mental limit, the limit of its basic essence, its spiritual person, and if it now gazes, as if beyond itself and through itself—in the sense of that spiritual direction "ever higher," in the sense of that deepest nucleus of emotions "ever deeper"—then it views, beyond its basic essence and yet as if shining and streaming into it, the divine essence. (As in, say, the sense of Plotinus' and Meister Eckhart's doctrine of emanation and the "sun-sphere" in Justinus Kerner's *The Seeress of Prevorst*,[53] as the primal force in "nature," from which ultimately all other powers "arising" in the basic essence stem.) From this ultimate layer in the deepest

---

52 See, Simmel 2010b, 144 ff., 153; 2010a, 96; Scheler 1973a, 351, 385 ff., 420, 489 ff.; Stein 1989, 100. Also, Conrad-Martius 1917 seems to drive at something similar. Unfortunately, we were only able to see her book *Metaphysical Conversations* (2024) during the printing of the current work.
53 [Justinus Kerner (1786–1862) was a German poet and physician. The work cited here, originally published in 1829, contains Kerner's descriptions of his patient Friederike Hauffe's medical condition that caused her to fall into spontaneous spasms and trances, and the alleged mystical experiences she had while in these semi-conscious states.]

inner limit of the basic essence all numinous[54] lived-experiences seem to arise consciously or unconsciously, or at least on the way to it. We shall hence call it the *numinous* or, following Pfänder, the *essential basic*[55] *sphere* in the self.

It is only from here that we can elucidate what is to be understood by the depth of a feeling and of a unification. For this notion can have a threefold meaning, two relative and one absolute. We can therefore describe the depth of a lived-experience of emotion, affect or unification:

1. according to how close its "point" of origin lies to the emotional nucleus of the basic essence, or, stated differently, to what extent the emotional kernel of the basic essence of a respective subject vibrates along with it, streams into it,[56] discharges itself in it;

2. {61} according to how close its "point" of origin lies in a yet deeper, numinous sphere, in which the subject, gazing beyond its own basic essence, views God, that sphere, in which God illuminates the subject and its basic essence, in which the latter, in the unification with him, lives from within it; or put differently: to which extent the ray of the divine essence, alighting the respective subject, in conjunction with the latter's deepest lived-experiences of its basic essence, thus the "divine spark" in this subject (to use a term from Meister Eckhart)[57] vibrates along in the respective emotive lived-experience;

3. or, besides these, according to yet an absolute depth of the subject or of its self that seems to exist. The basic essence itself also seems to be of a different depth in different subjects, more or less abyssal, so to speak. There are light-hearted, simple lads who live from their basic essence and are also united in it with God and who are, nonetheless, in their deepest depth, so to speak, less profound than other, weightier, profound human beings. (This is not to say that simplicity and a certain lightness are the same as lesser depth; heaviness and depth are the same as a great depth. Rather, these characteristics of a person seem to coincide ordinarily in certain combinations, without being identical.) The unification of different subjects' basic essences with each

---

54 Otto 1924. [The term "numinous," from the Latin *numen*, is coined by Rudolf Otto in this work to refer to that element of "the holy" that is distinct from the moral and is non-rational. See, Otto 1924, 5 ff.]

55 [Here Walther uses Pfänder's term *Wesensgrund*, an inversion of *basic essence* [*Grundwesen*]. See the Translators' Introduction, 33.]

56 Scheler's distinction between the different layers of depth, as well as the different spheres of the self, seems to us to arrive at the same result. Scheler 1973a, 328 ff., 345 ff.—The investigations found in Hildebrand 1922, 524 ff./62 ff., which are related to the above analyses, became known to us only during the printing of the present work.

57 [Meister Eckhart's sermon on Luke 10:38, "*Intravit Jesus in quoddam castellum…*," (1994, 158 ff.)]

other or of one and the same subject with the basic essence of other subjects also seem to be of a different depth, although they arise each time from the basic essence. The coming-forth from the basic essence is, hence, not always identical with the origination from the ultimate depth.

Based on these results of this analysis of source-points, we can also elucidate a few other points in the intentional analysis, which can only become comprehensible from the analysis of source-points. For there seems to be an essential interconnection between the sphere in the self and that dimension of depth from which the affect and the drive to unification of the unifying *subject* originates, on the one hand, and, on the other, of that part of the self, the sphere, in the *object* of unification, in which this unification finds its intentional fulfillment, in which it comes to rest or takes roots.

One could perhaps establish the law here, that the unification must always take root in its full and adequate fulfillment in *that* sphere and depth-dimension {62} of the *object* (insofar as there is such a thing in the case of a unification with non-personal objects) that corresponds to *that* sphere in the unifying subject, from which the unification in it comes forth.[58] Thus the unification originating in the bodily-vital sphere of one subject, cannot find adequate rooting or fulfilment in the spiritual person (if we are talking about a human being) or in the metaphysically-real basic essence of its object, and vice versa. On the other hand, the tendency toward unification coming from one's own, deepest basic essence, can seek in the object of unification always the essential, the absolute (thus the essential in the metaphysically-real sense, the *entelécheia,* the *ti ên eînai* in Aristotle's sense, not the mere general concept or conceptual essence, the "meaning" or the idea), also in non-personal objects. In the case of values and ideals, too, it will direct itself at what is essential, since the different depth-layers of the subject (in the relative sense) correspond to quite different value-spheres, respectively. (Scheler's *Formalism* has demonstrated this, among other things.) In the case of a current unification from person to person, *as* person, the unification (in order to find an adequate fulfilment), as it originates from the Ego-center of the subject unifying itself, also directs itself at the Ego-center of the personal object with which it unifies. Of course, it can never direct itself at this Ego-center purely *in abstracto,* but the unification from Ego to Ego always reaches through it, so to speak, behind it, into *that* sphere of the self, in which the foreign Ego currently stands, from which it lives, and takes root there. However, under certain circumstances, an Ego that seeks to unite itself with a deeper sphere of its counterpart than the one in which the

---

58 Scheler 1913, 70 ff.; 1973a, 328 ff.; Stein 1989, 101.

other's Ego currently lives, can penetrate beyond its Ego and its rootedness in that part of its self, into the deeper sphere of the other Ego and thus awaken that sphere—perhaps for the first time in its life. (So for instance, an Ego that seeks to unify itself from its sphere of basic essence or essential basis, with this same sphere of another subject, seeks that sphere within it through the other's Ego, and, if it has the power for this, it may, although the other's Ego does not live in it—perhaps never has—penetrate through to it, to awaken it with an "affective call," such that this sphere now sends a {63} responsive ray into its own Ego-center, after the other ("foreign") Ego has paved the way for this, so to speak. In such a "spiritual procreation" lies perhaps the enormous ethical, pedagogical and metaphysical sense of such a unification.)[59]

Besides this, there is, to be sure, also a unification with the basic essence of the other, a mere concrescence with him, which does not occur through the Ego of the other, but "from behind," so to speak, without its knowledge or participation; as if one grasps in a certain manner the other's basic essence and now unites oneself from oneself with it, without any current contact between the conscious Egos. This is not, however, a "mere concrescence" in the sense analyzed above, since this unification occurs through the Ego proper of the *subject* uniting itself. Only from the standpoint of the united *object* is it a concrescence, since the latter's Ego is not involved in this. Such a unification is, thus, necessarily one-sided, even if it may suffice for the subject uniting itself ("What business is that of yours if I love you?").[60] It is not an intentional (and real), *reciprocal* connectedness, but merely an intentional and real unification in *one* of the subjects. Only the latter is unified and communalized with the other in its innermost self. It is thus merely a community "for itself," no community "in and for itself," since indeed the *reciprocation of unification* on the part of the other subject is lacking.

2.3.7 The Reciprocation of Unification as Necessary Presupposition for Communalization

Here we arrive at one of the last essential insights concerning unification as a basis for the community: that the unification must also be reciprocated if a true communalization is to take place. For a grounding, for an innermost founding of a community, what is needed is not just the unification of *one* subject with all others and

59 Scheler 1913, 69; 1973a, 491.
60 [This is an allusion to the figure of Philine in Johann Wolfgang von Goethe's *Wilhelm Meister's Apprenticeship* (2024), who one-sidedly loves Wilhelm but whose love is not reciprocated. The quote is *verbatim* from Goethe 2024, 139.]

a reciprocal interaction between them, but instead a unification of *every* subject with *all* others, a *general "reciprocal unification,"* which is experienced from the standpoint of the individual subject in each case as a reciprocal unification. (This is not to say that the unification of one subject with the others must precede temporally the unification of the other members with this one subject and with one another. This may come to pass, but is in no way necessarily {64} the case. Rather, all reciprocal unifications can, in principle, occur simultaneously.) Here lies also the ultimate, deepest ground for why a communalization (and a social connection in general) of a subject with soulless objects is impossible—likewise, of course, a social connection of *soulless* objects amongst themselves. All communalization presupposes precisely unification *and reciprocation* of the unification, *reciprocal* unification. All socialization presupposes some form of intentional relation of *response,*[61] a reciprocal interaction. For the latter it is necessary, however, that the objects with which a subject communalizes (or socializes) itself are also capable of an intentional movement and relation of their own, thus that they are ensouled (spiritual) creatures, endowed with consciousness.

This *reciprocated* unification (and reciprocal unification) now also, to be sure, obeys the same kinds of modifications as all unifications already discerned, and it, too, displays all intentional, noetic differences and those pertaining to the source-point, as does the simple unification.

In this context, now, we must distinguish, especially:

1. that layer in the *subject* of unification from which *its* lived-experience of unification comes forth;

2. that layer in the personal *object* of unification to which the tendency toward unification on the part of the subject refers intentionally and in which *it* [that layer] takes root in fulfillment, in which *it* comes to rest;

3. that layer in the personal *object* of unification from which all *responsive* unification comes forth, and

4. that layer in the original, "first" (of course not necessarily *temporally* first) *subject* of unification to which this *responsive* unification on the part of the *object* of unification is directed intentionally, in which *it* [that layer] in turn takes root in its fulfilment, anchors itself, in which *it* comes to rest.

The intentional direction of these respective lived-experiences of unification now determines, as we maintain, certain relations between these four layers, although they are, in certain limits, independent of one another. This holds especially for the "first" unification and its anchoring in *its* object of unification in relation to the

---

61 Reinach 2012, 18 ff.; Husserl 2002.

responsive unification and *its* anchoring in *its* object of unification, the subject of the former unification. We attempted to show earlier that the unification at all times seeks to anchor itself in *that* sphere in its {65} *object* of unification, which lies "similarly located" and parallel to *that* sphere from which the tendency toward unification streams in the *subject* of unification. This, however, is *not* to say that therefore the responsive unification would *have to* stream forth from *that* sphere in the *object* of unification, in which the "initial" unification of the "first" subject is rooted intentionally, and that it, in turn, would have to fulfill itself in *that* sphere in the former subject, from which its initial tendency toward unification came forth. This does in no way always have to be the case and is in fact quite rare. It is yet another question, whether such a relation, according to the sense of unification ("as such") at least, is demanded at all for its adequate fulfillment. "Demanded" not in the sense of an explicit or at least conscious demand or direction of the subject's striving—this it is undoubtedly not—but as a postulate arising from the sense and essence of the unification, immanent to it. In this sense there may indeed exist very concrete, *a priori* demands, so to speak, regardless of how the unifying subjects fulfill or even can fulfill them. Thus, one would certainly deem it inappropriate if, say, a person loved another human being from their deepest, numinous sphere of basic essence, and that other person in their reciprocal unification only sought for empirical-external features of the other, such as bodily beauty, talent, and so on. Or if, say, a person was to feel connected with another on the basis of common interests, on the basis of their own and the other's unification with "common" ideas—and indeed *only* for that reason—while the other loved them for the sake of themself alone, as empirical or spiritual personality. Thus, undoubtedly, certain *a priori* demands obtain here for an adequate realization of such reciprocal unifications and thereby for the structure of a community on the basis of the members' relations of reciprocal unification.[62] But, at the same time, this is not to say that these unifications on the part of certain members with each other must all be of the same type. If this is true for the intentional side of unifications in relation to their rootedness in the different spheres of the self of its personal object, it holds even less for other elements of the unification, especially, e. g., for the rank ordering of the different subjects to each other. What is demanded here is certainly not the *same* rank ordering in the {66} reciprocations —this would only be the case in equally ordered unifications—but only the *corresponding* reciprocation. Thus, a higher-order unification does not demand a higher-order unification of its personal object, but rather one that subordinates itself, and vice versa. A unification that accommodates itself, puts itself into its right order,

---

62 Scheler 1973a, 535.

does not for the most part, demand such a reciprocation, but a responsive unification that takes up, takes in, "encompasses," and so on and so forth.

Every unification and, thus, every community has, in all these directions, its *a priori* delineated structure, although it may not always be empirically realized. It would be the task of an *a priori* typology of communities to investigate these immanent laws for the respective types of community. It would be the task of a social ethics and of a practical, perhaps political and legislative social activity, to realize these in its empirical factual being.

But let us now return to our analysis of the community and its essential elements.

2.4 The "Common" Life on the Basis of Unification

We have already seen that an essential part of a fully developed community is a "communal" life, which, as we can now say, builds on the inner reciprocal unification of the members and is simultaneously motivated by a common object in the sense specified above. Or is there perhaps no longer any need for such a common object for communal life in the broadest sense after introducing the essential trait of unification and reciprocal unification of the members of such a community? Without a doubt, we always have such an object wherever the unification of the members with each other is already in itself founded in the unification with any object lying outside of them. But we saw that the unification can also, without mediation, span from subject to subject, such that in many cases the members of a community unite themselves with one another purely as such, as these empirical or spiritual persons, without taking the detour of a common unification with a third object. What about the common object in these cases? Is such an object always necessary in order to impose meaningful norms on the life of the unified members? It is clear, at any rate, that the intentional founding of the unification and the common object are intimately connected, although they {67} perhaps do not always have to entirely coincide. But is it even necessary that there be a common intentional object, in or besides the intentional founding of the unification and reciprocal unification of the members, which permeates their common life as if a leitmotif? Is not such an object only found, as such, in purposive communities in the broadest sense?

2.4.1 Reflexive and Iterative Communities

Surely, there are also communities where a common, real or ideal, *"external"* object no longer seems to govern and rule throughout their common life, for instance, in a union of friendship, in marriages, family, and so on. This indeed seems to be the case at first sight. But if we look more closely at these communities, there is perhaps no *external* purpose that connects the members—the members here obviously only live for themselves and for the sake of their unification, without pursuing an *external* purpose. Yet here, too, the common life will be permeated and governed by a common meaning, and this meaning is here precisely the unification, the community itself: here the community and the life therein are ends in themselves. Here the goal of this common life is to "live out" the unification and the community of the members, to prove it, to deepen it, to unfold and to preserve it. However, we maintain that one cannot say—because here the community turns back upon itself in its meaning—that it does not have a common meaning, no guiding objective, even if beyond the community and its members as persons there is no external object or meaning. These communities—one could call them *reflexive communities* because of their being-related-back upon themselves—have such a particular object.

It is similar in cases where a part of the members of a larger community are connected, within its structural complex, to a community within this community and are now related to the encompassing community (say, for the sake of its preservation, dominance, organization, furthering, and so on). One could speak here of *"iterative"*[63] *communities.* For instance, political parties would be such communities insofar as they are true communities, not merely societal connections. {68} One could also count among these a community "for the fostering of the German spirit and German mind" within the German people, and so on.

Thus, it appears that an intentional object or meaning common to all members in their common life belongs necessarily to every community only if one understands this determination broadly enough, such that, under certain circumstances, instead of an "object" lying outside of the community and its members, the community itself or the intentional founding of the reciprocal unification of its members can, in the broadest sense, be this object.

But how should we construe the "common life" itself and its relation to the reciprocal unification of the members founding it? We must be careful not to narrowly conceive the concept of common life. We want to understand it, especially, as *not* necessarily a life that flows along *spatio-temporally*, alongside others. The

---

63 Husserl 2014, 105, 202 ff., 210–211; Stein 1917, 17–19.

members leading a common life in our sense, thus, do not have to live together spatially, nor do those current lived-experiences belonging to the common life have to come to pass concurrently—this only happens in the ideal cases of common co-lived-experiencing, especially, however, in the case of we-experiences (see below).[64] But the common life is in no way restricted to these ideal cases.

But how should we then conceive of the common life? Let us start out from Weber's definition of "common activity." As such, he believed (as we saw, see above, Section 2.1, 60/{21}, note 2) that every activity in the broadest sense, in which a subject of this activity directs itself to other subjects, directs itself in its activities *to* them. We had added that such an activity of different subjects must, in our opinion, relate in the same sense to the same intentional object in the broadest sense and that it must stand in a relation of reciprocal unification with those other subjects. But we do not merely want to talk of *activity* in the broadest sense, but instead of any type of intentional lived-experience, any manner of comporting oneself in general, internally or externally, passively or actively, psycho-physically, mentally-spiritually, in the broadest sense. The main trait of the common life, its most essential basis, was, in our opinion, the reciprocal unification of its subjects—no matter what type of unification this may be. Starting from this point, the common life in our sense is thoroughly guided by it, founded through it.

{69} But what does this mean? Surely this cannot mean that a lived-experience or a subject's comporting-oneself only belongs to the common life when it is accompanied by a current lived-experience of unification with one or several people. This would be too narrowly construed. We mean something else. The unification is, as we saw, not merely a current unifying-of-oneself-with-another, but it can also be *habitual*: a unified, habitual residing in the other or others—regardless of whether it has come about through an explicit or current or unconscious concrescence. *It is first and foremost the habitual unification, which (we believe) must serve as the foundation and fundamentally ground our entire communal life.*

2.4.2 The Category of "Human Beings, Who Also..."

How should we envision this founding through habitual unification? As a more or less clearly observed "being-there-as well"—albeit only a vague awareness in the background, surely not in an attentive knowing or representing—other people are always "given," "people, who also..." This is one of the most essential categories

---

64 [See below, Section 2.4.3.]

for understanding communities.—This "also" can be determined in very different ways, depending on the type and intentional founding of the unification, as humans, who "also" value thusly, who "also" have such goals, "also" feel this way, will, think, and so on, as the individual subject itself. Certainly, this "also" does not always relate merely to some *external* goals, manners of behavior, lived-experiences, and the like. Rather, it can also pertain to the basic stances toward life as a whole, the entire cosmos, regardless of its differentiation and expression in individual lived-experiences, opinions, actions, and so on. In the case of people who, precisely because of their essential differences complementing one another (as, sometimes, in the case of man and woman), unify each other, we have, of course, only such an "also," an "also," however, which perhaps points to a higher unity of both, which is potentially contained in them, but which only becomes realized when they form a community. (This will become clear in what is to follow when we speak about the community on the second level.)

These "people, who also..." are always somehow present in the background of the subject, albeit ever so indeterminately. The subject is not only vaguely aware of them but is also unified with {70} them in *those* layers, which the sense of the community demands. It resides in them and belongs to them, no matter how lose it may be and no matter how limited a part of the subject's total lived-experience —and they "belong to him"—it forms a "we" with them. The subject's life, to the extent that it is precisely a communal life, is not just *its* life, springs forth not only from *it itself,* as a single individual, but it arises, so to speak, from its unity with the other *in it.* Here, the lived-experience is characterized for the experiencing subject not only as "I experience thusly," but as "*we* experience thusly," "I *and the others in me* (with whom I am unified) experience thusly" and we are one in this lived-experience of ours. But how can we describe this communal lived-experience, in which the Ego comes forth living from itself and from the others in itself?

2.4.3 The Communal Lived-Experience (We-Experience) "For Itself"

It is not a "we" standing "behind" or "above" the individual person that experiences, a "we," say, that would be separated from the others and now breathed its lived-experience into them in a sort of emanation, such that in this way they came into their self and from there, for the sake of actualization, into their Ego-center. The "we" is also not a bodiless subject of its own that would be grasped by the individuals in a special type of empathy and whose lived-experiences they now make into their own based on this empathy, such that only those lived-experiences would be communal or we-experiences, which individuals would have taken over in such empathy from such a mysterious subject. Nor do things stand such that suddenly, say, a new, "communal" Ego-center, an independent, real "communal Ego-center" came to the fore (whatever one may imagine this to be), which in some mysterious way took up into itself the "communal" lived-experiences of the members of a community as "we" and actualized them. All of this has nothing at all to do with what we wish to mean by communal and we-lived-experiences.

These lived-experiences enact and actualize themselves in the *individual Ego*, in the Ego-center of the individual members. Also, such a lived-experience does not stream to them from a mysterious, peculiar communal-lived-experience-source-point behind their individual self and basic essence. Even if such a thing existed (perhaps in the case of some people's mystical lived-experience or mass suggestion through a speaker), {71} this would be, at best, a special case of we-lived-experiences, and yet the communal life would, in any case, be all too narrowly determined through a limitation to such (hypothetical) cases. Rather, one should picture this case, say, in the following manner: *my* lived-experiences currently enact themselves in *my Ego*-center, they stream to it from *my* conscious background, *my* self in which it is embedded. And yet, in this embeddedness, in this background, from which the lived-experiences come forth, I am not I alone as "I myself"—in the case of communal lived-experiences—but rather I have indeed taken the others into it, I have taken them intentionally behind my Ego-center into *my* self (or they have of themselves grown into it) and I feel one with them (unconsciously, automatically, or based on an explicit unification). "My" lived-experiences, to the extent and *only* to the extent they are precisely communal lived-experiences, do not merely arise from myself, from my isolated self, my I-myself-alone behind the Ego-point; instead, they arise simultaneously from the other *in me*, from the we, the "people, who also," in whom I reside and with whom I am one. I live and experience from myself *and* from *them in me* at the same time, from "us." Already *before* these lived-experiences enter into the Ego-point, are actualized within it, they are thus communal lived-experiences, for they arise already as stimuli from myself *and* the others *in* me. Let us illustrate this with an allegory! Above, we compared the mental subject with a light which receives its energy from a power source through wires or some such way, which it then transforms into light. Let us hold on to this image, then we could picture communal lived-experiences such that electrical currents from one lamp with *its* dynamo machine flow into the wires and from there into the light of the other lamp. Be it that they are concurrently illuminated, by its transformation into light, through the one lamp also from the other as light; be it that they only feed the wires of the other lamp with new energy and remain there, until they are also illuminated over there as light, perhaps much later—just as they with their own energy connected with that other lamp. Let us assume, say, that the energy of one lamp could be transformed, according to its essence, only into blue light, and that of the other only into yellow light, then, through such a mingling of energy, the yellow lamp will also be able to send out blue rays, the blue lamp yellow rays, or that both {72} (or just one of them) light up, and in addition to their own yellow (or blue) light, produce also a green light, light in a great variety of nuances, as a combination of their respective energies and forms of light. Perhaps one could—of course very much *cum grano salis*—picture communal lived-experiences in this way.

Thus, it is not the case that I have lived-experiences arising first from me as an *isolated* single Ego and individual self, that I then compare with those of others, grasped in empathy—especially if I then notice that the others experience the same as I too, just as them—and unite myself only then with these others in their lived-experiences, and grasp these lived-experiences only now retroactively as communal lived-experiences and call them such. Something like this may *precede* some communal lived-experiences, but these are *never* already genuine communal lived-experiences in our sense. These do not come about in such a manner. They also do not arise such that I would take up an individual lived-experience of others that I grasped earlier in empathy and had appropriated it such that it now would have become habitual within me and now, as if it were my own, arises in me anew. Here I could perhaps have the idea, based on a recollection, that I have taken over this lived-experience earlier from another person and how I now could *designate* it on the basis of this recollection as one that is common to me and the other, a "common lived-experience" on the part of both of us.[65] No matter how great the role of such lived-experiences may be for the genesis and consciousness of the community and communal lived-experiences, they are nonetheless in themselves never communal lived-experiences in our sense. Communal lived-experiences in our sense are rather *only* those lived-experiences that come about *on the basis of my unification with the others*, from them *in me* and of me *in them*, from us—*in me, as in them*—even before they enter into my (or their) Ego-center and become actualized in them. This, my Ego-center, is, to be sure, always individual (as is my pure Ego) and singular, it can *never* be "common" to me and others, and yet this in no way diminishes the fact of communalization, for the latter exists precisely behind the Ego-center, it has already taken place in that inner-mental layer from which the lived-experiences arise as stimuli, even before they enter into the Ego-center.

{73} Now one could think that such communal lived-experiences would always have to be limited at least to earlier or concurrent lived-experiences of others,

---

65 Stein 1989 and Scheler 1973a, 526.

whom I have grasped in empathy and taken up into myself. But this, too, is certainly not the case. From this *communal self*—let us thus call this layer—stimuli of lived-experiences can very plausibly arise, which those "people, who also" perhaps will never have. For what has entered into me from the others does not have to be limited to individual lived-experiences; rather, we are also talking about total attitudes vis-à-vis certain regions or life as a whole, even the totality of being (in the case of worldview-communities), or may also pertain only to the spiritual person, the basic essence of others (cf. also above, 55–56/{15–16}, 92 ff./{58 ff.}). (Then we have before us, perhaps, what Scheler calls the "collective person.")[66] Here, the lived-experiences spring from the "common spirit," they enter from the "communal self" into my Ego-center and from there push into the open, my total attitude, in this case, spring forth from the communal self; these are not merely singular current communal lived-experiences, which arise in me.

Let us analyze more closely this inner structure of the individual communal lived-experiences and of the entire communal life, in order to preempt all misunderstandings and false interpretations. It is extremely important to first get clear on the difference between mere *empathy*—as the grasping of any foreign lived-experiences—and communal lived-experiences. By empathically grasping the lived-experiences, states of mind, personhood (and so on) of another person, I have an entirely different originary experience from when I myself experience the same lived-experiences of the other as communal lived-experiences. (1.) In the case of empathy, I grasp through words, imitation and other forms of expression the lived-experience of others,[67] and yet I am immediately aware that *it is not I* who experiences these lived-experiences in an originary manner and in the flesh, that these lived-experiences belong to the other, that they arise from *his* self and are actualized in *his* Ego-center and are given to me only through phenomena of expression. They stand opposed to me as non-originary lived-experiences, grasped by me, objectified, {74} separated from my Ego and are not mine. Nothing changes, even when (2.) I now, by chance and in an originary manner and in the flesh, have the same lived-experiences as those that I grasp in the other. Despite this identity of the lived-experiences, *they stand alongside one another as belonging to different subjects.* I experience this way, the other that way, both might perchance be the same by accident and I am immediately aware of this identity in experiencing my own lived-experience and in the empathic grasping of the other's lived-experience. Nonetheless, *I stand for myself,* together with my lived-experience, stand within myself, *closed off and separated, next to* the other, who is equally

---

66 Scheler 1973a, 533 ff.
67 Stein 1989.

closed off and separated within himself. There is an intentional "wall," so to speak, an inner-mental "gap," an "in between" (only metaphorically, of course, non-spatial) between myself and the other. (3.) Also in the case of *sympathizing* (and co-lived-experiencing in the sense of Reinach)[68] things are no different. Here I grasp in empathy the lived-experience of another and experience it "with" him. I experience originarily the same as he, but "for his sake," the relation of my lived-experience *to him*, in this sense, is essential here. I myself, only *for myself,* would *not* enact this experience *in this way*.[69] I grasp in empathy, say, that another (now) feels joy about something. Perhaps the object of his joy is not a matter of joy for me, but is perhaps indifferent, if not downright unpleasant to me. But *because* he feels joy (this "because he" is essential), I now also feel joy with him and *for him*. (Also, we must not mistake an empathizing connected to one's own experiencing the lived-experience of the other belonging to the same type of lived-experience as *his* lived-experiencing; one may not mistake this for the following case, as when, say, someone feels joy and feels joy *about his joy,* by grasping in empathy his joy. This is again something completely different, as when I feel joy *with* him, *for* his sake, or when I feel joy about the same thing as he.) Of course, sympathizing presupposes a form of inner unity with the other, but it is a different sort of unity from the case of communal lived-experiencing, where the parties originarily experience, stemming from the same layer, in the feeling of their unity, the same thing or something similar, in the same or in a similar manner, concurrently or later. For in this case, I do not experience only *for the sake of the other* and *with* him. I concurrently experience {75} also *for the sake of myself,* for regarding and concerning the we, it also concerns *myself for myself as part of the we*, of the community, not only the other or "for the other."

Compared to sympathizing (and so on), communal lived-experiencing is, thus, something different in principle. Let us analyze it more closely! Let us grasp in empathy someone else's lived-experience. Now this lived-experience passes over into a communal lived-experience. (It could, of course, arise from the beginning as such, but let us assume, to work out the difference clearly, that it first passes over into a communal lived-experience.) What changes then? Let us say I view with another person a vista. Hereby, he explicitly asserts his enthusiasm about the beautiful vista. In empathy I grasp his lived-experience, it stands opposed to me as *foreign* lived-experience, not belonging to me originarily and in the flesh,[70] nonetheless I am perhaps equally enthused by the vista—or, I completely

---

68 Reinach 2012, 84–85.
69 Scheler 1913, 10–11.
70 Stein 1989, 10.

give myself over to his enthusiasm, I co-experience it *for him*. Here I do indeed experience something similar or I experience it *for him* and *with* him, partaking, of course, in his enthusiasm, and I also feel joy originarily, but *for his sake*. I, for my own sake would not, judging purely from myself, act in this way. Likewise, when I experience, from myself, something similar: here, too, his enthusiasm about the vista and mine stand *separately next to each other,* despite their similarity. Now, suddenly, a strange "merging together" of my lived-experiences into his lived-experiences and his into mine takes place. All of a sudden, we are "together," the intentional "wall," the inner-mental "in between" has been torn down, it is as if what he experiences, *I myself* experience, from me, as if he, and I, in him, experience it. (If he experiences *concurrently* originarily *exactly the same currently* as I, then we would have a "we-lived-experience" in the most intimate sense, this would be an especially distinct special case of communal lived-experiences.) His lived-experiencing *now also belongs "to me,"* although it is he who experiences it, I am in it as well, almost as if I am also concurrently and originarily "in it" in my own identical or similar lived-experience.

This strange "belonging-to-me" of the lived-experiences of another in we-lived-experiences and communal lived-experiences is something very {76} peculiar and should not be mistaken for other characteristics of a lived-experience which have, at first sight, a certain similarity with it. Thus, for instance, it may be similar to the consciousness of another person having a lived-experience "of me." It is possible that I felt joy at an earlier point at this vista and have expressed my joy at it at the time. Now the other has taken over the joy from me and now it repeats itself at the same time, or only later—perhaps unconsciously—in precisely the same manner and with precisely the same expressions in him. I remember in his joy my own joy and say, "he has that from me," "this belongs (now in *this* sense) to me." This is something completely different as the "leaping together," the "belonging-to-me," the communal life in which I am *unified* with the other and his lived-experience. For here his lived-experience is precisely his, he has not only *taken it over* from me *externally,* or if he had done that, only because it was adequate to him, such that it might as well have arisen in him without the mediation of one of my lived-experiences.

Communal lived-experience has equally little to do with *imitation* of the other's lived-experience. (Although imitation can play a role in the genesis of communal lived-experiences empirically-genetically.[71]) In the imitation of a current (or

---

71 Fischer 1914. [Aloys (Alois) Fischer (1880–1937) was a pedagogical theorist and member of the Munich Circle. He completed his dissertation, *On Symbolic Relations* (1905), under Theodor Lipps, was the private tutor of Dietrich von Hildebrand from 1903–1906, and was professor in Munich from 1915–1937 when he was forced to retire for having a Jewish wife.]

potential) activity or of the lived-experience of a (real or fictional) subject, I grasp in empathy its lived-experiencing and "slip," as one has said, "into it." In this way I can, say, in our above example imitate the joyous cries of the other, his gestures and his tone of voice, playacting, but without being *myself* enthused fully and genuinely as him—I am perhaps even completely unmoved, the landscape leaves me completely unaffected. The other's lived-experience covers me over like a mental cloak not belonging to me, it has not arisen in me from my primordial self. Likewise in the case of *suggestion*. This, too, is no communal lived-experience, and the latter is certainly not, as some psychologists assert,[72] only a "normal case of suggestion." In the case of suggestion, the other's lived-experience {77} grasped in empathy is immediately transposed into an identical lived-experience of one's own, without the experiencing subject realizing it. It is even the case that the subject for the most part takes the suggested lived-experience immediately for its own and does not experience it as embedded into the more or less clear awareness of the "people, who also...". Now, the other's lived-experience, which has called for this suggested lived-experience of one's own, in no way stands opposed to it as its cause or as a similar lived-experience on the part of the other. Thus, it can also not feel unified with him and his subject in that peculiar manner. The subject having experienced the suggestion lives entirely in the object of the suggested lived-experience, is fully and wholly intentionally turned to this object. It does not at all view and compare its own lived-experience and that of the one issuing it, and thus it can also not, in experiencing it, feel one with the issuer. Even if it would make the issuer of the suggestion and his lived-experience his own intentional object, it would stand opposed to him just as foreign as before, only that he would now realize that he experiences the same as the other and that it "has from him," in the sense above, its own lived-experiencing mediated by the suggestion. But never would this be an inner unification in the sense as we demonstrated it as the necessary basis for communal lived-experience. Indubitably, such an inner unification could build itself on such a suggestion, but then it would be an addition, as a peculiar *new* element, to this suggestive lived-experience, as to any other lived-experience; never would it be given from such a suggestion alone. Thus, suggestion is a special case of lived-experiencing on a par with lived-experience, characterized by its genetic origin, be it that an individual lived-experiences or a whole manner of attitude is being suggested, from which further individual lived-experiences could then come forth, which the issuer of the suggestion did not experience. It is similar to the case of compulsory life in another or several others *without* inner unification, which we will have to investigate later.

---

72 Lipps 1907.

Now one could think that everywhere where one or several subjects exist in one person, where he "lurks," so to speak, in all of them, then in all cases a communal life would have to obtain. Such would be the case when, say, during a lecture all the listeners are entirely enraptured by the lecture and the speaker's lived-experience. Here—at least in the ideal case—all listeners (compared with one another and with the speaker) would have {78} the identical lived-experiences that he picked up. One could think that one is dealing here with an especially adequate communal lived-experiencing. But this is not the case, for the listeners, or at least a part of them, can, despite being enraptured, surely distance themselves from the views of the speaker. It may occur quite frequently to sensitive people that other people penetrate them, so to speak, in a manner whereby they get into their momentary or even total attitude, such that they "see everything with their eyes," and so on, although it in no way corresponds to them. Who has not experienced returning from a gathering and not being able for a long time to shake its "spirit," its total attitude—also vis-à-vis objects to which this gathering, while he was with it, did not even relate? Perhaps this gathering still resonated in him, lived in him, although he experienced this attitude as in no way appropriate to himself, even resisted it and attempted to purge himself of it with all his might. But this, too, one could in no way consider a communal lived-experience, although here other subjects were taken into the proper self, so to speak, or have penetrated into it, such that here, too, my stimuli stemming from them, the others "in" me, enter into my Ego-center. But even if the respective subject would not feel these others as being opposed to itself, if it did not strive to "expunge" them from himself, if it rather allowed them and their attitude to silently hum on in himself without taking a position against it, or even *without counting it as part of himself,* without having that feeling of belonging and unification with them—even then this would not be a communal lived-experience in our sense. For here the others would indeed live in that subject, while it lived from out of them, but it would not thereby have the feeling as if it at the same time lived *from out of itself,* as if it lived, while living *with* the others, from out of the unity of itself and the others, and at the same time from itself as part of the community, of the We. Here it lives *only from out of the others* within itself, but not from out of itself and *the others* in itself, as in the case of true communal lived-experiencing. The latter, rather, only arises, when to that "living in the other" is added that peculiar feeling, that this lived-experiencing, although it takes place "in the others," at the same time belongs to the experiencing subject itself, as itself, and it to them, because it is itself also contained in the unity with them. But this experiencing belongs "to him," {79} not because it is "contained" in him, arose in him, or because it could experience it as similar or even identically so (rather, the feeling of indifference or distinction could be combined with this), but because it is precisely unified with the others.

Likewise, of course, pathological cases, such as split personalities, where for periods something other than the common, "normal" complex in the self (in the "subconscious") of a person is responsible for the meaningful order of his experience, have nothing to do with communal lived-experiences, because what is lacking is indeed the relation to other subjects and the unification with them, as also the conscious independence of the different split personalities in the respective subject as *independent* psycho-physical subjects, as well as their mutual unification. The fact that it might perhaps seem so to the subject of the split personality in a sort of hallucination, is of no further importance here.

Thus, the fact that a subject may be capable of grasping in empathy foreign lived-experiencing, experience it, imitate it or otherwise be enthralled by it, may indeed be the basis and precondition of communal lived-experience, but it does not sufficiently and fully characterize it. Likewise, as we saw, the communal lived-experience is not already given through a subject being capable of transposing the foreign lived-experience grasped in empathy into an originary lived-experience of one's own,[73] such that the "other" lived-experience becomes *"its own."* In contrast to Theodor Lipps, we could also, as mentioned, never acknowledge this as a communal lived-experience, although we do not deny that all of this is an essential *precondition and presupposition* of communal lived-experience.

In the case of the true communal lived-experience we have, instead, in relation to other subjects and their lived-experiencing, always that peculiar "leaping into one another," discussed before, the "belonging-to-me." Here, a "ray," so to speak, of my lived-experience directs itself to that of the other. (This does not mean, of course, that my lived-experiencing might have been, under certain circumstances, awakened by that other lived-experiencing, that I may perhaps never have arrived at the point myself to experience it *in this way,* originarily.)

On the other hand, the characteristic trait of unification in the case of communal lived-experiences is certainly not always bound to the fact {80} that one subject has previously grasped in empathy other subjects with similar or identical lived-experiences in originary experience. Instead, we could be dealing with a mere "empty representation" or even a fiction of such other subjects. For instance, on a trip through a foreign country, a subject may be enchanted by an unusually beautiful landscape. During this trip, he might think of any other *possible* subjects (although he is now completely by himself and might not even know any such subjects personally), others, who "also" would feel joy by experiencing this landscape, *if* they saw it, or who would

---

73 Stein 1989, 12 ff.

have felt joy, *if* they had seen it earlier, or who would feel joy, if they at some point later would see it—even if the respective subject has been dead for a while. And now this subject can very well feel as one with these imagined (potential or only fictional) "people, who also" and their joy, although he does not know them and knows nothing about them, not even if they exist. He only knows that they must be constituted *thusly* that they would precisely "also" feel this joy about this landscape, if... And in thinking of these people and their joy, in unification with them, the subject can now indeed feel its own joy as the joy of a fictional We, as joy, which it does indeed experience, but which is embedded in that awareness of the (perhaps only potential) "people, who also," with whom it is unified,[74] although now, as we said, it is completely by itself and perhaps even knows none of these people. Only later—if at all—it perhaps meets these people and they now occupy the place, which the "empty intention" of these "people, who also" assigned to them already earlier, *a priori*, so to speak.[75]

2.4.4 The Community "In and for Itself" and ...

2.4.4.1 The Knowing-of-One-Another of the Members
Here now arises the question of whether or not, in addition to the ontological constitution of the community, and apart from the inner unification (with all its {81} components), the characteristics mentioned earlier, such as knowing-of-each-other and reciprocal interaction on the part of the members, will have to be considered as well.

One could think that communal life in the sense characterized above does indeed contain everything necessary for a fully unfolded community. But this does not seem to be the case. Even if a given amount of people, without knowing of each other, had such communal lived-experiences, yet without knowing of each other (and in which they would live from out of them, and also if all these people related in this communal life in the same manner to a common object in the broadest sense of the term), even then there would obtain, as we believe, no *objective* community, if we did not secretly add more components to these determinations than they contain, strictly speaking. We would then have, to speak with Hegel, only a

---

74 Scheler 1913, 131.
75 Scheler 1973a, 535–536, 540 ff. Unfortunately, his *On the Eternal in Man* (2010) only reached us during the printing of the present work. We can therefore only briefly refer to the fact that therein he shares these views (esp. 373 ff.). Of course, for Scheler, other ethical-metaphysical considerations are at play here, which we shall not get into here and which we—at least *here*—do not wish to use as presuppositions for our investigations.

community "for itself,"[76] a community thus, which consisted in the subjective individual consciousness of one or several people.

The *putative* existence of identical vital contents and the *putative* coincidence in life and manners of activity with any other people, *mainly putative ones,* other human beings with whom one feels unified, but whose existence one only surmises or assumes, but of which one knows nothing for certain, would not be a *real* community. And likewise from the outside, for an external observer who saw that a part of the lived-experience of these people came forth from a layer of a "We" in each and every one, that a part of their lived-experience ensued with the feeling of belonging-together with any "humans, who also," but without these people knowing of one another and without them standing in a direct or indirect reciprocal interaction, this would nonetheless not yet be a full, real community.[77] What needs to happen for a fully constituted, *objectively real* community to occur is the fulfilment of the intention toward those "people, who also" through *direct or indirect real experience,* and the communal life {82} in each and every one of them needs to lead, through direct or indirect reciprocal interaction, into a life *with these others* in the community—and only then can we speak of the full *community "in and for itself."*

Now this knowing-of-each-other does not always have to be direct, it can also be mediate. The manner in which members know of each other, which is required for a community, would seem to be dependent on the respective essence of the community in question, especially on their intentional foundation in unification as well. The more a unification of people is conditioned upon the unification with certain objectives (purposes, goals, ideals, and so on) as such, the *less,* under certain circumstances, a *direct,* immediate, bodily (originary) reciprocal experience and givenness of the respective people to each other will be necessary. So, for instance, a community of scholars is very well conceivable, in which its members know of each other exclusively through their scholarly writings (and the like), without knowing each other in person, while an intimate alliance of friends[78] or a marriage is almost inconceivable where the members merely knew of each other exclusively through their relation to some object. (What is conceivable, however, is

---

76 Hegel 1991, among other texts (certainly also *Reason in History* (1975), *Phenomenology of Spirit* (1977), and so on), especially the distinction of the three levels of the state in "abstract law" ("in itself"), "morality" ("for itself") and "ethical life" ["*Sittlichkeit*"] ("in and for itself"). We are focused here, however, only on the different *ontic* characters of community on these three levels, not their ethical-metaphysical *value* character.

77 See, also, the reference to the subjective side of society as "potential society" in Giddings 1896, 18.

78 See also, for instance, Aristotle, *NE*, bk. VIII, the conclusion of ch. 4.

a friendship which rests exclusively on written correspondence (as for instance the relationship of Elizabeth Barrett and Robert Browning prior to their marriage),[79] but these letters would have to be of an intimate nature, the people would have to pour themselves, so to speak, their innermost self, into these letters. They could not deal exclusively with general, purely factual-objective, theoretical assertions about some external object. Things are somewhat different regarding the relation to certain values and so on, where the deepest personal layers come to the fore.) One could perhaps say: the more the unification of the members depends on the external objects, lying outside of them, the more the communal life rests on the mere behavior to these objects, the more the knowing of the members of each other is mediated indirectly and through many mediate links (likewise in the case of reciprocal interaction), the greater also can the spatio-temporal distance of the respective members be from each other.

Things are different, however, if the community is grounded in the persons themselves or a deeper or more peripheral layer of them {83} as such. This is especially the case, if the community of certain persons, their living together with each other, is an end in itself, as in the case of reflexive communities (see above, 101 ff. / {67 ff.}). Here, an indirect knowing-of-each-other mediated merely through a third party or through some objects and the relation to them would not suffice.

Things are different once again where the community is grounded entirely in the unification with the spiritual person and the basic essence of the other or others, instead of their *empirical-factual* existence and life. Here, the spiritual person has to have been seen just *once* unambiguously and clearly, be it directly in the basic essential intention and basic intuition of a person given in the flesh and standing opposed to me (even in occult or telepathic intuition, some believe to grasp something of this sort, yet in those cases the identification with an empirical person is not easy, to say the least), be it through works, actions, and so on, of the other, in which his spiritual person, his basic essence has expressed itself especially adequately, perhaps through reports of others about the respective person and his manners of behavior, from which his essence is especially clearly discernable. Something of this sort seems to play a great role especially in religious communities, if they are grounded in the spiritual person of the founder of this religion or another saint. In this case, many concurrent or also later members of the congregation cannot see the saint, either because they are spatially too distant from him or perhaps because he has already passed away by their lifetime. Nonetheless, the

---

79 [Reference to the British poet Elizabeth Barrett (1806–1861) and the poet and playwright Robert Browning (1812–1898), who famously carried out their courtship in written correspondence before meeting in person and eventually marrying.]

oral or written report of others suffices for a unification with him, or the knowledge of his works or the (real or putative) inner intuition of his essence, since all that matters is his spiritual person and its lived-experiences as expressions and revelation of that personality, but not its empirical-contingent, factual lived-experiences as such, just as little (mostly, at least) as its real existence precisely here and now or at any other point in time. What suffices, rather, is that one indubitably knows that this person has certainly been in existence as such now or earlier in the real world, that he is, thus, no mere figment. This seems to be the case, as we assert, in the case of communities rooted in a spiritual person of one or several human beings, thus especially those communities who, as Weber says,[80] rest merely on a real or {84} putative "charisma." Not only the person in which the community is grounded—thus the community of each and every member with the personhood grounding the community—it seems to us, has to be given in this communities of spiritual essences exclusively through such a knowing, but also to members of such a community amongst each other seem to require no other knowing-of-each-other. Likewise, the responsive and reciprocal unification can be limited to a minimum. What oftentimes suffices, is the immediately evident essential insight that the members of that spiritual type have to feel connected "in principle," without even knowing each other, as soon as these others belong to this community through unification with the person of leadership. (Every *genuine* Christian must, according to the meaning of Christianity feel *a priori* connected with all other genuine Christians, and they with him, albeit not as individual but "as a Christian."[81]) The responsive and reciprocal unification belongs here to the meaning of the object of the first unification and the actual unification with it. A knowledge of its actual, current enactment in every individual case is not required. (This will be further clarified in what follows in the unification with the community as such.[82])

Thus, it seems certain that the members' direct or indirect knowing-of-each-other as the fulfillment of the intention toward "people, who also" (despite every individual's living out of this communal self "for himself") is an essential constituent of communal life, which may not be omitted.

---

80 Weber 1946b ["The Social Psychology of the World Religions"], 295–296, among other writings. [All of Walther's references to Weber's *Collected Essays on the Sociology of Religion* I are to the Introduction of "The Social Psychology of the World Religions," which can be found in Weber's *Essays in Sociology* (1946a).]

81 See also, Scheler 2010, 373 ff., 266–267.

82 [See below, Section 3.2.]

2.4.4.2 The Analysis of the Current Communal Life in the Community "In and for Itself"

Now how should we picture for ourselves a *current* communal lived-experiencing, where the knowing-of-each-other is added to the unification of the members and their reciprocal unification? What is the inner structure of a *current* we-lived-experience like, in the narrowest sense, on this basis—where, thus, the different member live out of themselves, experiencing the same—and how must we understand here the communal lived-experience, even if we are not dealing presently with precisely the *same* concurrent, current lived-experience in the different members?

{85} What especially belongs to such a current we-experience in the narrower sense is that every one of the experiencing subjects, in conjunction with the unification with the lived-experiencing (or the whole personhood) of the other or others also in grasping of the other's, or others', lived-experience in empathy, is that they are aware of the fact that also the others *on their part* are aware of and have unified with his lived-experience—the lived-experience of the experiencing subject (or with it itself). (This is, of course, not to say [the experiencing subject] (or the others) makes this a *special* object of their own intentional lived-experience, or asserts it explicitly in a cognition, a judgment, or the like. It can be, rather, also merely a peculiar, immediate awareness in the conscious background, an empathic-unified living-in-and-with-one-another.) We thus need to distinguish in such a current communal lived-experience, indeed *perceived as unity,* the following moments: (For the sake of simplicity, we assume that the community, the We, is only made up of two subjects, A and B; in principle it can be, of course, more than that):

1. The originary lived-experience *of A*, which directs itself to a given *object* intentionally.

    1a. The originary lived-experience *of B*, which relates in the same or similar manner to *the same object* as the originary lived-experience *of A*.

2. The originary *empathized* lived-experience of A, combined with the first originary lived-experience of A, in which A grasps this lived-experience of B.

    2a. The same *empathized* lived-experience of B directed at the same first lived-experience of A.

3. The *unification of A* with the lived-experience of B, grasped in empathy (perhaps also with A himself).

    3a. The *unification of B* with the lived-experience of A, grasped in empathy (perhaps also with B himself).

4. The empathic lived-experience of A, in which he grasps the unification of B with his lived-experience (or with him himself). (This lived-experience is

thus grounded in part in iterative empathy.)[83]

4a. The same empathic lived-experience on the side of B.

{86} Perhaps one could visualize this highly complex structure of a current we-experience in the following schema:

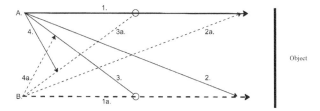

Figure 1: We-experience

Instead of communities and the We merely showing themselves and "living themselves out" only in such current we-lived-experiences, there is now also the possibility that the communal lived-experiences arising from the "common" layer in every individual member are spread out over the different individuals in which the community consists. Thus, not *all* members of *every* communal lived-experience must necessarily *concurrently and in exactly the same manner* experience currently. It is also possible here that *all* members experience only through empathy, communication (and so on) the *total* live of the community, that is, everyone experiences, at first, all those communal lived-experiences, which come forth from this communal "layer" *in him himself* and only then through empathy, communication (and so on) those communal lived-experiences, which come forth from this common "layer" *in the others.* Thus, not every member experiences *every one* of these lived-experiences in the same manner and in exactly the same manner originarily and in the flesh. It is especially the *originary-creative breaking forth* of the communal lived-experiences from the communal self and its sources of experience in the different subject, which is very differently distributed across the different members. The others then experience it only through empathy, communication, and so on, and will be enticed, under certain circumstances, to have the same or other *originary* communal lived-experiences in this or another field. The entire communal life and lived-experience then becomes, over time, a nearly inextricable web of one's own, self-created lived-experiences, or of lived-experiences,

---

83 Stein 1989, 17–18.

thoughts, ideas (and so on and so forth) only taken over in empathy or from the other members. But also, one's own lived-experiences are encouraged and necessarily determined through self-created lived-experiences (and so on) *of others*, as the latter in turn enter again through empathy (and so on) into *their* lived-experiences, such that they, in turn, also entice and determine *in the latter* self-created, originary lived-experiences, which would be impossible without the former. In this way, indeed, a type of total {87} life of a higher order arises, which *as a whole* is experienced originarily and as self-created in a certain sense only by the community *as totality*. Seen from the standpoint of the individual member, this communal life of the community dissolves, to be sure, into an immeasurable concatenation of empathized, self-created common lived-experiences, we-experiences, co-experiences, imitative experiences, and so on and so forth, which arise from the communal self of the individual members partly in the now, partly residing in it habitually, in part providing the substructure for future actualization and continuation of the communal life.

Thus, *that* layer in the self of *every single* member becomes ever more permeated, unfolded and enriched, from which communal life comes forth, through empathizing grasping from the communal lived-experiences of *the others* coming forth from the same layer in the others. Thereby, the concrescence and reciprocal dependence of the members becomes ever more intimate and steadfast in their communal self and communal life. Although in every individual member lived-experiences may come forth also from the communal self and *his* innermost Ego-self and their sources of experience, which are experienced by him as *his* new creations, these lived-experiences, too, are nonetheless determined and co-furnished in part through that common experiential ground within and outside of him and in turn enter into it again, newly creating and transformative, both in the respective person himself, as well as in the others. This common experiential ground becomes ever more a sort of "common" mental ground *in every individual,* from which the lived-experiences come forth as communal lived-experiences. In this sense—and *only* in this sense—all lived-experiences coming forth from this experiential ground are common, more or less, to *all* members, because they come forth the from the *total subject,* encompassing all of them yet *consisting of them,* the community as such, in *this* sense, although they can only become actualized by passing through the radically individualized Ego-center of the individual members.[84]

---

84 This is also the reason for the "communal guilt" and responsibility of all members of a community "for all" in Scheler's sense (Scheler 2010, 376–377).

(To counter here all misunderstanding concerning the metaphysical and empirically real interpretation of the community as "overarching total subject," we here refer to the section on "The Reality of the Community as Such" below.)[85]

{88} All leading sociologists who delved deeper into this subject matter have also all felt this way (thus Adler, Simmel, Scheler, and many others), although they could never quite bring into relief this phenomenon, precisely because they failed to clearly distinguish between the experiencing Ego-center of each individual, which is always and necessarily individual and singular, and the background, the self, from which experiential stimuli arise and in which (as we saw) communalization takes place. Due to this lack in distinction, it had to appear as if the community were a living organism, living, as it were, all for itself, separated, between or over and above the individual members, while the psycho-physical independence of the individual and especially the necessary individuality and singularity of its Ego-center clearly runs counter to this. Going off this fact, one reverts, then, to a complete denial of any communal life, of any "communal spirit," counting only singular individuals, which at best are able to relate to one another intentionally and can follow each other accordingly. (Thus, e.g., Georg von Below,[86] Weber, and others.) But this stands in opposition to the undeniable existence of the communal self *in every member* "behind" his Ego-center and the communal lived-experiences arising from this Ego-center.

But that dispute concerning the independent existence of the community as such can extend into the self. It concerns not only the individual. It concerns also members as psycho-physical individuals in their unity of Ego-point, self, and basic essence. For one could hold that the entire self of a person is, at bottom, a We, in which one's own and foreign lived-experiences are indistinguishably mixed together. This communal self, which alone exists, is now topped off in every single individual with an experiencing Ego-center as an individualizing moment—a position of which especially some Marxists[87] and Hegelians are fond, although they do not make these inner-mental distinctions. Here, too, the solution presumably lies in the middle. Certainly, *a part* of every person's lived-experiences from the most diverse spheres of his *communal* self enters into his Ego-center. Likewise, another part of his lived-experiences may be possible only through an empathizing, sympathetic and co-experiencing grasping of the lived-experiences of others. In this respect, thus, he is indeed dependent in his lived-experiencing

---

85 [This paragraph is printed in a smaller font; the section on "The Question Concerning the Reality of the Community as Such" is to be found below, Section 3.8.]

86 [Georg von Below (1858–1927) was a German historian and well known critic of sociology.]

87 See., e.g., Josef Karner (= Karl Renner) 1904, 151, 169. [Karl Renner (1870–1950) was an Austrian sociologist and socialist politician. He published under the pseudonym Josef Karner, among others.]

{89} on other human beings, with whom he is communalized or perhaps only so-cialized, and determined through them. But alongside these others there are cer-tainly also lived-experiences, which spring from the primal-original, most individ-ual basic essence as well as other, radically individual centers and sources of lived-experience belonging *only to him,* in the most diverse spheres of a person's self, which pertain *only to him,* which are his most intimate possession and his pri-mal-individual, spontaneous expressions of life, even before they enter into his Ego-center, no matter if other individuals have ever so similar and related lived-ex-periences belonging *only to them* and even if one may—by abstracting from their primal-individual proper quality (their mental moment of individuation)—sub-sume them under the same general concepts and categories of lived-experiences as those of other people as well. Along with Adler,[88] Simmel, and Scheler,[89] it seems to us, this differentiation of every individual into a communal and radically individual self, into an individual and a social or collective person, runs through his *entire* personality. This difference seems to us to obtain in every layer of depth, from which his lived-experiences may ever arise, to which objects they may ever direct themselves at (thus also in his numinous sphere)—at all times it experiences either a part of a We or also *only* as "*it itself.*" Going along with Scheler, this distinction seems to crisscross with all other distinctions and catego-rizations of the self-concerning its depth or its intentional relation to objects of any kind. It is thus not the case, we maintain, that communal lived-experiences are bound from the very beginning to certain intentional objects or regions of objects (this may be the case for current we-experiences: these can never be, according to Scheler, purely sensual),[90] nor are they bound to a certain layer of depth in the sub-ject, such that only the peripheral lived-experiences could count as communal lived-experiences, while the deepest lived-experiences are always necessarily only of an individual and radically private kind (as one could infer from some of Simmel's statements)—or also vice versa. However, {90} this certainly does not preclude that for certain founded communities, the communal self and its lived-experiences, according to the essence of that community, can necessarily in-tend only certain objects and touch only certain layers of depth of the subject. Like-wise, the number of people with whom a certain kind of communalization is pos-sible, may in certain cases be limited, by necessity, to a very small one.

---

88 See, among other writings, Adler 1913, 9 ff.; 1914, an offprint from Carl Grüneberg's *Archive for the History of Socialism.*
89 Scheler 1973a, 519 ff., 525, 543, 561; 2010, 373 ff., 382, 266–267, concerning the communal lived-ex-perience of spiritual persons; 1913, 127 ff., concerning so-called "life-communities."
90 Scheler 1913, 137–138.

2.4.4.3 The Communal Life and Reciprocal Interaction

The question now is, if—besides the unification and reciprocal unification of the members, the living-out from the communal self and the direct or indirect knowing-of-each-other—the element of reciprocal interaction is still required in order for the communal life to realize itself "in and for itself." (In these purely eidetic analyses, we are not, of course, interested in the empirical-genetic question, whether or not a reciprocal interaction of the communalized group has to have preceded every factual communalization and whether or not this is necessary— for empirical reasons. Though it is possible that in such an empirical factuality an eidetic law lies hidden, this does not seem to be the case here.)

It is, to be sure, presupposed from the beginning that this reciprocal interaction is intentional and reciprocal in the sense already discussed above and it is "equally intentioned."[91] Likewise, this intentional and equally intentioned reciprocal interaction in the broadest sense by no means has to be enacted by one or all subjects in question here, nor even intended.

Let us illustrate this reciprocal interaction in the broadest sense with an example. Let us imagine a medieval hermit, who haplessly and ineffectively struggles for his God and seeks to realize the life that he has deemed correct despite all the world's resistance. He feels entirely alone in his struggle, for even though he has been informed of similar struggles of others in the past, he nonetheless knows among his contemporaries not a single one who wages the same struggle as he. Then one day he sees, while walking through the streets of a city, in the throng of people, from afar another person whom he sees clearly and "empathizes" with him that he wages "the same" struggle as he, and imputes to him that he, too, is a hermit like him, feels perhaps just like him. They do not talk to each other, never again see each other in their lives, and none of the two knows that the other has also noticed him. Nevertheless, each of them takes with him {91} the deepest impression of the other into his loneliness; each of them now knows that "also" there is another person fighting the same struggle and feels fortified by this, and unifies with him, and feels himself—without ever coming in contact with the other again—connected in an invisible community of God-seekers, and knows that he, too, according to his essence as God-seeker, must feel connected with him *a priori*, as *embodiment* of the type "God-seeker." (This will only become fully understandable from the standpoint of the community on the second level and the unification with the community as such—see below.)[92] Here we find an intentional reciprocal interaction in the broadest sense as part of a community

---

91 ["*gleichsinnig.*"]
92 [See below, Section 3.2.]

in the broadest sense: here the mere knowing-of-each-other on both sides is already a sort of reciprocal interaction as element of the community, *if* and to the extent that it combines with the other moments already investigated. Such a form of reciprocal interaction in the broadest sense belongs, as is self-evident, to every community, for the latter is then the higher-order notion vis-à-vis our other determinants, such as reciprocal unification and knowing-of-each-other.

But what about the intentional reciprocal interaction in a narrower sense? This would be the case where a subject intentionally directs itself in his current behavior and lived-experiencing directly or indirectly *toward* other subjects, refers to them, as is the case, say, in the "communal action" of Weber,[93] if it is construed reciprocally, not just one-sidedly. Likewise, there would be something similar in the case of so-called "social acts" as analyzed by Reinach[94] and Husserl[95] (request, communication, instruction, command, and so on), where one's behavior is not just directed *by* the other, but also *at* him. It should be beyond any doubt that such a reciprocal interaction in the narrowest sense is compatible with the essence of a community; yet it is the question whether it *necessarily* belongs to its essential traits. That a reciprocal interaction of *all* members of a community must necessarily obtain, in which they also directly or indirectly (through oral or written communications, requests, commands, agreements, and so on and so forth) orient themselves *at* each other and are not just oriented *by* each other, does in no way seem necessarily to belong to *every* community "as such." Yet it seems to us that {92} a fully developed community is hardly conceivable in which the members are not more or less, directly or indirectly, oriented *by* each other. Likewise, it is the case that in a community indeed not *all,* but at least *some* members are directed *at* others or the community of the others as such. This will obtain especially in the case of functionaries, leaders or representatives of the community, especially when they direct themselves "in the name of" the community (see below, the section on "'Social Acts' in the Pregnant Sense")[96] to the other members and these direct themselves through them to the community as a whole. (Thus, for instance, in the case of issuing laws, announcements *of* the government of a community to the members or a part of them; inquiries, decisions, petitions *to* the government, and so on and so forth.) We shall get back to this later.

But apart from that, a reciprocal interaction between *all* members, whereby they direct themselves *at* each other, does *not* necessarily seem to belong to the community "as such," if we exclude the special cases above. We can, thus, perhaps

---

93 Weber 1981, 159–160.
94 Reinach 2012, 19.
95 Husserl 2002.
96 [See below, Section 3.3.]

decide that a direct or indirect reciprocal interaction, in which the members orient each other *to* each other, necessarily belongs to every form of communal life, *to the extent* and in *that* way, in which the sense of the community, the common leitmotif in the broadest sense of its communal life, demands it. It seems to us, however, that the members *can* thereby very well orient each other *to* each other, that perhaps the objective reality of the community and the real connection of the members, the objective "probability" for the creation of the communal life becomes very much augmented thereby, but that they do not *necessarily have to* do this. We believe, rather, that it suffices that the members in the communal life in the above sense orient each other in their relation to the common object and in their reciprocal interaction *to* each other, to the extent, precisely, that the meaning of the community demands and allows it. (But if, say, the life in the sense of the communal leitmotif becomes threatened or made impossible through some or several members—perhaps unconsciously—with their behavior, then it is obviously the others' duty not to orient themselves to them, if otherwise the community shall be preserved—although perhaps not with *these* members.)

Now this orienting-oneself-to-one-another can also be, as indicated, mediated in the highest degree, such that, say, all {93} members orient themselves to a common norm or the like, in the "expectation"—to speak with Weber[97]—that the others follow suit. (The fulfillment of this "expectation," the objective "probability," as Weber calls it, of its realization does demand in many cases here too, that the members direct themselves *at* each other directly or indirectly.) The more a community is founded in an object lying outside the personhood of the members, the more, as in the case of knowing, an indirect reciprocal interaction of this sort suffices; the more, however, it is grounded in the factual, current life and behavior in the broadest sense of the individuals as such, the more a reciprocal interaction of the members in an immediate relation to each other is required. In the first case the acts, lived-experiences and manners of behavior, and so on, of the members in their reciprocal interaction are merely means to the fulfillment of the objective meaning of the community in relation to certain objects. In the latter case the relation of the members to the most diverse objects is only the means of bringing their subjective lived-experiencing and behaving, in reciprocal interaction toward each other, to full bloom and to reciprocal recognition. All types of empirical-personal communities of *life* require therefore a *direct* reciprocal interaction of the members toward each other in the intimate and most intimate sense, likewise their spatio-temporal coexistence, while, vice versa, with the increasing grounding of the community in objective, extra-personal formations and objectives, the im-

---

97 Weber 1981, 159–160.

mediacy and spatial proximity of their reciprocal interaction, as well as their spatio-temporal dependency decreases. The more the community rests on the relation to such objective formations, the more the latter are decisive for their membership and their reciprocal unification, the more the individual members also become "representable" through random other subjects. (With the exception that the relation to these objects demands very special, individual, purely personal qualities.) The representability of the members seems to stand in intimate connection with the mediacy and spatio-temporal independence of their reciprocal interaction, at least within the communities anchored in the unification of something objective-impersonal.

Things stand differently in the case of the rootedness of the community in the spiritual person, the basic essence, of the members. Here {94}—and here alone—it seems that the highest irrepresentability of the individuals can be reconciled with the highest mediacy and spatio-temporal independence of reciprocal interaction (as in the case of the knowing-of-each-other), thus for instance in the case of the supra-temporal "community of all mystics" or "the hallowed," to the extent that they know of each other, as far as, thus, the future ones were presaged by the earlier ones, that messages of the earlier ones reach the later ones through tradition or written documents, and so on, and it follows from the essence as spiritual types of this sort, that they feel as one, *eo ipso* and *a priori*, with all representatives of this identical spiritual type as such.

Thus, we can say that what is necessary for the constitution of the community "as such" is only the intentional reciprocal interaction in the broadest sense between members (which, thus, can coincide perhaps with the knowing-of-each-other and the reciprocal unification), while reciprocal interaction in the narrower and narrowest sense is certainly indispensable for certain types of communities, but not for the community "as such."

3 The Community "In and for Itself" on the Second Level

3.1 The Knowing of the Community Itself, As Such

But have we, in our earlier discussion, exhausted everything belonging to a fully unfolded community? Is what we described a community, but despite everything, only a community of a lower level, a community in the "childhood" stage, so to speak, a community *without* an actual *self-consciousness?* Does not more belong to a fully unfolded community, to the "mature" community (as one might say), namely, above all else, the self-consciousness *of the community,* thus the members' *knowing of the community itself, as such?* Thus, not only a knowing of the members of each other—and likewise: *their unification with the community as such,* not just with each other and ultimately, as strange as it may sound, a *reciprocal interaction and reciprocal unification between communities themselves and their members,* not only between and amongst these members? What can we make of the foregoing claim?

It is not only the knowing-of the other members as "people, who also…" that plays an important role in the community, but also the knowing of the community itself, as such, which is to be {95} distinguished from the former. It seems to us that, without further ado, together with the communal life, the knowing-of this lived-experience and with this the knowing-of the community itself are given?

This is by no means the case, however. Indeed, every current lived-experience, as we know, can be accompanied at all times by a reflexive knowing-of this lived-experience, yet (as especially Moritz Geiger has shown)[1] mental life, conscious life, and life that is self-conscious, life that is *known,*[2] that is, where there is reflexive knowledge of this lived-experience, all of these are by no means identical. If this is already the case for current lived-experience, then all the more for habitual lived-experiences and the lived-experiencing and behavior founded in them. Thus, it seems we must further investigate this point.

To the extent that communal life in the sense above rests on a factual, *current* unification (see above, 73/{36}, the section on "The Inner Unification as Essential Constituent of the Community"), it seems likely that it is for the most part con-joined with a knowing of this unification. Already where this current unification

---

1 Geiger 1921.
2 [Here and in the following paragraph, Walter contrasts *bewusst* (conscious) with *gewusst* (known).]

transforms into a habitual unification, it is, however, questionable whether the communal life as such founded through it always has to be *known*. This is all the more the case where the communal life wells up from an unwanted, unconscious concrescence (present or past), as this is especially the case in what Scheler calls "vital communities."[3] But even the *consciousness of "people, who also…" and the consciousness of the unification with them* is by far no *knowledge of the community itself, as such,* or even *a unification with it.* For, in the case of this knowing and this unification, the intention directs itself, to be sure, always only at the individual, separate, other people, or their sum, and perhaps at the unification with them, but not at the community as such, as the case in a certain sense a supra-individual mental-spiritual formation. The latter is, to be sure, necessarily inseparably connected with its members, a formation that can only exist and be embodied in them and through them, but which indeed has its own essence, its own existence, its own life, and its own rules, norms and laws, which are by no means identical with those of its members or their sum.

{96} Above, we spoke of the community "in and for itself,"[4] which constitutes itself the moment when the member, not only each for himself in his innermost self, unifies himself the other or others and lives from out of them, but where to this community "for itself" is added the direct or indirect knowing-of-each-other, the reciprocal unification and reciprocal interaction. And yet this was not already, strictly speaking, a true community "in and for itself," it was not even —from the standpoint of the *community as such*—a community "for itself" in the strict sense of the term. For what the consciousness of the individual members referred to, were always only the individual members as *individuals* or their sum and their relations to each other, but never the community as supra-individual, spiritual-mental being embodying itself in it. The "subjective" spirits knew, to be sure, "in and for themselves," of each themselves and each other, but they had not yet seen the "objective" spirit (to speak with Hegel), which embodied and formed itself in them, in their reciprocal unification and their cohabitation. The latter was at best visible in this communal life on the first level "in itself," for others, for external observers, but it had not yet come to "self-consciousness" out of the objective spirit "for itself" in the consciousness of the members and their communal life.

How often does it not happen that one lives along with random people in trusted exchange, entirely unconsciously in reciprocal connectedness, that friends in their life together completely flourish, without ever reflecting on their relationship to one another: they go about their lives, are immersed in it, but they do not think

---

3 Scheler 1973a, 430 ff.; 1913, 126 ff.
4 [Above, Section 2.4.4.]

about it, until one day they become aware of this friendship *as such* with one stroke—perhaps through an escalation of the same in an especially strong communal lived-experience, perhaps also through a threat to their unification, be it through strife, separation, through an attack of a third party, and so on. (It is especially the latter, which, it appears, first awakens many communities to a consciousness of themselves, as such, its members to a communal consciousness in this sense. This is oftentimes the case in times of war, which first awakens a people to a self-consciousness,[5] or through the repression of one tribe through another, one class through another.) Be these empirical-factual {97} reasons as they may, what is shown in these examples is that all other traits of a community may very well remain, without, however, the members knowing of *it itself* and their connection within it. It is, thus, something completely novel, which is added through this knowing of the members of the community *as such*; it is only through this that a community becomes a community *"for itself"* in the fullest, truest sense, that in addition to everything else it also attains this knowledge.

It is an essential aspect in this ontological classification, to ascertain, in the developmental history of the community, the degree and range of *this* knowledge. This point is of such eminent importance that we shall remain here with it a bit longer.

As indicated, it is a peculiar, novel object, a synthetic, collective object,[6] which constitutes itself here in consciousness. This object (as the consciousness of it) is built upon the community on the first level, which grows out of it. It is not only A+B+C..., of which I know in the case of knowing-of the community itself, as such, and of its unification with me and amongst each other at the same stage. It is also not the sum of these relations of A, B, C...—this all exists and can be an object of intentional lived-experiences of the most diverse sort. But it is not yet the community as such, as new object, which penetrates all this, which is built on it and at the same time reigns throughout all of it, giving all these relations a peculiarly modified meaning, if they now are now no longer viewed as such and for themselves and from their point of view, but precisely as expressions and utterances of the community as such. It is the connectedness of people as such and the meaning of this connectedness, which now separates itself, so to speak, from the people as its bearers, as a new, peculiar object *sui generis*, having its own meaning, its own existence and its own laws, although it is undeniable that it can consist and be grasped, on the other hand, only in the individual members and their reciprocal interaction—both from within and from without (see

---

5 Weber 1913b, 51.
6 Husserl 2014, 240.

below, the section on "The Phenomenological Constitution of Communities").[7] Only where this knowing of the connectedness, the community as such, as, in a certain sense {98} higher-order and all-penetrating totality, arises in a community in its members, it is only then that we can speak in the most intimate and fullest sense of a community "for itself." What the Ego-consciousness means for the individual vis-à-vis the manifold of changing lived-experiences, goes likewise for the consciousness of the community as such vis-à-vis the sum of the members and their connectedness and reciprocal interaction for the community. This consciousness is, to be sure, most intimately connected with the members' knowing of each other and their connectedness—and yet it is something particularly novel. What we have here is an inversion, so to speak, of the earlier, "natural" attitude of the members. For, if the consciousness of the members takes its first point of departure from itself and the others and their relation as what is concretely given, and if the points of departure (phenomenologically, not historically) are for it also for the most part itself first and these other subjects, and if it values everything only from their standpoint—then what takes place here is a spiritual summersault, so to speak, in its intentionality—the "Copernican" Turn in sociology! —by taking as its point of departure the connectedness of the subjects and the meaning of this connectedness while observing and valuing itself and the other subjects, as well as their relations, from that point of view alone.

(It seems that herein, for instance, one finds the main differences between a crowd and a community. A member of the crowd does indeed know of the "others, who also...," but is neither capable of positing the connectedness of itself and the others as existing independently of itself nor of intentionally relating to it. It lives blindly and is carried along with the crowd—at least as it lives in and with the crowd. Later, when it is no longer subjected to mass suggestion and looks back at it, perhaps at times such reflections may come to pass.)[8]

Only where this attitude is enacted—both in the case of the external observer and the members of the community itself—a genuine sociology seems to be possible, especially a sociology of the community.[9] Scholars who, also in sociology {99}, again and again take their point of departure *only* from individuals and at best

---

7 [See below, Section 4.]

8 [This paragraph is printed in a smaller font.]

9 Credit is especially due to Karl Marx and Marxism (and some of the positivist followers of Auguste Comte), for having repeatedly placed this thought front and center, although the individual— in psychological, ethical, and metaphysical regard—ultimately got short shrift in spite of this, if it was not denied altogether (see above, Section 2.4.4.2, 119/{88}, note 87). Indeed, it seems to lie in the essence of the historical dialectic that one view first has to arise in an extreme form in order to be recognized at all.

from their sum and the sum of their relations, seem to us to not at all have taken the genuine sociological attitude, not at all have viewed its genuine realm—or at best from an inadequate viewpoint.

One could also think, however, that the knowledge of the community as such could come forth necessarily only from the previous intention toward the individual person as such, toward the members and their connectedness. But this, too, is not at all the case, although this may be the case at times on a lower level of communal consciousness (also, see below the section on "The Unification with the Community as Such").[10] Quite often it is, in a certain sense, precisely vice versa. Especially in an historical sense, the knowing of the community precedes the knowing of the members as individual persons and their unification and reciprocal interaction. Oftentimes, an individual knows of others *merely as members*, thus even before it becomes aware of their existence as individual persons. Indeed, oftentimes, the behavior of certain members (especially the communal organs) becomes understandable only through knowing of the community and its meaning and purpose. (One may think here of diplomats, missives, military organs, fiscal organs, the administrative staff of states and communities, clerks and cashiers in clubs, and so on and so forth.) Here, too, the relation of the knowledge of the members and their sum to the knowing of the community as such is determined especially through the meaning of the community.

The more the community is founded in individual persons and their personal existence and life—be it as empirical or as spiritual vital community—the more, to be sure, the knowing in relation to the community as such will presuppose the knowing of the members and of the unification with them and will be founded in it. The more, however, the community derives its meaning and purpose from an objective formation, which is objective, that is, lies outside of the individual members as individuals (material, spiritual or otherwise), the more it is founded in it, the more the knowing of the community will be independent of the direct knowing of the other members and of the unification with them as individual persons.

3.2 Unification with the Community as Such

Just as the knowing-of the community as such clearly differs from the knowing-of the other members and the {100} "communal life" with them, we must likewise distinguish the unification and reciprocal unification with the other members as

---

10 [See below, Section 3.2.]

an intentional act of its own kind from unification with the community as such. This unification with the community as such is, by the way, indeed analogous to unifications with any other object and obeys also precisely the same modifications as these, as already discussed. It may be grounded in the unification with the other members, or also ground the latter, but it can also obtain entirely independently of them. It is not especially necessary that the order, the conservation of the inner-mental contour and the inner-mental source of lived-experiences must be of the same sort in the case of the unification with the community as it obtains in the case of the concurrent unification with its members. Indeed, it can also obtain entirely without a unification with the other members as individuals: the respective subject, then, is only unified with these as a constituent part of the community, constituting them.[11]

The earlier relation can even reverse into its opposite to the extent that one only becomes aware of the other members of this community as "people, who also…" on the basis of a previous knowing-of the community, its meaning and its essence and a unification with them, ultimately unifying with them. Thus, it is not the case here that one first knows of other people with whom one has something "in common" and whom one likes for this or that reason, as one unifies with them for this reason and comes together as a community, but rather vice versa: one knows of a community, its meaning and essence, one is unified with *it*, and only on the basis of this unification with the community the other members appear to one as "people, who also" and only now one unifies with them. Such a relation may obtain, for instance, by joining a religious community other than one's original one, by joining a political party or by obtaining citizenship in a different country. One could object, however, in these cases, that by a new entry of a foreign subject into an already existing community, this may occur from time to time. {101} But this unification, too, must have necessarily come forth from the previous unification of the other members with each other for their own sake or on the basis of their unification with an independent object and from their knowing-of this unification, which ultimately has constituted itself as independent object and now has become an end in itself.[12] But this is by no means necessarily the case. It is very much possible that, say, a person first conceives the idea of a community

---

11 Such a dialectical reversal of the originary relation is also to be found in Hegel's view of the marriage, when the parties of the marriage enter into this relation through an insight into the objective value of this institution: to love each other, because they form a marriage community, instead of forming a marriage community because they love each other. Hegel 1991, § 162.

12 In the sense of Simmel in his "Proto-Forms of Ideas" [later reprinted as "The Turn Toward Ideas"] (2010c, 37 ff.) (where he, however, does not refer especially to sociological questions). We do not, however, wish to thereby identify with Simmel's epistemological stance.

of which type whatever (vital, artistic, scientific, religious, and so forth), works out its meaning and purpose, structure, constitution, and so on, and only once he has completed this task, seeks out other people who should realize this community with him.

One could be tempted to think here, however, that it is here still only the common interest in the purpose of the community, not the mere unification with it, what joins the members together. And yet one can meet this objection with clear examples such that in some cases it is really *only* the belonging to a community which combines the different subjects and nothing else beyond this. Such cases may indeed be very rare, but they do happen. Let us take, say, a member of a family, perhaps of a royal dynasty (one could also think of Thomas Mann's *Buddenbrooks*),[13] having an unusually strong and encompassing sense of family. Now this member of the family joins with another member, who perhaps is not even known to the former—for whom it, thus, apart from his belonging to this family, cannot even have any special sympathy—through marriage with another family. Based on this joining of his family, his community, with this other family, the new member can feel conjoined with all living and deceased members of the other family, with the entire dynasty, purely based on his belonging to a family with whom his own family has joined itself. In this case, it is not necessary that any interests may have been common to the members of the two families, it is indeed alone the belonging to a community, which is now conjoined with one's own, that unites them. But the history of the familial politics of royal dynasties, as well as the history of unions and legal relations (blood vengeance!) of primitive clans and tribes show that {102} this type of unification, today, is always only a mere formality, but it can also be genuine and deeply rooted.

There are, however, also cases where it is very much so that a person is unified with the community, or at least the idea of it, or its essence, as such, without at the same time being unified with any single or all other members. This is the case when, say, this member is of the opinion that the other members do not conform to the meaning of this community of the behavior demanded by it in individual manners of behavior or their total behavior. In this case, the subject in question does know of these members as such, but it is by no means unified with them, but instead finds itself, in certain cases, in a strong inner opposition vis-à-vis and separation from them.[14] In this sense, Luther, for instance, may have related to the other members of the Catholic Church, at least to its official representatives, once he had already seen its flaws and had begun fighting against it, while he was

---

13 [Mann 1993.]
14 Pfänder n.d.-b and the negative emotions in 1913, 1916.

still a member of it. Taken to the extreme, however, this opposition for the most part, and necessarily so, leads to an exit from the community, perhaps "in the name of its true spirit," strictly speaking: "in the name of its idea," its ideal essence, to which the community as empirical formation does not correspond.[15] (Here, as everywhere, one must distinguish between the knowing-of and unification with an empirical-factual, concrete community and the knowing-of and unification with its idea and its essence. (See also below, the section on "Inauthentic Communal Lived-Experiences.")[16] This distinction is especially important to understand reformations, splits, dissolutions with or without new formations, and so on, of communities of all sorts.)

Thus, it is possible that despite the most intense knowing of the community and in the most intimate unification with it, concerning the inner unification with the other members, a complete indifference, indeed a pronounced inner separation, may obtain.

From all of this we can now derive a new, extremely significant, meaning of the notions "social act," "social self," "communal {103} life." We understood by these, following (among others) Husserl and Reinach, those mental *relations of individuals to each other,* from which *emerges* the community, relations which, in a certain sense, thus form the basis and premise for communities on the second level. These were the acts, lived-experiences and manners of behavior (and so on), in which people come into reciprocal interaction toward each other, in which they know of each other, orient themselves to and after each other, unify with each other; then the inner-mental sphere in the self of the individual, in which they are unified with others, and finally the communal lived-experiencing and behavior emerging from this sphere. Following what we have just analyzed, we can now, following Pfänder,[17] understand by "social acts" and "social self" all those acts, which *direct themselves at the social communities as such* (as well as other social formations), knowingly, willingly, through position-taking, unifying, acting, and so on, as well as to the sphere in the self, from which these acts (and so on) come forth and in which they, once they have become habitual, reside in the subject.

---

15 See, among others, Kautsky 1916.

16 [See Section 3.4 below.]

17 In Pfänder's lecture courses on the *Fundamentals of Human Psychology* (n.d.-b) and *Introduction to Philosophy* (n.d.-a), the expressions "social self" and "social acts" have *only this* meaning.

3.3 "Social Acts" in the Pregnant Sense: Acts "in the Sense" and "in the Name" of the Community as Such

The members' lived-experience and behavior—and under certain circumstances also that of other people—with respect to the social communities once constituted as independent objects in consciousness does not, however, end with the lived-experiences in the broadest sense, which—in different ways—direct themselves intentionally and purely in the interest of knowledge at these communities as their objects.

We have discussed above how someone can have another person "in" him and can live "from out of him," by compulsion, against his will or also on the basis of a unification, perhaps deliberately. If one of them inwardly was unified with this or these other(s), from out of whom he lived, then we had communal lived-experiences in the first sense. Now it is also possible that a subject live in this manner *from the "spirit" of a community itself,* and here too by compulsion, with or without his will or also deliberately. And here, too, the experiencing subject can separate these experiences {104}, which arise from his conscious background, from his self, but yet from the "spirit of community" *in him,* while it enacts them, inwardly from himself as individual person and his "own" lived-experiencing. Or it can stand opposed to them indifferently, or can also feel as part of the community connected with them, can count himself as belonging to them and they as to him. This latter type of behavior can, however, extend even further, and in that case the subject by no means longer lives as "it itself," albeit in the sense of the community, but yet merely as a "representative" of the community, "in their name," it views itself merely as a point of actualization and passage of that other, here the community, in whose name it experiences, as its "mouthpiece."[18] These lived-experiences in the "sense and name" of the community, once it has constituted itself as an independent formation, can be enacted, under certain circumstances, also by people who do not count as among its members, thus by "mere" employees and representatives of the community who are not at the same time members. But then they have to be empowered by the community regarding the type and duration of such manners of behavior in the broadest manner in "the sense and in the name of the community." (Compare, for instance, the regulations concerning citizenship of ambassadors, employees of embassies in different countries, and so on and so forth.) This form of intermediate stance between these manners of behavior "in the sense and the name" of the community in non-members and members form perhaps those cases of such lived-experiences, where the entire meaning of the com-

---

18 Reinach 2012, 25, 27, especially 83 ff.

munity rests on the unification with the personality of the leader and its life. The latter here stands, so to speak, beyond the membership of its community, and yet especially their forms of behavior are to an especially distinguished (perhaps norm-giving) extent manners of behavior (and so on) "in the sense and name" of the community (as also of itself, since the latter, in its behavior and so on, first gives meaning to the community). All lived-experiences, activities, and so on, of this sort in the broadest sense are enacted, to be sure, by the respective subject itself, they actualize themselves in its Ego-center, but experiences and enacts them not as "his own" lived-experiences, but precisely as lived-experiences "in the name," "in lieu of" the other—regardless how "the subject itself" may stand with respect to these. With these lived-experiences "in the name of..." the experiencing subject can unify itself, and yet thereby they do not become his own {105} lived-experiences in the strict sense, attributed *only to it itself*, but perhaps it takes a position (although it itself enacts them—and yet not) to them, assenting, negating, unifying, separating, as to any other lived-experiences that another subject enacts (of course it can also take a stance toward lived-experiences, which it enacts *as itself*, but that is again something else). Hence, for the enactment of these lived-experiences it is indeed not necessary that the experiencing subject also assents to and "goes along with" its lived-experiences itself "in the name" *as it itself*, freely from itself—as individual. Rather, it can very well negate them, as, say, when a police officer "as police officer" apprehends a pauper because of theft, although he, "as himself," "as human being," and so on, would perhaps prefer to let him go. Indeed, it is even conceivable in principle that these lived-experiences "in the name of" turn against the enacting subject as such, as when, say, an especially dutiful judge judged himself, as a private citizen, guilty "in the name of the law" or "of the state," and so on. (See, for instance, *The Judge* by Conrad Ferdinand Meyer.[19] Or one may also think of the Carl Lindhagen's proposal in the Swedish Parliament: The king of Sweden, as executor of parliamentary decisions, may decide to abolish monarchy in Sweden and to introduce a republic.)[20] Here arises the concept of the "private citizen" vis-à-vis the "public persona" or "social person." (Whence also the peculiar feeling of irresponsibility, which some people display toward their activities "in the name of" a community.)[21]

---

19 [Conrad Ferdinand Meyer (1825–1898) was a Swiss poet and novelist. His novella *The Judge* was first published in 1885.]

20 [Carl Lindhagen (1860–1946) was a Swedish lawyer and politician. On more than one occasion he put forward a motion to abolish the monarchy of Sweden and establish a federal constitutional republic.]

21 For example, the excellent description of the psyche of the judges during the revolutionary tribunals by France 1797. [The original French novel, *Les dieux ont soif*, was published in 1912.]

Yet, it would be quite erroneous to think that we are dealing here with two strictly separated, spatio-mechanically distinct spheres of reality and sides in the inner-mental self of the experiencing subjects as social and private persons, because the lived-experiencing, living and effecting arising from one of these two spheres is indeed distinguishable and distinct from that arising in the other. It would be quite wrong to infer from this that we would be dealing here, always and necessarily, with two spheres of the person's self that stand side by side and completely irreconcilable. That this cannot be the case one can already see from our previous discussions. Only in a few cases, especially those dealing with communities anchored in objective formations, {106} in which the community's life "in the sense" and "in the name" is limited to a sharply delineated sphere of objects, is a relation to a limited circle of objects, only there the two layers of "minds" and lived-experiences in the inner life of the respective person are separated at timessharply and immediately for the external observer, as well as in their own consciousness. This is the case, of course, in the case of mere "employees" (and so on) of the community, who are not at the same time its members. There can also exist an unbridgeable contrast between both spheres in the mental life of the individual and their demands in the case of conflict between the duties as a private and public person. But apart from that, and in general, the communal "soul" (the "social self" in *this* sense) and the individual "soul" (the private or individual self) in the members as well as the lived-experiences arising from them, are so closely woven together and intertwined, that it is almost impossible for both the external observer as well as the experiencing subject itself to discern where one of them "begins" and the other ones "stops," which lived-experiences (and so on) have their origin in one, which in the other. This is, to be sure, the case to an exceptionally high degree in the communities founded in the spiritual or empirical personhood of its members. (Marriage, friendship, certain religious communities, and so on.)

In the particular case of the "born" leader personality, who seems to be, so to speak, a unique, especially adequate incarnation of the communal spirit, both are woven together in an indistinguishable unity.

(The leader of a community may be grasped in a fourfold sense:[22]
1. It can be the leader's personality as such and his life and work, which form the meaning and foundation of the community. It is the unification with the leader that binds the members together. The life with the leader in loyalty, love and adoration is the purpose of the community. (As is the case, say, in the purely personal partisanship with the leader of an army (as, e.g., Dietrich

---

22 [The following four bullet points are printed in a smaller font.]

von Bern, Alaric, and so on),[23] saints, and so on. This is the purest case of "charismatic" leadership in the sense of Weber.)

2. The leader can also be a person in whom the "spirit" of the community is most adequately embodied, whose proper essence has the greatest inner kinship with the essence of the community. (One man think of so-called "national heroes" of certain peoples, tribes, and so on, who combine and embody in their person their "ideal" or "typical" traits in the most encompassing and perfected manner.)

3. The leader can have the greatest understanding of everything that is required *in communal affairs,* be it

    a. {107} because the leader—to speak with Weber[24]—knows best the handed down and conventional, the *"traditional"* course of the life of the community, be it

    b. because the leader has the best *"purposive rational"* understanding—in the sense of Weber[25]—of the essence of the community and the realization of its tasks in general and in particular.

4. Finally, the leader can be but a type of symbol for the personality of the community (as, perhaps, the Dalai Lama in Tibet), say in the sense of Hegel's view of the monarch as the "dot on the I."[26])

But even where we are not dealing with a leader as the incarnation of the communal spirit, there obtains here too the most intimate connection between the member and the community inside as well as outside the individual person. Not only *can the community not fully unfold its essence, if it does not count the individual persons as among their members demanded by this essence,* but the same holds vice versa: *only when a personality finds or creates the community demanded by its basic essence, can it fully unfold.*[27]

---

23 [Dietrich von Bern is the name of a character in Germanic heroic legend originally based on Theodoric the Great (454–526), king of the Ostrogoths. Alaric I (ca. 370–410) was the first king of the Visigoths.]

24 Weber 1946a, 296 ff., among other writings.

25 Weber 1946a, 296 ff.

26 Hegel 1991, addition to § 280.

27 See also, Scheler 2010, 374–375.

3.4 Inauthentic Communal Lived-Experiences and Social Acts in the Pregnant and Most Pregnant Sense

Now there exists the danger of a fateful misinterpretation of lived-experiences in the "sense" and in the "name" of the community, which we should reject outright. For, one could think that we are dealing here with "nothing other than" certain lived-experiences, which are *apprehended* or *designated* as lived-experiences by the subjects experiencing them or by an external observer, or both, as such lived-experiences.

For a lived-experience to become a communal lived-experience "in the sense" or "in the name" of the community, it would accordingly be required merely that the experiencing subject explicitly grasped, intended, or called it as such in *reflexive turn of regard,* or that another subject—grasping these lived-experiences from without—did so. To qualify a lived-experience as communal lived-experience would hence be nothing that were to be attributed to it *eo ipso* through its own immanent sense and the manner in which it arises in the experiencing subject {108}, through its origin in its communal self; but rather it would be appended to it only afterwards, from without, so to speak, when one's own or foreign lived-experiences direct itself at it intentionally, marking it as communal lived-experience. How erroneous such an interpretation is, is already clear from our previous analyses concerning communal and we-experiences. In many communal lived-experiences and lived-experiences "in the sense" of a community, the experiencing subject is oftentimes not completely aware of the fact that it now lives in communal lived-experiences, especially when it is entirely directed at its intended object instead of reflexively observing the manner of its lived-experiences. In the case of lived-experiences "in the name of" of a community, it indeed seems to be the case, if such a reflective consciousness of the manner of the lived-experiences must at all times be present. Nevertheless, however, here, too, one is not the cause of the other.

This is especially clear from the fact that there are indeed lived-experience that are grasped by the experiencing subject "for itself"—as also in the case of external observers "in themselves," oftentimes by both—as lived-experiences "in the sense" or also "in the name" of a community, without being thus. This is especially the case in *inauthentic communal lived-experiences*—inauthentic not from the standpoint of the experiencing subject (this occurs as well, but is something else), but from the *standpoint of the community,* or its essence, itself. Let us focus on this case in some greater detail.

If we find in a subject lived-experiences and manners of behavior, which are indeed real but do not correspond to the meaning and existence of his personality, in which a personality, or a side thereof, expresses itself, which may be appropriate in itself or in the case of other people, but not in *this* particular personality, precisely because it is another personality with a different character—or because it has not yet reached the height of development on which it otherwise could enact these manners of behavior (and so on) *authentically* (as when, e. g., a child takes a position which corresponded to it, according to its essence, but only as an adult—an "inauthenticity," which is, to be sure indeed different from the former and perhaps less "morally appropriate"), then we speak of *inauthentic lived-experiences,*[28] manners of behavior, and so on, from the standpoint of the *individual person.* (And, indeed, they also can be, in another sense, "inauthentic": inauthentic in the above "authentic" sense, with respect to the experiencing *subject,* {109} or else inauthentic with respect to the object of the lived-experience. (It would certainly be better to speak, in the latter case, of "deceptions" or "illusions.") So, for instance, some people always create for themselves a false image of their fellow humans by identifying them based on a certain trait simply with certain personality types and, accordingly, behave with respect to them in this manner, although these others are "in reality" very different. Here, the behavior of the experiencing subjects indeed corresponds to the behavior demanded by its essence vis-à-vis such personality types, and in this respect, it is "subjectively" authentic. On the other hand, it is, once again, "objectively" inauthentic, because the objects (the other human beings) precisely do not correspond to the image that the subject makes of them. But here we wish to speak only in the first, authentic, "subjective" sense of inauthentic lived-experiences.) The lived-experiences, manners of behavior, and so on, of a member (or of a "mere employee" or the like) of a community "in the sense" or "in the name" of the latter now can indeed be inauthentic from the standpoint of the respective subject as private or individual person. The essence, the character manifesting itself in these lived-experiences and behaviors, is by no means their essence and their character. Nonetheless these lived-experiences may be, from the standpoint of the community itself, downright authentic: in every respect there manifests itself in them fully and adequately the manner of lived-experiencing, apprehending and manners of behavior, as they correspond to the meaning and essence of the community. Here, a contradiction arises between the being and the essence of the member as an individual personality, as a private person, and the existence and essence of the community to which it belongs. (If this contradiction is exacerbated, if it reaches deeper layers, then it leads, in the consistent behavior of the member, to the member's exiting the community, perhaps to the latter's dissolution, if we are dealing with a greater number of members.)

---

28 Pfänder 1913, 75 ff.

On the contrary, it can also be the case that lived-experiences or manners of behavior on the part of a member, understood as private person, can be completely authentic, while they are equally inauthentic the moment they are supposed to hold as lived-experiences and manners of behavior "in the sense" or "in the name" of a community. The individual in this case mistakes oftentimes what is right for itself, as private person, with what it ought to do as a social person, as a member, perhaps as a representative[29] of the community. This can be because it consciously deviates from what is demanded by the meaning and essence of the community, or because it is lives in {110} good faith to really act and experience "in its sense," while it has not at all yet fully grasped the meaning of essence of its community to such a degree, while it not yet has unified itself with them, has not yet embodied them in itself, such that it is in general capable of experiencing and acting from out of them in an adequate sense.

(It is perhaps the greatest tragedy in the development and unfolding of communities that their history has been directed onto wrong paths through such inauthentic communal lived-experiences. In the case of leading personalities in communal life, such a danger of inauthentic communal lived-experiences is, of course, especially great and fateful.)[30]

Now we can, moreover, speak of yet two different further senses of inauthentic communal lived-experiences—similar also as in the case of the individual personhood—for the inauthenticity can be measure both in the *empirical* being and behavior (up to now) of the community, as well as in its *essence*, its "*idea*—or also in its metaphysically-real *essence*." Inauthentic in the first sense are all those communal lived-experiences that do not correspond to the behavior of the community, as it has played out empirically-factually so far, thus its "traditional" behavior in the sense of Weber. In this case, it does not correspond to the norm that have governed the communal life so far. Inauthentic (and false) communal lived-experiences in this sense identify themselves for the most part as such in that they contradict the tradition and practice dominating the community, the governing conventions and customs and the governing (perhaps fixed) law. The inauthentic lived-experiences in this sense can now be inauthentic additionally from the standpoint of the essence, the idea, the community, when they also do not correspond to the manners of behavior and so on demanded by these. This will be all the more the case, the more the empirical-factual being of the community corresponds to its essence. But if there is a schism between the empirical being of the community and its essence, then it is conceivable that precisely those commu-

---

29 Reinach 2012, 85.
30 [This paragraph is printed in a smaller font.]

nal lived-experiences and manners of behavior which are inauthentic in light of its *empirical* being up to now, present themselves from the standpoint of its *essence* as especially authentic and adequate—and vice versa: that lived-experiences and manners of behavior, which are completely authentic and justified in light of its *empirical* being, are, in the sense of its *essence*, its idea, entirely inauthentic and despicable.

(These three types of inauthentic communal lived-experiences are extremely hard to distinguish and all-too oftentimes {111} confused in theory and practice. Very often those manners of behavior of leading minds in a community are mistaken for subjective opinions and idiosyncrasies, because they contradict the current, traditional, conventional and legal norms of the communal life, while, in truth, they originate in deeper insight into the ultimate meaning, the metaphysical essence, the idea of the community. Vice versa, to be sure, oftentimes also subjective opinions and manners of behavior on the part of leaders are taken for intuitive expressions of the true communal spirit, without being so.)[31]

Now we can call the *authentic lived-experiences* and manners of behavior *"in the sense" and "in the name" of the community communal lived-experiences on the third level, communal lived-experiences in the pregnant sense.* They are typical especially for those members, who are *"organs"* of the community, either super- or subordinate organs. It is especially this type of lived-experience that the community constitutes itself vis-à-vis its own members as well as strangers: the members and the strangers grasp this community through these lived-experiences. These are therefore *"social acts" in the most pregnant sense.* By empathizing grasping of such acts, manners of behavior and total attitudes, the subject grasping them is necessarily referred beyond the experiencing, acting (and so on) individual subject toward the community "in whose sense and name" all of this takes place. (See the Appendix below.)[32]

(How these lived-experiences "in the sense" and "in the name" arise in a subject, how they are determined by it and are triggered by it psycho-genetically, is a completely different matter. They can be ordered by command from other communal organs or the totality or at least the majority of the other members[33] (as for instance in the case of an elected mandate of a representative), furthermore by permission[34], empowerment to act in general or certain cases "in their name." They can also arise by empathetic dedication to the communal attitude of the communal life or its attitude with respect to certain objectivities (for instance, in the

---

31 [This paragraph is printed in a smaller font.]
32 [See below, 182–184/{156–158}.]
33 Reinach 2012, 25.
34 Reinach 2012, 84 ff., 94 ff.

case of division of labor), as they are common in the community (tradition)—or as they arise from its sense and essence. Be it that they are fixed in different norms ("guiding rules," "resolutions," "constitutions," "statutes," and so on) or that the individual must first accomplish all of these for itself. Most likely, subordinate organs will lead these lived-experiences, manners of behavior and so on, back to commands or an explicit empowerment or at least to "tradition" and "purposive rationality"—to use two terms by Weber.[35] The latter type will most likely be reserved for the higher organs, especially the leaders of the community. But all of this does not belong to our ontological problem.)[36]

3.5 The Question Regarding the Personhood of a Community As Such

{112} From the vantage point reached now through our previous reflections we can also decide the question of whether or not communities as such are, or can be, in their essence, *actual* persons. They undoubtedly have a life and behavior of their own, which comes forth from the social self (in the first and third sense)[37] of the members and expresses itself in the lived-experiences and modes of behavior, which enact themselves "in the spirit" and "in the name" of the community. Communities thus have, in a certain sense, (1) a "self" of their own in the *self of the members.* (2) We must attribute to at least some communities a metaphysically real basic essence, which is, however, contained in a peculiar manner in the basic essence of the members and in the unification of their basic essences. However, merely those communities seem to be able to have a metaphysically real basic essence (Aristotle's *dunamei on,* as long as it is not unfolded; the *entelecheia,* as soon as it is fully unfolded), which are founded in the unification of the basic essences of the members. Here, too, the basic essence of the community does not simply coincide with the mere sum total of the individual essences; rather it constitutes a "spiritual collective person" in the sense of Scheler and Hegel, which, like all metaphysically real basic essences, are rooted in the divine essential basis[38] (in

---

35 Weber 1946a, 296, 299.
36 [This paragraph is printed in a smaller font.]
37 [See above, Sections 3.1 and 3.3.]
38 [Here again Walther uses the term *Wesensgrund* rather than the usual *Grundwesen.* See the Translators' Introduction, 33–34.]

Hegel's "absolute spirit")[39] (even if the members of the community are not aware of it at first). Such communities are, thus, not only a unity via the *"terminus ad quem,"*[40] as Simmel calls it in such cases.[41] They are also a unit via the *goal* of their development, which ultimately ends up in a unified behavior of the members in the sense of some guiding objective and the organization of this unified behavior, as some sociologists, such as Weber as well, believe.[42] In our opinion, they are rather, also a unity as *"terminus a quo"*; that is, the connectedness of the members here consists not only in a *unified* (external) *telos*, at which lived-experiences aim, but *in them themselves,* in their self, in certain cases in their basic essence, from which lived-experiences arise. This unity, which lies potentially already in their inner {113} being, becomes unfolded in them only through the striving for a unified telos and guiding motive along with the organization of the behavior arising, and is *elevated to the consciousness* of the members. Yet, the connectedness of their basic essences does not *arise (realiter)* through this. This connectedness, to the contrary, lies already in the basic essence of the member themselves, where, in its sense, it is already present in embryonic form.

(This is not to say, of course, that this is in fact the case in all *empirical* communities, for instance in all nations. In the case of many *factual* communities, the basic essence of the members may be absolutely irreconcilable with the basic essence of a community, and the behavior and lived-experiencing may correspond to the behavior and lived-experiencing demanded by the community only through a conscious or unconscious imitation and adaptation in inauthentic communal experiences (in the subjective sense), but not because it also corresponds to the basic essence of the member as individual. Here, it is indeed possible that the community has come to be a unity *in fact* only through the identical external goals, fates, and so on, over the course of history. Thus, only through the *"terminus ad quem,"* not the *"terminus a quo."* Yet this does not rule out that a community's unity is not also possible *in principle* as a *"terminus a quo,"* a unity that is embodied and realized in the real world through empirical fates in the course of history. Whether or not the unity of a community is based on a *"terminus a quo"* or a *"terminus ad quem,"* respectively, may nonetheless be impossible to decide for the external ob-

---

39 We also wish to remark that Scheler, too—2010, 375 ff., a work that has only become available to us during the printing of this book—takes this position in his "sociological proof for the existence of God."

40 [The conceptual pair *"terminus a quo"* (concept from which) and *"terminus ad quem"* (concept toward which) stems from Scholasticism.]

41 [Simmel 2009, 45–49.]

42 See, among others, Weber 1913a ["Contribution to the Discussion of Ferdinand Schmid's Lecture," *The Law of Nationalities*] 74.

server, for instance, the historian, especially when the latter does not himself belong to this community, or at least when his own basic essence is not itself actually related to the basic essence of the community. Of course, it is also possible that someone's individual basic essence, who is *in fact* not a member of a community, is related to the latter's basic essence in a much profounder way than to the community of which he is in fact a part. (As, for instance, the Englishman Lafcadio Hearn in his relationship to Japanese identity.)[43] Perhaps even his basic essence was much more intimately related to the basic essence of that community, to which he does not in fact belong, than that of many of the factual members of that community.)[44]

On the other hand, those communities that are founded merely in an external guiding objective or the empirical existence of their members do not necessarily seem to have such a metaphysically real communal basic essence. For the most part, it rather seems to be lacking, in any case it is not in the least demanded by the meaning and essence of this communal type. (A community's metaphysically *real* basic essence is not to be mistaken, to be sure, with the *notional* essence and the idea of a community, which can pertain also to those communities that do not · (or cannot) have an actual basic essence in the sense expressed above. This conceptual essence, {114} this idea of a community is, according to its sense, something completely separate, something that is in no way founded in the conceptual essence, in the idea, but also not in the metaphysically real basic essence of the individual members—nor in the conceptual essence or the idea of their sum total— as individual persons.)

We must, however, completely reject the notion that all communities—of any type whatsoever—have *their own Ego-center of will and self-control*. In this, they are rather completely dependent and rely on the existence of psycho-physical individual persons—the members. There is not, as we already indicated, a separate center of an Ego and of self-control of a community over and above the Ego-centers of the members, which would be separate from the latter. Neither is there, properly speaking, a separate communal Ego-center, which would somehow be *realiter* contained *in* or next to the individual Ego-centers of the members in their inner mental total existence (similar to the social self in the individual self, the commu-

---

43 [Patrick Lafcadio Hearn (1850–1904), later known as Koizumi Yakumo, was, contrary to what Walther indicates here, born on the Greek Island Lefkada to a Greek mother and an Irish father, and later emigrated, via the US, to Japan, where he remained until the end of his life. Hearn came to identify Japan as his spiritual home and attempted to assimilate into Japanese culture. He is most well-known for his work on Japanese folktales and ghost stories. His writings on Japanese culture were much read in the West at the time of Walther's dissertation.]

44 [This paragraph is printed in smaller font.]

nal basic essence in the individual basic essence). Likewise, there is equally no such thing as a *communal lived-body of its own*—which also does not belong to every actual psycho-physical personality—next to, behind or above the lived-bodies of the members and their sum total. In this respect, too, the community is entirely dependent and relies in its being on the being of its members.

What exists, thus, is only a separate communal life, behavior and lived-experiencing, which has its origin in the members' social self. This presumably pertains to *all* communities—no matter which type—without exception; on top of this some communities have, as we have seen, a basic essence. But these expressions of the communal self (and perhaps of the communal basic essence) do not penetrate into the open through a separate, individual communal Ego-center as actual lived-experiences. They are also not transmitted through a separate, individual communal lived-body into "external" actions and manners of behavior. They rely, rather, in rigorous essential necessity, on the Ego-centers and lived-bodies of the members. We can, thus, well maintain that the community is a *supra-personal*, psycho-physical (and spiritual) *unity*, but not a *separate person*, since what is lacking here is the essential trait of a person, the center of consciousness and will. Rather, a community depends on the Ego-centers of the members, as also on their lived-bodies.

{115} But this is not to say that *every* communal lived-experience must now actualize itself also in the Ego-centers of *all* members (cf. already above, 117 f. / {86 f.}), that every "external" communal action would have to be enacted through the lived-body and the bodily organs of *all* members—rather, this is quite different in the different communities.

(Depending on circumstances, special eidetic, empirical, traditional, or also stipulated, legal (and so on) rules obtain here. These stipulate especially, how many and which members have to make those decisions regulating the behavior "in the spirit" or "in the name" of the community. Moreover, decisions pertain, in certain circumstances, to certain especially important individual lived-experiences or manners of behavior on the part of the community (e.g., peace treaties and declarations of war in the case of states). One can especially notice this in the different state constitutions. Here, in certain cases, it is precisely stipulated for different manners of behavior "in the spirit" and "in the name" of the community, in which way and to what extent these manners of behavior must actualize themselves in the totality or in a more or less defined, more discretely or more generally characterized or qualified number of members, or perhaps in only one or several communal organs, in order to be actually valid for the community. So, for instance, in all decisions of a state requiring a plebiscite, the actualization of the respective communal lived-experiences is in principle required for the totality of all full members, although not the agreement of all members (as it was demanded, for instance, in the earlier Polish *szlachta*),[45] but for making decisions it is required only of a certain majority. In many constitutions (and statutes of clubs, clerical constitutions, and so on), the number and range of members, in which certain communal lived-experiences must be actualized in order to count as communal lived-experiences, are limited quantitatively or qualitatively, traditionally or more or less according to certain principles, as this is shown, for instance, in constitutions of republican or monarchic democracies, of constitutional or absolute monarchies, of aristocracies, ochlocracies, and so on. Here, it is extremely important for the structure and type of community, which rules it stipulates as internal and external criteria, which lived-experiences, manners of behavior (and so on) of their members should be enacted "in the spirit" and "in the name" of the community. These rules can be identical, at first, for all manners of behavior and lived-experiencing, yet some manners of behavior of an especially important sort require, occasionally, a different quantity and quality of members for their actualization than other, less important ones. Likewise, the principles of selection that decide which members are suited in all or only certain cases to actualize communal lived-experiences can be radically different according to the characteristic sense and essence of the community. To these cases belong, for instance, the principles of selection contained in the regulations of certain constitutions to decide someone's active or passive right to vote. (So, for instance, it is very important, whether the active and passive right to vote is made dependent upon the respective members' ownership of capital or land, upon taxation, level of education, political leaning, {116} class status, and so on and so forth.) These criteria likely depend ultimately on the inner founding of a community in the unification of its members and through the teleological objective to which the total life or the respective part (the respective "department") of communal life relates.)[46]

In these cases, no special type of actualization of communal lived-experiences is prescribed by the general essence of the community "as such"—from the latter one can only infer that the communal lived-experiences necessarily do not actualize themselves in a communal Ego-center lying outside of the members, that the communal actions cannot be enacted through a separate communal lived-body, but that they, instead, always have to be enacted through the Ego-center and the lived-body of one, several, or all members. How many members there must be and in what way they must be qualified, in each case, can, however, not be inferred from the essence of the community "as such." Only this much is clear: that the

---

45 [The *szlachta* was a legally privileged noble class in Poland, ruling from the early Middle Ages until the 15th century.]

46 [This paragraph is printed in a smaller font size.]

individual members or the majority of members who are relevant here, must be intimately knowledgeable of and unified with the sense and essence of the community as a whole or with the part in question, such that no inauthentic communal lived-experiences can be attributed to the community itself. Yet even if the general essence of the community "as such" does not and cannot establish more precise criteria, the special and "individual" essences of the different communities do perhaps contain here (as we believe) very specific, essentially necessary norms that are to be investigated respectively.

Perhaps one can say that the more the significance and purpose of a community concerns the life of the members themselves as empirical persons (as in the state) or as spiritual persons (as in the church), the more is demanded from the essence of the community, such that all communal lived-experiences—or at least all the important ones—actualize themselves in as many members as possible and that only their collaboration in certain manners of the community's behavior can come about. This demand exists, at least as an ideal, in certain communities, although in fact they sometimes can and must not be fulfilled, since the members do not—or do not *yet*—have the necessary inner maturity and necessary insight into the significance and essence of their community, which forms the highest presupposition for this maturity.

On the other hand, in communities where the significance and purpose of the community, the norm of the communal life, relate back to some objective {117} beyond the members themselves, of which sort whatsoever, here, under certain circumstances, the participation of all or as many members as possible may be not only unnecessary but perhaps even harmful and must be prohibited. In such cases, this participation is necessarily restricted to political, military, juridical, religious, artistic, scientific (and so on) "experts."

(Also, we can glean the answer to the eminently important problem for a democracy, whether the will of the community regarding a certain issue can be identified with the will of the totality, or at least the majority of the members concerning this issue. This answer can be inferred from what has been said before, without, however, discussing it here in greater detail, since it does not, to be sure, belong to an eidetic-ontological treatise. We can well say that the will of the community (of a state) can only correspond to the will of all members to the extent that this will emerges from the communal self (in the first and third sense)[47] in them, thus from that stratum of their mental life, in which they live based on the unification with the community with the other members and with the normative guiding objective of the communal life "in the spirit" of the commu-

---

47 [See above, Sections 3.1 and 3.3.]

nity. The more the individual and the totality of the individuals live "in the spirit" of the community, the more clearly and insightfully are they able to consider and solve the issue in question "in the spirit of the community," the more the communal will and the majority of the members' wills converge. But unfortunately, this relation is factually and commonly by no means always so. At first, and generally speaking, only a few members have grasped the "spirit" of the community to such an extent that they would be capable of correctly judging and acting in its sense. More commonly, they mistake the opinion they have formed as a private person with the one that they should gain through immersion into and unification with the communal spirit and essence. Or they follow merely blind impulses and instincts, which perhaps come about only on the basis of a previous or concurrent, direct (through orators, and so on) or indirect (through press, pictures, movies, and so on) mass suggestion.[48] Only where the majority of the members truly live from and in the spirit of the community does its will correspond to the ideal (i. e., demanded by its significance and essence) or empirical (i. e., corresponding to its empirical being up to the present) will of the community. If this is not the case, then an individual or a small minority, who are *actually* "inspired by the spirit of the community," are much better suited to bring it to expression than the majority or the totality of members could. This is also the case in communities where the members themselves, their lives as empirical or spiritual persons, their development and their welfare (perhaps in their "spiritual salvation"), are the purpose of the community. On the other hand, it would be the ideal of every community that an interpenetration *of this kind* took place with the spirit of the community in all fully valid members (to be sure, only in *those* sphere of their lives, {118} in which the spirit of the community demands it), such that the will of the community at all times coincides with the reflective will of the totality or at least the majority of its members.—Yet it is, to be sure, also a legitimate postulate on the part of all individual persons, that they never be forced to belong to a community whose significance and purpose is irreconcilable with the demands of their own general, special, individual, and so on, basic essence.)[49]

---

48 Le Bon 2002; 1910. [Gustave Le Bon (1841–1931) was a French polymath and is widely considered to be the founder of group psychology. His writings had a profound influence on many sociologists in the early 20th century, especially Weber. The original French version of *Psychologie de foules* was first published in 1895. Le Bon's *Psychologie politique et défense sociale* has not been translated into German or English.]

49 [This paragraph is again printed in smaller font.]

3.6 Reciprocal Interaction and Reciprocal Unification

3.6.1 Between the Members and the Community as Such

We saw, thus, that the knowing-of, "directing-oneself-toward," and the "unification-with" are not restricted to the relation of the members amongst each other, but there is also a knowing of the community as such, a directing-oneself toward it and a unification with it on the part of the members. But here, too, the fully unfolded communal life does not come to a halt, but to all of these is added the reciprocal interaction and reciprocal unification between the members and the community itself, as such.

But how are we to conceive of these [reciprocal relations]? How and in what sense are they possible? (Of course, also in this case of the reciprocal interaction we are dealing here, once again, with an *intentional* reciprocal interaction.) On the lowest level of communal life, in which the community is not understood and encountered by the members as an independent object, where not yet organs, no actually conscious life and behavior "in the sense" and "in the name" of the community have formed themselves, there, to be sure, one cannot speak of an intentional reciprocal interaction between the members and the community in the strict sense. At best, there can obtain an unconscious reciprocal interaction "in itself," which perhaps the external observer can grasp, but which, when seen from within, by the members, coincides with the reciprocal interaction between these, or parts thereof (in the context of the community). For the external observer, it can already be grasped as something proper, because the reciprocal interaction between the members in the communal life here (in the sense and on the basis of the community) is already distinguishable from the other reciprocal relations between the members, which may take place outside of this context. Thus, it is conceivable, for instance, that some members of a family are yet at the same time members of a scientific society. Then they are in the relation of reciprocal interaction and perhaps even in reciprocal unification {119}, both as members of the society as well as family members (and perhaps also in other ways). And yet their reciprocal interaction and reciprocal unification in the scientific society never is in question for an investigation of the family as such and the reciprocal interaction of its members *in it*, likewise vice versa—even if the family, in this case, has not yet constituted itself as an independent object in the consciousness of the members. Thus, already here, the reciprocal interaction of members *within a community* is indeed clearly distinguishable from its *other* reciprocal interactions. For, to the external observer already here the seed of a reciprocal interaction between the community as such and its members reveals itself.

One can only speak of an authentic reciprocal interaction and reciprocal unification between the members and the community, where the community is also a community "for itself,"[50] where the members know of it as an independent formation, where some or all members live *consciously* "in the sense" or "in the name" of the community, especially on the highest level of communal life, when a formation of proper "organs," "institutions," and so on, of the community has occurred. We find a *transition* from the reciprocal interaction between the members amongst each other as individuals to the reciprocal interaction between the members and the community as such, where the majority or totality (all-ness) of the members as such (thus not yet as a unified independent community as such) takes on certain manners of behavior in the broadest sense, which direct themselves[51] at certain individual members of groups thereof. (As when, for instance, a part of the members of a city condemns, bans or also honors, greets (and so on) a fellow member in the name "of the citizens" of this city (thus not yet "the city").) Here, the sum of the members as such, but not yet the community as such, takes a stand as a unified formation. The borders between both of these forms are, to be sure, very fluent.

In reciprocal interaction between individual or all members and the community itself, the latter meets the members as if it were a person (we already saw in what sense it can do that), especially mediated through manners of behavior on the part of certain of its members (perhaps organs) in its "sense and name"—be it now that these members have such a function {120} only intermittently, or are employed permanently as organs of the community, or that they represent it, or finally that they embody, so to speak, the community and its power (perhaps its self-importance, its sovereignty), such that the latter is incarnated in them, so to speak. (As is the case, say, in some secular and clerical leaders.) In this way, through missives, calls, demands, manners of behavior of any form (and so on and so forth), the community directs itself at all times through its representatives and organs at its members, as well as under certain circumstances at other people and communities. But the members, too, direct themselves in all kinds of possible ways, through organs and representatives or by addressing other members—*as* members—or their totality in general (as in, e.g., newspaper articles, calls, speeches, and so on and so forth) at the community.

Something similar occurs in the case of reciprocal unification (and severance) between the members and the community itself, which is but a special case of the

---

50 On this topic (besides the other literature already cited in a different context), see Holzapfel 1903, 7.
51 [Reading *"wenden"* for *"wendet."*]

reciprocal interaction between them. The latter, too, is enacted through manners of behavior in the broadest sense "in the sense" and "in the name" of the community on the part of all or some of its members, its organs and its representatives—be it spontaneously, be it on the basis of very distinct rules and ceremonies regulated by tradition or statute. We would count as belonging to this especially the acts of the (ceremonial) acceptance of a new member into the community (baptism, confirmation, and so on, as acceptance into the church; acceptance into a state, a guild, a club, and so on) which is, indeed, in a certain sense a unification of the community with the respective member or members. Also, in this case of unification and reciprocal unification we find all the same modifications, which we found in the analysis of unification and reciprocal unification on the part of the members with each other. What is likely to be especially important in the unification of the community with its members is the relation of equi-, super- or subordination of the community with respect to the members in the unification. This unification, too, requires merely the corresponding, but not the identically same, unification of the members as reciprocation. (We certainly do not have to emphasize that this unification in terms of equi-, super- or subordination *with the community itself* is not the same as a unification of the members amongst each other, or of one or several of its members with one, a group, or the sum of the respective other members, or of the members with the organs or representatives of the community, although especially the latter case can be a *symbol* or a preliminary step for the unification with the community itself.

{121} Likewise, there is a separation of the community with respect to its members, which likewise occurs through manners of behavior in the broadest sense "in the sense" and "in the name" of the members, organs, and so on. It comes to expression especially in phenomena such as exclusion, ban, excommunication, and so on.

3.6.2 The Reciprocal Interaction and Reciprocal Unification of Communities with Each Other

Yet, the higher communal life itself does not come to a halt with reciprocal interaction (and reciprocal unification) of the community itself with its members. Through the lived-experiences "in the sense" and "in the name" of some or all members, as well as the organs and representatives of the communities, the latter can indeed take a stand as persons and are thereby put into a position of relating to each other like other persons, be it in mere reciprocal interaction (albeit a reciprocal interaction also of a "higher order"), be it in a reciprocal unification. It is a presupposition for this reciprocal interaction and reciprocal unification, however, that they mutually recognize each other as *real* subjects, who are capable through these subjects and in the Ego-centers of their members—especially of their organs, representatives, and leaders—of their own willed actions. Thus, it does not suffice here that a community stands as an independent, autonomous formation in the consciousness of *its members*, that it forms in this sense, "for itself," an independent unity, but it must function as such also for the *other communities*, with whom it comes into contact, and their representatives, organs, and a part or all of their members. From this we derive a new meaning of the concept of a community "*in* and *for* itself."

In the case of the reciprocal unification of communities, we also see the relations of super-, sub- and equi-ordering, likewise the modifications of the inner (and outer) contours in the unification. From here we can begin to understand, we believe, also phenomena such as the heterocephaly and autocephaly of communities—to use two concepts from Weber[52]—in relation to other communities, to the extent that they arise in the unification of communities. (One may also think of merging and overreaching in the governance and territories relating states and the State (here the former unify themselves with the latter in a subordinate manner, while they are equi-ordered with each other); of protectorates and colonies with respect to their protective or colonial leaders; of lands of the Empire (Alsace) to the Empire;[53] of members of a federation of states {122} to each other (here we have an equal ordering), and so on.) The intentional modifications of the unification are also to be found in this sphere. (Personal unions, real unions, military alliances, customs unions and so on between states, who are each founded intentionally in different ways.)

3.7 Communities of the 1st, 2nd, 3rd, 4th, ... nth Power

Just as a community as a higher unity with its own life arose from a unification of several individuals with one other, likewise, under certain circumstances, from the unification of communities with each other, also *new communities of communities* come forth as higher unities with their own life, perhaps with their own organs, representatives and leaders. (For example, states of a union in contrast to union states, perhaps the "league of nations," also societies of societies, "central councils" and so on and so forth.) These communities, too (one could perhaps call them com-

---

52 [Weber 1981, 164. Weber uses the terms *heterokephalen* and *autokephalen* to mean extraneously-directed and self-directed, respectively.]
53 [Up until 1918, Alsace was part of the German *Reich*.]

munities of the 2nd power) can now, of course, in the same sense as communities of the 1st power (thus communities of individuals), through *their* members, especially *their* organs and representatives (who are now either organs or members of their member communities, or else mere "employees" and "organs" (and so on) of communities of the 2nd power), who here thus *cannot* at the same time be *members of the communities of the 2nd power*, as in the case of communities of the 1st power, since the communities of the 2nd power for the most part only accept communities but not individuals as members, [these communities] can come into reciprocal interaction and reciprocal unification with respect to their members and in turn their members. We shall call this an *internal reciprocal interaction* and reciprocal unification. But they can also come into the relation of a reciprocal interaction and reciprocal unification with individuals or with other communities of the 1st and 2nd power—we shall call this *external reciprocal interaction* and reciprocal unification.

But new communities can also arise from the reciprocal unification of communities of the 2nd power with communities of the 1st and 2nd power (as, say, in the case of the unification of a state of a union with another simple state or with another state of a union, for instance into a league of states), and they would now be communities of the 3rd power. These, too, can in turn display an internal and external reciprocal interaction and reciprocal unification. From these, in turn, higher communities of ever higher potencies can arise, up to the nth power. For *in principle* and, perhaps also in fact, there is no limit to this process.

3.8 The Question Concerning the Reality of the Community As Such

{123} In connection with what we discussed previously, we would like to address the important and controversial question of whether communities as such, in terms of their meaning and essence, are *as a reality* separate formations, existing for themselves, or instead only as the sum of its members—although this problem actually transcends the competency of an ontological-phenomenological work. That a community as an independent object of intentional acts of the most various forms, sharply distinguished from its members and their sum and reciprocal interaction, can very well be *meant* and indeed must be meant for the sake of a formation of a higher social life—this we have already demonstrated. But what about the reality of this intentional formation? Is it a mere product of abstraction of theoretical thinking, or a mere summarizing of similar traits in the givennesses of human realities for the sake of the "economy of thought"[54] or a fantastic idea that people just happen to make use of in their practical behavior—as some extreme individualists in the field of sociology believe? Or is it rather a peculiar formation existing for itself, which is the *actual,* true *real* being, while its members are merely ephemeral products and embodiments of this *"ens realissimum"*? These two views stand juxtaposed to each other starkly opposed in sociology and history. According to one view, there exists "nothing other than" a sum of separate individuals, which may be subsumed, for theoretical reasons of purposiveness, under the concept of different communities, but these concepts do not correspond to a reality existing in itself. On the other hand, one finds the opposite view, held especially by some socialists and Hegelians. Which stand should we take toward this issue? Is a community—as *reality* (thus not merely as concept or idea)—merely the sum of its members, or does it exist apart from them, independently of them, by way of "objective" spirit (and so on), an independent "communal soul", and so on? Is it more or less than the sum of its members?

First, this question cannot be answered in the same way for all types of communities. A community founded exclusively in the individual, thus as "irrepresentable," empirical or spiritual personality of its members, will certainly coincide in a higher degree with its sum {124} than a community, which rests on something objective and on a general, position-taking and creative behavior toward it, whereas the individual members as individual persons are more or less "replaceable."

Yet, despite these important distinctions, the following holds, most likely, for *all* communities of whichever type, namely, that they are in one respect more, in another, however, less than the sum of its members and their lived-experiences. For in the first respect, certainly those real and ideal formations and objects, in which they are founded or at least co-founded, also belong to the being of a community. Thus, for instance, it is indubitable that a territory belongs its state;[55] moreover, a great part of varied cultural, scientific, religious, and so on, formations, which were created by its members in its "sense," perhaps even in its "name," on its soil and from out of its "spirit," belong to many communities. Also, as "spiritual" or physical possession, many such formations belong to certain empirical, real communities as such (clubhouses, administrative buildings with all of their equipment and so on and so forth). To this extent, the community is thus certainly more than the sum of its members and their communal lived-experien-

---

54 [Walther here alludes to the principle of *"Denkökonomie"* found in the works of Richard Avenarius (1843–1896) and Ernst Mach (1838–1916).]

55 For example, Kjellén 1917; Simmel 2009, 445 ff. [The year 1917 here refers to Margarethe Langfeldt's German translation of Kjellén's book. The original Swedish text, *Staten som lifsform*, was published in 1916.]

ces. On the other hand, and indubitably so, the entire circle of existence, lived-experience, and behavior on the part of the individual members of a community and their sum, in which they do not live, experience and act from out of their social self "in the sense" or "in the name" of this community, but instead as private persons "in the sense" or "in the name" of *other* communities. All of this certainly does *not* belong to the being and life of the respective community. In this respect, thus, the latter is less than the sum of its members and their lived-experiences.

But now, wherein lies its existence, its real embodiment, since it also cannot be *realiter* entirely independent of its members or their sum? Without a doubt, a community is and exists, to be sure, *realiter:*

1. When it is a community having a metaphysically-real basic essence—in the *metaphysically-real basic essence* of its members and the connectedness of their basic essences (be it in an intentional unification of basic essences; be it that the inner connectedness of the members reaches into their basic essence, although they might not be aware of this).

2. {125} Mainly in that "sphere" (or whatever one wishes to call it) in the self of its members, in which they are unified with the other members, with the main object of the community and perhaps with the latter itself, thus with the "*social self*" (in the 1st and 3rd sense), from which they live "in the sense" and under certain circumstances "in the name" of the community.

3. In all lived-experiences, manners of behavior, activities, and so on, which the members enact, living from out of this sphere, thus, in their "social acts" of all sorts. (The reality of the community, thus, consists by *no means only* in these lived-experiences, and so on, as one could surmise according to, for instance, Wundt's theory of social actuality.)[56]

4. The reality of the community with the basic essence, self and Ego of its members, as the basic essence itself, *grounded in the lived-body and bodily life* of the members. This is especially the case in those communities, where the unification of the members is intentionally anchored in their lived-body and their bodily life. But also *those* communities in which this is by no means the case, are rooted as reality (in *this* earthly world at least) in the lived-body of its members, since the members as psycho-spiritual individuals themselves depend, in their *existence* and in their empirical reciprocal interaction with each other and with the spatio-temporal, organic-inorganic world, on their lived-body. (A correct kernel of historical materialism is ultimately based on this grounding of communities in the lived-body and in the bodily life.)

---

56 [Walther does not specify to which of Wundt's works she is referring here. Elsewhere, she refers to Wundt's *Völkerpsychologie* (1900–1920).

The last point of access for the reality of the communities lies in the *objective, material and spiritual formations* of all sort, *which are created by the members for the communities* (such as buildings, scientific, militaristic, religious, and legal institutions and organizations with all of their equipment, and so on) or "in their name" or at least "in their sense" are created by the members as *products of their communal life.*

The highest, most authentic and most important point of access for the reality of communities is undoubtedly the social self (esp. in the 1st and 2nd sense) of the members, and then also, in certain communities, their basic essence. There they are, so to speak, incarnated in a "bodily" manner, their reality is rooted most firmly here, even if at any given moment the totality does not live from out of it currently, or perhaps even {126} none of its members. (As when, for instance, all members are sleeping[57]—if Wundt is right, then in such a case the communities would cease to exist for that period of time.)

The reality of communities of higher potencies is grounded in a more complicated manner, namely:

1. In the member communities, thus indirectly in the same real points of access as those organs, representatives and leaders, who enact the reciprocal interaction and reciprocal unification
   1. between the member communities *amongst each other,*
   2. between the member communities and the *community of higher power on the part of the member communities.*
2. In the life, lived-experience, and behavior of the organs and members of the member communities, to the extent that it is grounded and regulated through the meaning and the leitmotif of the community of higher power and the unification with it and taking place in *its* "sense and name."
3. In the organs, representatives, and so on, of the community of higher order as such (in the same sense as in the case of the members of communities of the 1st power), who are not and cannot be *their immediate members,* but instead only their "employees," "delegates," and the like, be it that they are
   1. members of their member communities, or
   2. not even that.
4. In the lived-experiences and manners of behavior (and so on) of these organs (and so on), which take place "in the sense and the name" of the community of higher power.

---

57 Holzapfel 1903, 9. This is a treatise with which, however, we do not agree, despite its many valuable analyses, to the extent that it is based on positivist assumptions and on the theory of analogous inference concerning the grasping of the mental life of an other.

5. In the real objects (and so on), which are the property of the communities of higher order (for instance, the weapons and such of the army of the old German Foreign Legion), or in the products of the organs (and so on) of the community of higher power, or even the products of the members and organs (and so on) of the member communities, which arose "in the sense" or "in the name" of the community of higher power.

{127} We shall not delve deeper into the first four points of access of the reality of communities, since everything to be said about them is already clear from what has been said above: We could merely repeat it here. However, we wish to investigate the fifth point more closely.

This fifth, most indirect point of access for the reality of the communities was their accomplishments, their products and "works" of all sorts of the communities,[58] that is, all those products, formations in the broadest sense or modifications of objects of nature, and so on, which are brought forth from the members *as members* of the community (or, respectively, in communities of higher power: from their mere organs, who are not at the same time their members, or also from the members of the member communities) for these themselves, or at least in their "sense and name," be it explicitly or not, conscious or not. These can be: spiritual formations (such as languages, sciences, legal orders, and so on), religious formations (such as confessions and cults and everything belonging to these), technical formations (such as trains, bridges, canals), artistic formations; also material formations and tools for the sake of spiritual or practical purposes of all sort (edifices, and so on and so forth) or also modifications, and the like, which communities make in the material or organic objects (in the broadest sense) of their surroundings, be it that they are co-founded in them (state territory, and so on) or that they perhaps own these, and so on. (One may think here of all the changes that a state territory, a landscape, and so on, undergo through the life of the communities living in them, through the building of cities, villages, through agriculture, forestation, mining, horticulture, through trafficking (building canals, railways, cattle breeding, and so on and so forth).) In all of this—although in a less immediate manner as in the members of members (or the mere organs, and so on, or the members of member communities in the communities of higher potencies) and their vital, mental and spiritual life—lies and authenticates itself the reality and ontic manner of many communities. Indeed, in the case of many long extinct communities, of whom also the last members and organs, and so

---

58 Husserl 2002, which contains important reflections with respect to these problems from the manuscript for *Ideas* II (1989) (unpublished and unknown to us).

on, have died a long time ago, these are the only testimonies of their {128} reality, which still inform us of their existence and being. (One may think here of the pyramids and the sphinxes with their inscriptions, the ruins of cities and villages, the stilt houses, kitchen waste piles, graves, jewelry, weapons, tools, and so on, of prehistoric cultures.) All of these formations, upon closer immersion into their meaning and their ontic mode, show up as *"works."*[59] They did not come about on their own or through the mere interplay between physical, chemical, biological or mental forces of nature, but in their meaning and their being they refer back to the purposive, creative activity of mental-spiritual subjects, and indeed not only of individuals, but also of communities. Or we are talking about products of nature or culture to which are attached "predicates of achievement,"[60] bequeathed to them by individuals or communities (such as letter symbols, monuments, signals, public buildings, and so on). These are "predicates of achievement," giving them sense and meaning, which they would not have as *mere objects of nature*. (One may think here of the black dots of printer's ink on paper, which form the "natural" (chemical-physical) basis of a book, or of the mere chemical, physical or mineralogical meaning of stones, glass shards and the like, and of wood, which are involved in constructing a church.) In all of this is manifest and proven the existence and the manner of being of those individuals, of which the community consists and, ultimately, the community itself. All of these "characters of work" and "predicates of achievement" refer back to the thinking and creating of human subjects and through these once again to the communities, from whose spirit, in its "sense and name," these subjects perhaps creatively acted. In such manner, in the building style of churches, castles and cities, but also in the patterns of traffic, economy, and agriculture becomes manifest the spirit of a community and it embodies itself in them.[61] (In Gothic or Romanesque churches, in Greek temples, in the frame houses of Rothenburg and Nuremberg, in the modern tenement buildings and streets, and so on and so forth, in each case is manifested the spirit of a different community.)

---

59 Husserl 2002 [*Hua Mat* IV, 103–110.]

60 Husserl 2002. [In this text, Husserl uses the word *"Prädikat,"* and its cognates, such as *"Wertprädikat"* or *"Zeitprädikat,"* more than 90 times. The specific term *"Leistungsprädikat,"* which Walther uses here, is not in Husserl's text.]

61 Also, in Spengler 1926, we find pointers (albeit not more than that) in this direction. Likewise in the unpublished part of Stein 1989. In the field of literature, Friedrich Gundolf, among others, has shown this in his writings. [Friedrich Gundolf, born Gundelfinger, (1880–1931), was a German-Jewish literary critic and poet, and a member of the George Circle. Walther would later attend his lecture course on 19th century German literature at the University of Heidelberg.]

{129} Certainly, one has to distinguish the emanations of the individual creative and original power from those of the communal spirit. And yet they are intimately unified and mutually permeate each other. Even for the most individual artistic creation of the most individual personality it is conceivable, that it would not have come forth at least in part from the meaning and spirit of one or several communities, of whom the creator of the work was or is a member (be it a community of a people, a culture, a union of friends, or whatever else.

(Likewise, no communal product is conceivable, of course, which not somehow, at a certain place, a most original spark of an individual spirit would have ignited, even though it may never become known from whom and at what place. (One may think here of the origin of proverbs, folk songs, indeed language itself.))[62]

Here, too, one has to distinguish what is authentic and inauthentic, purposive and its opposite, but of course in a different sense than in the case of authentic and inauthentic communal lived-experience. For these works and such can be genuine or false:

1. from the standpoint of the work or the object of accomplishment and its meaning and its sense. (The meaning of an artwork may, for instance, "not be expressed correctly" by the artist, one feels what it is supposed to mean, but the representation somehow does not "do it.")
2. from the standpoint of the creative individual (as in the case of lived-experiences) and
3. from the standpoint of the community itself;
4. in the communities of higher power: from the standpoint of their member communities (and perhaps *their* members).

So, for instance, an edifice (say, a church or a city hall, and so on) may very well correspond to the spirit of its builder and the community to which he belongs— and yet it can very well be purposive. Or it can, conversely, be adequate to its purpose and the creative manner of its individual creator in every manner, yet without corresponding to the essence (or the empirical being) of the community, whose spirit is to be manifest in it (as when, for instance, one would transpose a city hall in medieval-gothic style into a city like New York). At times, once again, something is adequate to the taste and the essence of a leading personality in the community and of an artist, while it positively mocks the spirit of the community as such, which it is supposed to express. (One may think here, for instance, of the Siegesall-

---

62 [This paragraph is printed in a smaller font.]

ee in Berlin, and similar things.)[63] It is also inauthentic when a community, which does not have enough creative power of its own to create something of this sort expressing its proper essence, or which is forced through membership in a community of higher power—perhaps in order to conform to those other {130} member communities—when such a community simply takes up architectonic, artistic, legal, scientific, and so on, styles and formations, perhaps also the mores and customs of communities and cultures of an entirely different type, and "grafts"[64] them onto themselves. Yet, this may not be justified by a deeper essential kinship of its own spirit and essence with that of the respective cultures and communities. Here we have merely a semblance of reality, not the true reality of the community, which expresses itself in these formations. The same holds, of course, also to a certain extent, in the case of inauthentic communal lived-experiences (in every sense). All these dangers of an ethical or aesthetic derailment, to which already individual persons in their real existence in relation to each other are subject, repeat themselves here in an extended manner in the relation of communities to each other, to their members, to other people and to any objects "as such." It is the task of a general, specific and individual, ontological, historical and political investigation of the essence of communities, to find here what is appropriate for a community and its essence and its respective level of development, and to show up and reject all that is inauthentic and mere semblance.[65]

We spoke above of a "faux reality" of communities in inauthentic communal lived-experiences and inauthentic communal products. In so doing, we of course do not wish to deny that these lived-experiences and products exist *in real life* precisely in the same manner as the authentic ones. Only spoken from a metaphysical point of view, they seem to us, in a certain sense, less real and more ephemeral than the authentic ones. It was Hegel who coined the famous-infamous phrase: "Only the rational is real, the real is rational."[66] He meant by this that only that is truly real, according to the "concept" (by which he typically understands the metaphysically-real basic essence, without sharply distinguishing it from the ontological and conceptual essence), only that is of a *metaphysically* lasting existence and value, because only the embodiment of the "concept," of the metaphysically-

---

63 [The *Siegesalle* (Avenue of the Victors) was a boulevard in Berlin that stretched from Kemperplatz to Königsplatz. In 1895, Kaiser Wilhelm II commissioned 32 sets of 3 neo-baroque sculptures to be erected along the boulevard, each one depicting a member of the German nobility, from Albert the Bear to Wilhelm I. At the time of Walther's dissertation, the sculptures were widely mocked, and the boulevard was dubbed "puppet alley."]

64 Pfänder n.d.-b, concerning the idea of "grafting onto" in the case of *individual* persons.

65 [This paragraph is printed in a smaller font.]

66 Hegel 1991, 20; 1975, esp. sec. 1.

real essence displays an absolute, eternal, supra-temporal being, while everything else—spoken in a metaphysically-absolute sense—perishes like a mere semblance. We, too, do not wish to say anything else, when we designate the inauthentic communal lived-experiences and communal products as "faux reality."

Now, if the basic essence and what corresponds to it is truthful, absolute, and eternally "real" in the individual, it is the individual's responsibility to realize this absolute kernel of his personhood {131} in his behavior toward the world,[67] then it is also the responsibility of communities to unfold *their* basic essence, and accordingly everything what does not correspond to it—spoken from a metaphysically absolute and eternal standpoint—is mere semblance. Only a community, which corresponds to the basic essence of its members (be it as rational creatures, as human, as species, as type of individual)—only a community, whose members have truthfully, from within, according to their basic essence unified themselves with the community and embody it, instead of merely taking up and grafting onto themselves what is demanded from the community from without (perhaps in good faith that it be genuine and rooted in them), only such a community, whose true essence (in conjunction with the metaphysically-real basic essence of its member) expresses and embodies itself in genuine communal lived-experiences, manners of behavior, actions and the like, and communal works, only such a community is metaphysically absolute and metaphysically real, only it is an *ens realissimum* in this sense and no mere "faux reality."

3.9 The Question of the Identity and Preservation of a Community Despite the Change of Its Members

We saw that the reality of the community, while not coinciding with that of the sum of its members, but that nonetheless the social self (perhaps the metaphysically-real basic essence) of the members is the main point of access of its reality. Contrary to this, the difficult question now arises: how it is possible that a community *realiter* can remain identically the same and as such preserve itself, while, at the same time, the members constantly change through death, exit, relocation, and so on?

It is the question which ontologically-constitutive traits of the community need to be preserved under all circumstances, such that it can still be called "the same" community despite the change of other traits, which, however, can change perhaps entirely or within certain bounds. In the different communities of different kinds,

---

67 Heiler 1921, 19–20; Pfänder n.d.-b and n.d.-a.

it seems impossible to find a unified standard here {132} that would be valid for all kinds and types. Let us see, nevertheless, if we cannot derive such a highest and most general standard from the general essence of the community "as such."

Let us, for this purpose, summarize the main ontological essential traits of social communities! We distinguished here: (1) a given number of people who (2) knew-of-each-other, (3) were unified with one another and whose unification (4) was intentionally anchored in any given object in the broadest sense or in any other intentional manner. These people came into (5) reciprocal interaction with one another which (6) took place in certain manners. On the basis of this reciprocal interaction they (7) led a common life, which (8) was guided by a highest paradigmatic object or at least a unified sense, which was, in ways not yet fully investigated, most intimately tied to the intentional rootedness of the unification. On a higher level what constituted itself there was (9) a knowing of this common life and the inner unity of the members, from which (10) issued forth a knowing of the community itself as a higher, unified structure. To this was added (11) a unification with this formation and (12) a living, lived-experiencing, comporting-oneself "in the sense" and "in the name" of this formation, (a) in a given individual or in all members (or in the members of the member communities, insofar we were dealing with communities of higher potencies), (b) in certain organs and representatives and (c) in the leaders of the communities. From this issued forth (13) a reciprocal interaction of the community (a) internally with its members (or member communities and their members), (b) externally with other people and other communities. (14) From all these arose certain products, symbols, and so on, of the communal life.)

Now which of these essential traits must necessarily, most generally, remain identical for a community (perhaps despite the change of its members), remain "the same," even if it perhaps changes, develops further, unfolds, and so on? The people forming the members of the community seem to be able to change, perhaps also their number, if not, indeed, the precise sense of the community requires a certain number. The "meaning" of the community! In what is this especially revealed? What does it rest on? It would seem on the intentional grounding of the unification of members amongst each other, furthermore on the "leitmotif," the "guiding 'object'" in the broadest sense, {133} of the community. Do we perhaps have here the foundation on which rests the identity of the community, such that, when it vanishes, the community also suffers breakdown?

Indeed, this is how it seems! If, for instance, a community is intentionally grounded in the individual, psycho-physical person of its members, if the leitmotif of their communal life is precisely no other than the living-with-one-another of these individual members and the expression of their unification, then the community perishes when these perish. If the community is *merely* or *also* grounded in the empirical person of its members as individuals (thus not merely as representative exemplars of the species "human" or of a certain type, and so on), then the community perishes with the death of these psycho-physical persons (just as in the case of a marriage, family, some association of friendships of this sort, purely founded in the empirical being of its members). But if the community, on the other hand, is anchored in the spiritual person, the basic essence of its members, then it perishes only when the latter does; if one, thus, assumes a further life of the latter after the physical-physiological death of the respective people, its immortality and its further life beyond this earthly existence, then their community can continue to live despite their death.

Things are similar where objectives lying outside the individuality of the members provide the unifying foundation of the community. (Say in a scientific community. If the latter has posited for itself merely the task of, for example, to solve a particular problem and if that problem has been solved—with all problems belonging to it—then the community, too, ceases to be.) If a community turns to entirely different things *in duration,* things which have nothing at all to do with its first guiding objective, also not as preliminary work, transitional phases (and so on) for it (one may, of course, not take the concept "guiding objective" in too narrow a sense), then, strictly speaking, the community would no longer be the *same* community, although its members and their reciprocal interaction remained the same. (This presupposes that their unification was really grounded *only* in the common manner of behavior with respect to this guiding objective, something that indeed occurs rather rarely.) Such would be the case, when, for instance, the members of a philological community "for the study of the Hebrew language" dropped this area of research and instead turned to the nursing of flowers. Or when, in a marriage, which essentially rests on the unification of a man with a woman, *as* man and *as* woman, this unification transitions into a unification, {134} which is merely grounded in the essence of its members as humans and individuals, while the male-female element (spiritual, mentally, physically) completely falls by the wayside—then it is no longer a marriage—in the sense of its essential type—although it may retain the external forms of marriage, instead it has become a friendship.

Thus, the further existence of the guiding object and of the intentional foundation of the unification and of the common life of the members of a community is surely necessary for the further existence of the community itself. But does it also suffice? Certainly not! The objects (say a scientific problem in need of solving) may further exist—but when the unification with them and the unification of the members with each other based on it and their common life does not continue to exist, the community nonetheless ceases to exist. The unification itself and the common life must thus also continue to exist! But how? Under certain circumstances, the subject of the unification and of the common life can change and perish—but the unification and the common life must necessarily continue to exist for the community itself to continue to exist—but how can both be reconciled?!

One could perhaps once again try to find a way out by thinking that it would suffice when the contents, the noematic part of the common life and of the unification, remain identical, but not the common life and the inner unification itself, from its experiential-noetic part. But is this correct? Let us assume there was a community, say a scientific society for the sake of the solution and discussion of a certain problem. The purpose (the problem and its solution), the organization and the results of the research attained so far, the path of the individual discussions and their problem-setting, and so on and so forth, has been fixed in the most precise manner and in all details and set down in writing—at this point, due to an accident, *all* members of this community die at once. After a while, other scientifically-minded people—who *never* stood in the relation of reciprocal interaction with the perished members of the community—discover their notes and reports and form a new community, with precisely the same purpose, the same organizations and even has—as we shall assume for the sake of completing this thought experiment—the same number of members. These would immerse themselves into the reports (and so on) of the previous community, appropriated their insights, lived entirely "in its spirit" and would continue solving the problem at exactly *that* place, where {135} the former community left off—would it then be the identically same community? Of course not! It would, at best, *renew* the life of the previous community, link up to it and continue it in *its own* life—but never would it be, for that reason, as we maintain, *the "same," identical* life and exactly the same community. At best, this community would be the heir, successor, completion of the previous community, but never *itself* the same.

Let us assume, on the other hand, that the members of the first community had not *all* died at once, only some had died, but in their stead new members had entered who had been introduced by the other extant members into the life of the community and continued it together with them. This process continued until all the "old," "first" members had died and had been replaced by new ones, who perhaps had entirely different views on the problem and its solution, and carried these out, such that their life, its noematic content, would be very different in many respects as that of the first members. Nevertheless, we would have here *"the same"* community. But why is that? Because the life of the community, *as life*, had not been interrupted and then had restarted, because in this case, despite the change in members, its continuity had been preserved, something which was not the case in the previous case. (Unless we want to assume that those first members, those who had suddenly died, of the first community had communicated with the founding members of the new community who continued the life of the old community, through telepathy or as spirits; but—for now—we have no reason for such assumptions.)

As we saw, the communal life could only be realized when mental stimuli arose from the communal life of the members standing in a relation of reciprocal interaction, entered into their Ego-center, and then existed as current lived-experiences—but communal lived-experiences—of these subjects as actual lived-experienced. It was not necessary, however, as we also saw, that *all* communal lived-experiences were realized in the Ego-center of *all* members and originarily sprang from the sources of lived-experience in the self of *all* members. Rather, it sufficed that the communal lived-experiences actualized themselves in the Ego-center of *some* members (and perhaps only sprang from the experiential sources of some members originarily, while they were present in the other members only as lived-experiences grasped in empathy, perhaps taken over through imitation and so on—perhaps not at all {136}). Indeed, it was even possible that intermittently (as during sleep) no communal lived-experience whatsoever was actualized in the Ego-center of any of its members, if *only the communal life* in habitual lived-experiences *in the inner-mental "self" or any or some members was connected with its vital stream of life and its own sources.* In these habitual or current lived-experiences of the members and their communal "self" alone, the communal life could exist and embody itself; it thus had to perish, when they—all of them—perished. Yet, for this reason it is indeed not identical with them, it is rather, as we already showed, nonetheless something primally original, a primal phenomenon of its ownmost type, which we can at best show up, but cannot further define. The communal life lay in all of this (and its sum) and yet was not *only* all of this, taken *for itself*—if one is not inclined to assume it already existent.

But as we have already seen (see above, "The Analysis of the Current Communal Life in the Community 'In and for Itself'," 116 ff./{84 ff.}), this communal life can be transferred from one subject to the next in lively, direct, or indirect communication, if one of several of the members direct themselves *at* other people, members or non-members, and in this way, *standing in this life,* trigger it in others and transfer it over to them. Presupposition for this is here only that we are dealing with a *live* transmission (albeit perhaps indirect), that thus the continuity of life is preserved, that life never completely perishes, that is, that it is never (and even just temporarily) completely cut off from the mental stream of life of all people and its sources, that it, thus, be it in habitual or current lived-experiences, no longer resonates in the mental life of *anybody,* such that only its *dead* (noematic) contents and products remain, which might, however, ignite *new* life, which connects to the old. Let us *illustrate* this in our analogy from mechanics (knowing full well the abysmal essential difference between any mechanical *power* and

life, of whichever type!), an analogy, which, to be sure, cannot and shall not explicate and prove anything.

Let us assume, an electric current from a dynamo flows through a wire into a
lamp and causes it to light up. All of a sudden, something breaks in the machine,
such {137} that it can no longer produce electric power and now electricity stemming from another machine were made to flow through the same wire into the
same lamp, which caused it to light up in the same manner. Here we would
have an analogy to our first example: despite the external sameness of the light,
the lamp and the wire would nevertheless have a different electrical current
and, in that sense, a different light. But let us assume that the earlier electric current, from the same machine, leapt over from the end of one wire through a spark
to a somewhat spatially distant end of another wire (if such a thing were techni-
cally possible, is irrelevant here) and would now flow into the same lamp, then we
would have *the same* electric current and *the same* light—and also, if it were to
flow into a different lamp, we would have, at the least, the same current, although
perhaps not entirely the same light. This is similar to the community, when the
members do not die at once, but the life is continually transferred from one mem-
ber-generation to the next, without ever expiring completely.

With Simmel we could thus say: "If the totality of the individuals or other life
circumstances of the group could be described as a b c d e in one moment, but in a
later moment as m n o p q, one will still speak of a preservation of its unified self,
provided the development maintains the following course: *a b c d e—m b c d e—m
n c d e—m n o d e—m n o p e—m n o p q*, so that each step is only separated from
the neighboring ones by one member and each moment shares the same main features with its neighboring moments."[68]

We believe that, in the case of individuals, it is enough, to be sure, that only
one is identical in order for the continuity of the (habitual or current) communal
life not to be interrupted, but this life must be transferred to *at least* one other
subject for a unification and reciprocal unification (which, to be sure, necessarily
belong to a community) to be possible. (Analogously in the case of a community of
higher power. Here, at least two people of at least two member communities have
to be present, thus at least four people.) Otherwise, we believe, the community is
annulled. At best, a similar or related *new* community with a *new* life could con-
nect to it. {138} Likewise, as we said, the intentional grounding of the unification
and the guiding object of the communal life must be preserved.

A middle thing between these extremes would obtain, however, when the last
member, upon his death, or also the entire community as such, while still alive, for

---

68 Simmel 2009, ch. 8, esp. 451.

the case of its perishing, would transfer its rights and duties (and so on) to any other people or communities, not yet living or perhaps already present, who do not yet belong to the former, with the task that they should continue its life and then should count as "it itself." Yet, what we would have here, it seems to us, would be merely a seeming or derivative identity with the earlier, original community.

For the sake of the preservation of its identity, besides the guiding objective and the foundation of unification, the continuity of the communal life, as we described it above, must also be preserved. However, we do not think that the individual reciprocal interactions between the individuals amongst each other and the members and the community must at all times remain the same. Also, the forms of this reciprocal interaction (such as unification and reciprocal unification) seem to be able to change, without thereby annulling the identity of the community (for instance, constitutional changes, changes of status, reorganizations, and so on)— if not a special form or at least forms of any discernible type issue forth in essential necessity from the type of the unification and its intentional foundation, as from the guiding objective (the "motivation") and the continuity of the communal life and thereby from the essence of the community. In that case, they can, of course, vary only within these limits.

It is not particularly necessary that the products, manufactured goods, symbols, and so on, of the community continue to exist for the latter to do so, since it can surely perish despite the continuing existence of these products, and so on. This would only be the case when the community petrifies in its life in the preservation, conservation, and care of its spiritual and material products, and so on, of all types, and would therein see its *sole* life purpose.[69] For then it would also lose, with the perishing of these products, its own purpose and legitimation of existence.

3.10 The Task of a Systematic and Historical Sociology of Communities

Now a systematic sociology would have the task of working out a pure typology of communities of all kinds, according to the 13 (or 14) {139} essential constituents of communities indicated above. Within each of these 13 points we find, depending on their manifestations, very different types of communities in need of investiga-

---

69 [The sentence is grammatically incorrect in the original. We have added "und darin" after "aller Art" and translated accordingly.]

tion. Again, new types arise depending on the connection of the different aberrations from the individual essential traits. However, an empirical-historical sociology would, we believe, have to investigate, apart from the unitary development of a community (or several) and their meaning and essence, to what extent these eidetic types have realized and developed in reality; and this means, both how the individual essential traits and their complexes were developed in a specific epoch, concurrently besides each other—in the same community or in different concurrent communities—(this would result in a sort of "lateral" rows and "cross-sections" in the sense of Franz Carl Müller-Lyer's "phaseological method"),[70] as well as how these essential traits and their complexes have developed from each other and have converged into each other. (This would result in "vertical rows" and "lateral-sections" in Müller-Lyer's sense.) One would arrive at a formal typology, if one investigates the types of reciprocal interaction of the members amongst each other and together with the community and between communities, their relation of order in the reciprocal interaction (and reciprocal unification), the *a priori* "chances" of these coming about, their rules, and so on, as this is already essentially done by, among others, Weber, also Simmel and Rudolf Holzapfel and most sociologists interested in legal matters.

On arrives at a material typology, however, when one starts out from the common intentional guiding objective, which lends, directly or indirectly, meaning and normativity to the reciprocal interaction and the common life, and from the intentional grounding of the unification.

What stands in intimate relation to this is, under certain circumstances, a distribution, which investigates and classifies the communities and other social formations according to the symbols and the products (and so on) of reciprocal interaction and of the common life, furnished with the "character of work." In attitudes and investigations such as these has to, as we already indicated, be extremely careful not to lose sight, among the symbols and products of common life, of its bearers and this common life itself; a mistake that occurs more often than one would think.

{140} One could also distinguish different communal types depending on the degree and the type of the knowing-of of the member of a community: of each other, their connectedness in the community, and the latter itself, as such—a principle of order which, as far as we know, has nowhere been clearly and consistently followed through, although one may find hints thereof in different sociological systems. Thus, we find in Weber's terminology a hint in this direction, when he starts

---

70 Müller-Lyer 1915, 44, among other writings. [This book was originally published in 1908, but the pages Walther references here correspond to the 1915 edition.]

out from the aspect, which "expectation" of the behavior of others guides certain people in their own behavior, and which "chances" of fulfillment these expectations have. Simmel, too, points to this in his sociology.[71] Also in Marxism, the "self-consciousness" (following Hegel) of a class plays a great, albeit not expressly methodological role in Marx' distinction between "constituted" and "non-constituted" classes.

One ordering principle, which encompasses knowledge, reciprocal interaction and unification, could arrange communities and other social formations according to the role that the *conscious* will (in contradistinction to mere automatic strivings[72]) plays in the coming-about of reciprocal interaction and reciprocal unification of the members amongst each other and with the community. Such a standpoint is taken up, we believe, especially by Scheler in his distinction between life-community, society and spiritual personal community,[73] although he does not strictly and consistently adhere to this principle, but he seems to relate it in part to other ordering principles (according to the grounding of the unity and the type of the common life). We also find this aspect in Weber and Tönnies,[74] but, to be sure, especially in Jean-Jacques Rousseau's theory of the *social contract*, likewise in Hegel's *Philosophy of Right*.

One could also wish to order communities according to the common life (so for instance Scheler in his *Formalism*). Such an order often leads back, however, to other ordering principles, so for instance to the type and grounding {141} of the reciprocal unification, the guiding objective, to the types of reciprocal interaction, and so on. This classification of communities sometimes also starts out from the genetic question how the "common" vital contents (noematically) and the "common" lived-experiences (noetically) come to be what they are and on what they rest.

For the specific problems of the *community* certainly *that* classification is the most important, which starts out from the unification and reciprocal unification and their respective elements. We have already indicated this above.

As an aside, it is certainly immediately obvious that all these different ordering principles and the types derived from them supplement each other and are intertwined, as we already indicated. A systematic sociology would thus have to take into consideration *all* these ordering principles, whether and how according to essential necessity or empirically-factually these different sides of communities can vary independently of one another, or if a certain quality of one or another mo-

---

71 Simmel 2009, 307 ff.
72 Pfänder n.d.-b; 1916; 1910, 67 ff.
73 Scheler 1973a, 525.
74 Tönnies 2002.

ment can only exist from one or another element with a certain quality of some or all other elements or develop from them.

3.11 Toward the Tasks of a Social Ethics (and so on) of Communities

Now that we have sketched in broad strokes, through working out the essential traits of the community "as such" as well as individual typical traits of communities, the *ontological* structure of the community, as it can be inferred from its ontological essence and sense, we are now also in a position to derive from these essential insights, certain norms, not merely for the theoretical-substantial *Being* of the community, but also for its value-laden-practical *Ought*. To the extent that this Ought can be *forced* into being through the external means of power on the part of a community, it belongs into the sphere of *right*; to this extent it is ruled through *custom, tradition* and (explicit or tacit) *agreement* in the sphere of conventions and "mores"; but insofar as it pertains directly to the *morality* of the individual as social and individual person, to his *voluntary behavior* writ large—and thereby no less binding—it belongs into the sphere of *ethics*. The boundaries between these three spheres are, of course, extremely fluid, and it depends, for the most part, on the historical-factual "contingencies," which depend on what is regulated {142} by the one or the other. But empirical factors not only play a role here, but it certainly also lies in the essence of certain aspects of communal life that they are never explicitly *able* to obey an external legal force, and this according to an eidetic *a priori*. To this a priori belongs the entire sphere of inner unification (and reciprocal unification) with the "leitmotif"; with the "others, who also…" and with the community itself, as such; likewise, also the living-out of the "we," the communal self. Of course, it is possible that certain external manners of behavior "in the sense and in the name" of the community and certain forms and manners of reciprocal interaction, which would have to stem, according to their sense, from inner unification (and so on), can be more or less necessarily enforced by external legal, conventional (and so on) means of power under certain circumstances. But what never will allow itself to be enforced (albeit demanded and desired), is the inner unification (and so on) itself. The latter indeed belongs exclusively to the inner, subjective realm of the individual as such—even if, *after* having entered into this unification on his own, *once* he completely posits himself on its ground, perhaps purely through this unification, he has to succumb to certain external commandments of power. (This is, of course, not to say that every unification always stems, and *must* stem, from a free act of the will on the part of the parties involved. Rather, we already saw above (73 ff. / {36 ff.}), especially in the case of "mere concrescence," that this is by no means always the case.) These pure inner manners of behavior, thus, obey in their essence a part of ethics: namely *communal ethics*. (But we do not claim that the *entire* ethics would have to do *exclusively* with this "social" behavior of people toward each other in society and communities and toward these themselves. Rather, apart from this, as has already been emphasized by many sides, there are ethical norms relating to peoples' behavior to non-human living or dead creatures and things, to their behavior toward themselves (perhaps to their basic essence), to cultural and natural formations, and so on.)

Likewise, another part of social behavioral manners, to the extent that it can be regulated from outside, obeys the communal *right* (perhaps the "societal right"), but with the difference that *legal* responsibilities *can* only obtain within a social grouping of societal or communal type—because only here we find external means of power for their enforcement—while the ethical imperatives (albeit not all their material {143} *contents*), as we believe, also obtain, in part, for individual, isolated people beyond all social binds.

Now these ethical and legal norms, to the extent that they arise from communal life and perhaps relate back to it, can pertain to the most differentiated sides of communal life. In part, this is undoubtedly also, in form and content, dependent upon empirical and historical circumstances. But we also believe that some of these norms, according to their sense, point beyond all empirical circumstances, regardless of their type, and back to the ontological (as also the metaphysically-real) essence of the community "as such" and its aberrations.

According to the essential elements and developmental steps of communal life we stipulated earlier, we can distinguish here:

1. Ethical and legal norms that relate to the *behavior of communalized* (perhaps merely socialized) *people amongst each other* in their reciprocal interaction and unification; thus. related to the "social acts" and inner and outer manners of behavior (morals, actions, and so on) in our first, broadest sense.

   These are grounded ultimately in the general-human, typical and individual *basic essence of the respective subjects themselves*, furthermore in the *sense*, especially of the intentional grounding, *the unification and reciprocal unification and the "leitmotif" of communal life.*

2. Ethical and legal norms that relate to the *behavior in the broadest sense of the members* in reciprocal interaction and unification *to the community itself,* as such (thus to the "social acts" and so on in the second, narrower sense) and

3. Ethical and legal norms that relate to the *behavior in the broadest sense of the community itself,* as such (mediated by its organs and so on) to *its members* (or member communities) in reciprocal interaction and unification.

These two sorts of norms (2 and 3) lead back, ultimately, to the *sense and essence of the community* (especially to its leitmotif and its intentional unifying grounding), but also to the *general, typical and individual essence of the members* as such {144} (or of the member communities and the essence of *their* members), to the extent that they are affected by it. It is especially their task to delimit both realms from each other and to avoid conflicts between them or to arbitrate between them (cf. also above, the section on "Inauthentic Communal Lived-Experiences," Section 3.4).

4. There are indeed ethical as well as legal norms related to the *internal and external manners of behavior*
    a) of the members (or perhaps the member communities and *their* members) or
    b) also "mere employees" *"in the sense and in the name" of the community* (cf. above, Section 3.3 "'Social Acts' in the Pregnant Sense"), be it that they are directed at the other members themselves and at the inner communal life, be it that they are directed—externally—to other communities lying outside of the community or reaching beyond them, or also other people, living creatures, products of culture and nature, God, and so on and so forth.

In the first case, they have the same material foundation as in the second and third cases. In the second case, on the other hand, it is based either on the sense and essence of the community and of its leitmotif and "purposes," or on the essence of the "objects" in the broadest sense affected by this behavior and on the essential relations between both.

Formally speaking, this foundation is particularly determined by the degree of the knowing-of and the unification-with of the members in relation to the community and its sense and purpose, thus, in other words, through the developmental level of the "self-consciousness"[75] and the "autonomous power"[76] of the community in its members (or its member communities and *their* members) as well as in their "mere employees."

Thus, it turns out that the social communities are independent, real, mental-spiritual unities of a higher sort. We saw how they—without their own lived-bodies and their own corporeal life—lead their own mental and spiritual life in the lived-body and the corporeal life of their members (and organs, representatives, and so on), and at the same time growing out from this life and beyond it. A men-

---

75 [*Selbstbewusst-sein.*]
76 [*Selbstmacht.*]

tal-spiritual life that does not just flow about automatically and blindly, which, hence, does not merely exist in the realm of spiritual existence, but at the same time carries the members over into the realm of norms and {145} values, of position-taking and Ought. Similar to the human being, we witness them growing into all spheres of the cosmos—into the material boundedness of nature, as well as into the realm of free spiritual creating and forming—through their persistence over time, as well as through their differentiation and their combined powers enabled for a higher calling and for hearing a vocation as individual—through the absence of a lived-body of its own and its own spiritual Ego-center, yet again more independent and more bounded than such a lived-body; in any case combined with this Ego-center in inseverable essential connectedness.

> So far the secret lore may be discovered
> *More than the sum of parts the total counts*
> *And through the circle new élan is ushered*
> *So that the strength of every member mounts.*
> And from this source of love which never shallows
> *Each tyro-templer will, in turn, attain*
> *A greater force* which tides into his fellows
> *And washes back into the ring again.*
>
> Stefan George, *The Star of the Covenant* (1974), 342.[77]

---

77 [Emphasis is Walther's own.]

4 Appendix on the Main Traits of the Phenomenological Constitution of Communities

{146} Now that our ontological investigations have come to an end, we want to address the question, briefly and in conclusion, how these peculiar formations, the social communities—about whose *ontological* constitution, its construction from its essential traits, we wanted to gain a degree of clarity—how these formations can be known and grasped *by consciousness*, how they build themselves up and constitute themselves in it. We wish to investigate the main elements according to which the different essential moments of the community must be related to each other in their layeredness and within each other, such that consciousness can penetrate into the community contained in these elements and grasp them as adequately as possible.

It is a cognitive attitude of a special sort, with an *intentionality exclusive to it alone,* in which social communities can be grasped and exclusively so. It cannot be derived from the attitude toward, say, cognition of mental life or of the person of individual members as individuals or as a sum of them—although it may stem from it empirically-genetically. If *every type of object has a special type of cognitive act related to it*—as it is demanded by the parallelism, ranging throughout the entire consciousness, of noesis and noema, of the conscious lived-experience and its intentional "content"—then the grasping of communities has its own cognitive attitude of a special type, even if its constitution and grasping may be intimately grounded in that of the mental life of the members and the latter themselves. Whoever does not take this attitude will never move beyond the individual members and their sum, or the sum of relations between them, and will never break through to grasping communities themselves.

Of course, things are similar with respect to the existence and reality of the community in the case of their phenomenological constitution {147} in consciousness. The way in which their being is founded in the being of its members and "representatives" (and their works), the same goes for their constitution in the consciousness of their members and strangers (and also in "pure" consciousness to be sure), in the phenomenological constitution of its members and "representatives" and so on. The existence of communities is primarily anchored in the social self (perhaps in the basic essence) of the members, and its essence is first and foremost embodied and realized in it, but only secondarily in the life, lived-experiences, manners of behavior, and the like, which stem from this social self or which others enact "in the sense and in the name" of the community. But in the case of the phenomenological constitution of communities, things are, in a certain sense, the *reverse*. For just as the total being, the essence of a personhood does not constitute itself in consciousness severed from all individual lived-experiences and so on of the person and independently for itself, but in and through all these individual lived-experiences (albeit not as their sum—that would be a fateful mistake!). Likewise, the community also does not constitute itself only in the social self of the members, for itself and independently and without foundation, and *besides* this, say, in the individual lived-experiences arising from this social self; rather, only in and through these lived-experiences does the social self of the members constitute itself, and in the latter and through it, once again, the community as such. However, these three steps in the individual acts of lived-experience (and so on), directed at communities cannot be sharply distinguished; rather, the gaze of the cognizing subject breaks, in the attitude toward the grasping of the communities, oftentimes immediately through to the lived-experiences of the members and their social self, and to these themselves.

Here, too, one could perhaps, as in the case of the absolute (in Heiler's sense)[1] speak of a "transparency" of communal lived-experiences and of the social self of the members for the community. To be sure, we are talking here of a transparency, of a "shimmering through" of a very peculiar sort, which may not be mistaken with other sorts of transparencies. *We are not dealing here* with a shimmering-through of an *independent* object through another object, which is *independent*, autonomous. It is also not an appearance of an independent object, autonomous in its existence of another, which is held in a certain sense in existence by it and is dependent of it (as it is perhaps the case in the transparency of the absolute throughout the world—in the metaphysical sense). Rather, things are {148} the opposite here: in independent "objects" (the members and, in certain circumstances, the "mere" employees and so on) something dependent appears, which realizes itself only in them, something which could *not* also exist independently and in separation of them, and which they yet again—despite its dependence on them—holds them in their existence and especially their *manner* of existing, and permeates it. The relation of the object, which is transparent *for* the other, to this object shimmering through is, in this case, much more intimate as in other cases of transparency. They thus permeate and hold each other, so to speak, reciprocally, although the members can, to a certain extent, more likely exist outside of the community than vice versa (at least without considering their community in and with God).[2]

---

1 Heiler 1921, 26, 41 ff., 50 ff., 70. We also owe important aspects here to a discussion in Pfänder's seminar on the different meanings of the word "appearance."
2 [This paragraph is printed in a smaller font.]

Now, it is indeed extremely difficult to decide whether the social experience here is and must be inductive-*a posteriori* or *a priori*, if it construes the members and their lived-experiences merely as transparency for the communities. To the extent that the cognizing subject must already approach the objects with the attitude toward the supra-individual society (objects, which are transparent for the community in which they are founded) in order to grasp them, one can indeed speak of a certain apriorism, although, on the other hand, the real grasping of an *actual* community is only possible, where this attitude can fulfil its intention a posteriori in the given material of experience. Likewise, it seems that in order to distinguish the authentic and inauthentic communal lived-experiences, as well as the individual ("private") experiences of a subject from the lived-experiences in the sense and in the name of the community, already the community and its essence, in some cases at least, must be given *a priori* in part or also in a form of total intuition. The sense and the idea of a community, its ontological essence (not, however, of course, its metaphysically-real essence—if it even has one), one seems to be able to intuit and grasp at all times *a priori*, that is, independent of all empirical-individual experience (thus perhaps also in mere phantasy images, and so on)—just like other ideas and ontological essences as well.

Now, an understanding of the ontological essence of the community can also be merely grasped a posteriori, and only when one has gained it, can it serve the now following experiences as "*a priori*" foundation (in *this* sense!). But this is not a genuine *a priori*, to be sure. For this experience of the community can only be gained, when the cognizing subject successively pictures the more or less adequate appearances of the community in the members and also the "employees" (and so on) and their communal behavior as well as in their communal works, {149} until the subject, penetrating ever deeper into the meaning of the community, finally arrives at a clear grasping of the total essence of the community by penetrating through it, a grasping which now, retroactively, sheds light on the adequacy and authenticity or inadequacy and inauthenticity of the manners of behavior and works, which earlier led up to the grasping of the members as appearances and expressions of the community and its members. Likewise, this grasping can then be the normative basis for all future experiences of the community.

In grasping a community, especially in the intuition of its metaphysically-real basic essence, this can also be a sudden total intuition in a flash, so to speak, which, to be sure, takes its departure from an empirical givenness. But it does not grasp in successive *continua* of givennesses, gradually through its different manners of appearance, the metaphysically-real essence of the community, but it intuits it in *one* grasp, so to speak, in a particularly adequate expression. It is as if one intuits in an intimate gaze and inner flash of light in two or more people—in which their metaphysically-real basic essence seems to rest, so to speak, together currently within each other—their unity in their deepest, undefinable metaphysically-real essence as primal phenomenon, as it were substantially. In this case, their community is divorced, so to speak, from all its other manners of appearance in the behavior of the members toward each other and to the most diverse other spheres of objectivity. Of course, it is for this reason that one can barely see in such an intuition alone the behavior, which would otherwise correspond to this unity and its essence, its (so to speak, external) meaning and its (so to speak, external) norms. (One can very well, however, by taking its standpoint inwardly, so to speak, quasi living out of it—although one otherwise does not belong to it—imagine all kinds of real and fictional situations and can attempt to grasp now, which manners of behavior toward the most diverse objects in the most divers situations are, or would be, the most adequate to this unity and its essence.) But here this unity in the intuition is given, as it were, absolutely, naked, "for itself," divorced from all relations to any other objects. Such a givenness is for that reason no further reducible to other givennesses or derivable from them, it can only be intuited, demonstrated or described indirectly. But ultimately it seems to be the case that one can only either have it or not have it, as in the case of most of ultimate intuitions of metaphysically-real essence, since they relate to primal phenomena. {150} But once one has grasped a metaphysically-real communal essence, one will also see it shimmer through more or less adequately in all of its other expressions. Yet, such an intuition is, to be sure, no real givenness *a priori*.

Apart from this, there does seem to exist another type of *"a priori"* givenness of communities, to be sure only of potential and not actually existing communities —and this goes especially for basic essential communities of "spiritual persons." Thus, in rare cases a person may intuit in oneself the essence of one or several other persons, with which it is or would have to be connected in *their* basic essence, in immersing oneself in the latter, may intuit the specific metaphysically real basic essence of the respective person and what lies in it potentially in a sort of divinatory vision as primal phenomenon and would have to feel immediately unified and communalized with the essence of this person or persons, and all of this despite the fact that these personal basic essences which this person views, perhaps coincide with the basic essence of none of the persons he has known before in any empirical way.

(It is indeed possible where such lived-experiences occur, that we are dealing with deceptions. For instance, in such manner that the respective actual persons to whom these intuited basic essences belong, have indeed somehow—perhaps in earliest youth, such that the experiencing subject can no longer remember—been given at an earlier time to this subject. Or perhaps these are modifications of one's own or of the general human basic essence grasped through immersion into one's own inner life, or modifications of the metaphysically-real basic essence of people actually known to the subject—"modifications" which would be especially congenial to this experiencing subject and for which it yearns. But this is irrelevant in this context, where all we wish to show is what such an *a priori* communal consciousness as ideal possibility would look like.)[3]

A subject may also live in such a (perhaps potential or imagined) "*a priori*" community, until it finds the actual persons, in which these "visions" (or whatever one chooses to call them) find their fulfillment. Scheler, for instance, seems to have had something like this in mind, when he speaks of the communalized "collective person," which exists *a priori*, belonging to every "spiritual person." (Whether it, too, can have an "*a priori*" givenness, he does not discuss, however.)[4] In any case, it is likely that this belongs to the actual or putative "*a priori*" givenness of religious, mystical and similar {151} communities (as also Dante's visions in the *Paradiso*). In any case, one can only speak in cases such as these of a truly *a priori* cognition of the metaphysically-real communal essence and it, too, is in need of concrete-a posteriori givennesses, in order to be legitimately applied to any *empirical-actual* subjects and communities. Apart from this, it is plausible that all experience of communities (apart from intuition the "idea," the ontological essence of a community, which can, as we already indicated, take place as phantasy modifications, and so on), at least to the extent that its intention is originarily fulfilled, is "a posteriori" and must first form and confirm itself in actual givennesses. It is thus not a theoretical or practical *auxiliary construction, arbitrarily* brought to bear on certain groups of people and their manners of behavior, which intuits them, "as if" they formed a communal unity, without the bodily-*actual* givennesses ever being able to demand or fulfill this intention toward a community on their own. This ontological and phenomenological-epistemological atomism concerning communities, it seems to us, is hereby ultimately rejected, both for its actual and metaphysical and eidetic existence as well as for its constitution in consciousness, and it is this latter alone which matters to us here.

Already in the Introduction,[5] we distinguished between the *inner constitution* of the community *in* peoples' *consciousness*, people who feel and experience themselves as *members* of the community, from the *external constitution* of the community in the consciousness of the *non-members*, to whom the community stands opposed as a closed-off totality, to which the former themselves do not belong. Of

---

3 [This paragraph is printed in a smaller font.]
4 His newest reflections on this subject (Scheler 2010, 373 ff., among other places) one may well read as supporting such an *a priori* intuition.
5 [See above, 56 ff. / {16 ff.}.]

course, this does not preclude that both manners of constitution overlap, that elements of the one enter into the other. This is especially the case in inner constitution, insofar as it is a constitution of the community "in and for itself," not merely of the community "for itself." So, for instance, the *inner* constitution of the community here *always* presupposes the *external* constitution of the individual members, or at least parts thereof as individual people or at least as "people, who also…," or as members or organs (this depends on the respective essence of the community in question). Likewise, also in the empathic grasping of the mental life of a community through non-members in external constitution, essential moments of inner constitution are on display. Both {152} manners of constitution form—mutatis mutandis—an analogy to the constitution of the human personhood in its own consciousness and in the consciousness of other subjects. We now wish to sketch first the inner constitution of communities in its main lines.

4.1 The "Inner" Constitution for the Members

If one gains an overview over the intuiting-experiencing Ego-center, the pure Ego of a subject in reflective turning-back upon its own mental life, its own entire present and past "stream" of lived-experiences, then it grasps itself as a subject of the most diverse position-takings, manners of behavior, and so on, in relation to the most diverse spheres of objects, and it thus cognizes its "empirical essence"[6] (see above, Introduction, 54/{15}), its "person" as it was and as it acted thus far empirically-factually in the actual world. From this, it may induce general, empirical rules for its future behavior, *if* it henceforth remains "the same" empirical person. But if it investigates more closely its past (and in a given moment respectively present) lived-experiences, then it will attribute to and count as *its own* some of them as less its own or in different manners. Some may seem to him having gone awry or deceptions, in which his "true self," his metaphysically-real basic essence did "not really" express itself; other lived-experiences, in turn, seemed to him as especially adequate expressions and pronouncements of the same (see above, 55f./{15f.} and 91ff./{56ff.}). Other lived-experiences, once again, do not at all, or merely mediately, seem to stem from "himself." They point to the empathically grasped mental life or mental total existence of other people, whom the experiencing subject has gotten to know,

---

6 See Walther (n.d.-b); 1923. [The former text that Walther refers to here is an essay that she presented to Pfänder in 1920 in honor of his 50th birthday. It can be found in her *Nachlass* under signature Ana 317 A III 2.1. This essay served as the base for her *Phenomenology of Mysticism* (1923).]

whose lived-experiences it perhaps also shared, imitated or perhaps even appropriated. Among these lived-experiences, once again, one type shows itself to be exceptional, in which an inner "horizon" of other people, the "people, who also..." (see above, 102/{69}), resonates, people, with whom the subject is unified, with and *in* whom it lives. This, once again, leads it to the {153} total complex of its life, lived-experiencing and behavior, *with* and *from out of* these people, but then also to the unity, as such, with them, to the community itself. Here we find that a part of his lived-experience are, or have been, carried out "in the sense," yes even "in name" of this community (see above, 133 ff./{103 ff.}). By observing and comparing these communal lived-experiences, it will find a certain continual sense, certain rules in its course, and thus constitutes itself in him the empirical life of his community and its empirical meaning. Perhaps it will then also find within itself—taken over from others in empathy or found on its own—empirical or absolute norms for this communal life, which stipulate what "holds" in the community, what "one" "does" in it, what one "expects" of one another, what in it counts for "mores," what counts as "customary" or "legal."

A part of these lived-experiences (perhaps also some of the rules) will appear to him perhaps as aberration, as inadequacy, as something he shouldn't do—not because they contradict necessarily the course of communal life up to the present and, say, its empirical rules, but because he understands, looking from out of a deeper layer of his inner self, of that deepest spiritual sphere of insight of his metaphysically-real basic essence (see above, 92 ff./{58 ff.}), that they do not correspond to the deeper sense and essence of this community. Likewise, he feels and understands here, living from out this essence, that some of his communal lived-experiences correspond especially to the metaphysically-real as well as the ontological essence of his community, while others in no way do so. Here, he immerses itself into his own metaphysically-real basic essence and lives concurrently in the metaphysically-real basic essence of the "others, who also," in harmony with them, contained within them in unification, grasped in empathy or intuition (or perhaps both) (but *to the extent* and *only* to the extent that both enter into the community in their connectedness), and here, too, he grasps the metaphysically-real basic essence of his community, what is adequate to it and the norms and imperatives of ought following from it in the most diverse situations, position-takings, manners of behavior, and so on, and vis-à-vis the most diverse objects and regions thereof.

If the subject currently lives from out of the deepest layer of his "we," the "collective person" in the sense of Scheler[7] (perhaps in a concurrent empathic-unified

---

7 [Scheler 1973a, 520 ff.]

reciprocal contact with the other subjects of the we, who thereby also live from out of this deepest layer in *their* interiority), then it attains in this we-experience {154} in the pregnant sense (see above, 116 f. / {85 f.}) from within an essential intuition of his community and of the communal life streaming forth from it, as it presents itself "naked" and uncloaked, so to speak—in its pure, metaphysically-real essentiality beyond space and time, although streaming back into them—in its ultimate, absolute sense. This is the adequate intuition of its metaphysically-real communal essence, which is in principle possible for a cognizing subject—of which type whatsoever. And here, too, it attains the most adequate grasping of the idea, of the ontological essence of its community, although it can attain it of course also through an "ideating abstraction" from those more difficult manners of givenness (through its empirical manners of behavior, and so on, as member) or through phantasy-"modifications."

In this manner, then, does the experiencing subject attain a givenness of its community, through turning back upon its own mental life and immersion in it, to the extent that it streams forth from the communal self. But we saw that things do not stop with this inner constitution, as the "people, who also…" who are in tune with its own communal lived-experiences and their we- and communal lived-experiences, grasped in empathy and perhaps also taken over, also refer to the external transcendent constitution. We therefore wish to turn to the latter now.

4.2 The "External" Constitution for Non-Members

First and foremost, what is given to the external observer is here a given number of *corporeal* things, which he apperceives as *lived-bodies,* that is, as *bodies of living creatures,* and furthermore also as bodies (lived-bodies) of *ensouled* (and spiritual) *living creatures.* These mental-spiritual living creatures constitute themselves in him through intuition as well as through grasping of their lived-experiences through the expressive phenomena stemming from their lived-bodies (and so on) as human beings. Through and in these intuitions as well as through these expressive phenomena this external observer grasps their current lived-experiences and mental states in the broadest sense, in these certain uniform rules and motivational directions, which govern their lived-experiences and manners of behavior in their temporal run-off (to the extent that it is accessible to this external observer). Going off the current lived-experiences and these rules and motivational directions given to him, he grasps the empirical being and self of the respective {155} individuals and of a plurality of them. Through being intuitively in tune with one's own metaphysically-real basic essence as well as in certain of their lived-experiences, or also with unconscious gestures and expressions, in their facial expressions, and so on, he further intuits their metaphysically-real basic essence—perhaps in a flash-like intuition through a lived-experience or a state, in which the respective other currently lives especially adequately out of himself—or also through a look, a gesture, a movement, and so on, in which it is especially clearly expressed.[8] If he now compares what he grasps thusly in different people, then this external observer finds certain similar bodily, mental or spiritual traits in these, perhaps also all together, which may also yet be amplified by a common external get-up (clothing, tattoos, and so on) and common symbols or signs for something common which is to be found in all. Likewise, he also grasps, perhaps in their (bodily as well as in their) mental-spiritual life and behavior, in all members the same habits and attitudes toward life.[9]

Yet, such common traits of all kinds do not suffice, as we already saw (see above, 57 ff./{18 ff.}) for an ontological as well as a phenomenological clarification of communities, going off on their consciousness.

If the main starting point for the reality of the community was the metaphysically-real basic essence and the members' social self, and only subsequently the lived-experiences, manners of behavior and actions (and so on) of the members issuing forth from them, and finally their lived-bodies transmitting all of this to the outside, then things are in reverse order in the external, transcendent, phenomenological constitution of the non-members.[10] For here we have (with the exception of their intuition) given at first the lived-body of the members and their bodily (and so on) expressive phenomena, only then in and through them their lived-experiences (and so on) and through the latter finally the self and the basic essence of the members as individuals. In order to, from here, {156} bring fully to givenness the social communities, it is now necessary that the external observer puts himself into a "social" attitude in empathy (as well as in intuition), that is, that he directs himself intentionally at the grasping of the communal life and the community, wherever an opportunity for a fulfillment of this intuition seems to present itself.

But who grasps in this attitude the mental life of the members will soon realize how they are at all times surrounded in their interiority, in a part of their lived-experiences, manners of behavior, actions (and so on), by other "people, who

---

8 Stein 1989; Pfänder n.d.-a; n.d.-b.

9 We owe valuable pointers to private evening discussions on problems in the philosophy of history facilitated by Dr. Edith Stein.

10 It seems to us that here might possibly lie an eidetic law: that the order and layering of the *phenomenological layering of constitution* (from the outside moving in) always presents an *inversion of the ontological layering of constitution* (from the inside moving out).

also…," how they here live out of one layer in their interiority, in which they are connected with other subjects to a unity, in which they perhaps experience "in the sense" or " in the name" of these others and this unity as such with the others. Or he grasps how the lived-experiences (and so on) of some people lead back to other people and to communities, as whose "employees" and "representatives" they live, behave in their "sense and name." By grasping the peculiarity of these lived-experiences of the members so designated as communal lived-experiences, then the sense and type of unification with others constitute themselves to the community. And in the community, the experiential (noetic) structure of the communal lived-experiences constitutes itself, their directions of sensing and motivations, their guiding ideas and their goals, their relation to the most diverse regions of objects in general and to individual regions of objects and objects in particular. Grasping these communal lived-experiences in as many members as possible yields what is typical for the community, in these manners of behavior it becomes possible to separate the individual excess—a peculiarity of the respective individual, which always still plays its part in communal lived-experiences—from that which pertains to the community itself. This is similar as in the case with lived-experiences (and so on) of certain "employed" or "specially tasked" (and so on) non-members. (This is especially the case, as we saw, where we are dealing with communities of higher potencies.) We can also understand in this way the inauthentic communal lived-experiences and distinguish them from the authentic ones. All of this is, to be sure, not easy to discern, for what is communal in the communal lived-experiences of the members is distinguished, as we saw, not always by that token from that of the individual side of their lived-experiences, such that it would now necessarily be common to all or the majority or a great number of the members, {157} or through the fact that it would in all of them as possibly identical in terms of the intention and the experiential-noetic characteristics. Also, *those* lived-experiences are not always communal lived-experiences, which are reflexively meant and claimed consciously by the experiencing subject or others as communal lived-experiences—as we already saw (see above, 137 ff. / {107 ff.})—for the experiencing subject can either completely lose itself in such a way that it is not at all reflexively conscious of the fact that it now has a communal lived-experience. Or, on the other hand, it can take subjective lived-experiences to be communal lived-experiences or claim that they are thus. In all cases, however, the other subject who empathically grasps the communal lived-experiences, will at all times expand the horizon of the "people, who also…," of the "we." On a higher level: the feeling of the community itself, as such, resonates in these lived-experiences, alongside that which is radically individual in the members. In the members, the connectedness, the unification with the others, to, in, and with the community as ontic manner (not only as *current* lived-experience), as habitual "state" (or whatever one wants to call it) of the members, from which these communal lived-experiences issue forth, all of this runs through the entire being and the entire sense of these lived-experiences, activities, manners of behavior, and so on. From these norms that are valid in the community and that the external observer can infer from the rules running through the lived-experiences (and so on) of the members of the community as such, as well as of the "employees" and "representatives" of the former, likewise from the consciousness of the members, and so on, from the morals, the laws, and so on, governing the community, furthermore especially from these deepest communal lived-experiences, in which a few or a majority or the totality of the members lives from out of the metaphysically-real essence of the community, or also from one's own metaphysically-real basic essence and its connectedness with the basic essence of the others in the communal basic essence—from all of this, the external observer may finally, in analogy to the inner constitution of the community (see above, 179/{153}), see the basic essence of the community here as well—but from the "outside"—intuitively, naked, so to speak.

Finally, the community constitutes itself also from the outside in consciousness (as also its reality in the ontological constitution), in the different objects (and so on), which point to the community and its members as its producers. Here, the work- and meaning-characteristics are layered upon the mere objects of nature, characteristics, which point back to the creative activity of individuals and of {158} the expression of the creative spirit of the individuals in their works. As we saw, all of this does not just refer back to the creative work of individuals as private persons (see above, 156 ff./{127 ff.}), but also to the community, in which—"from its spirit"—with which, and for which the work (say) came about. Likewise, the characteristics of meaning of some spiritual, material (and the like) creations point to the meaning and purpose for itself and others, whom the creator connected with this work, a meaning and purpose, which sometimes can also point back to communities, not just individuals. The community in a manifold interwovenness[11] of transparencies, thus, constitutes itself in this most complicated manner of givenness. Upon the object of nature lies the reference to its economic (money!), scientific (books!), artistic (monuments!), religious (churches!), legal (prison!), political (building of the *Reichstag!*), and so on, meaning and its respective functions. These in turn refer back to one or several conscious subjects, who gave these natural things these meanings and perhaps created and modified them in purposeful activity. These achievements, activities, manners of behavior, and so on, of individuals now in turn refer back to the communities, in whose

---

11 [*In-ein-ander.*]

"sense and name" the individuals acted thereby, and only now does the community come to appearance through all these layers in the constitutive structure of its givenness to consciousness.[12] This, of course, does not rule out that the intention and the cognitive gaze of the subject immediately breaks through all these layers in their complex layered structure and aims at the intended final object: the community, without running through consciously one by one or even paying attention to the other layers and their respective givennesses individually and separately as objects of special intentions. (In spite of the great complexity of these particular manners of constitution, this complexity is nonetheless unavoidable, especially where we are dealing with past developmental steps of a community or completely extinct communities. For the historians of all fields, this complexity is indispensable.)

---

12 Husserl 2002.

Curriculum Vitae

{159} I, Gerda Walther, was born on March 18, 1897, in the Nordrach Colony in the Baden region of the Black Forest. I am the daughter of the late owner and head physician of the lung clinic there, Dr. Otto Walther and his deceased wife Ragnhild Walther, née Bayer. I was raised without religion and am a citizen of Baden. I enjoyed private tutoring from 1904–1909, because my father deemed the Nordrach village school inadequate. From fall 1909 until summer 1911, I attended, as an internal student, the higher school for girls in Prinz-Ludwigshöhe (close to Munich) of Mrs. Dr. Himmer. From 1911 until 1912 I enjoyed, once again, private tutoring. From spring 1912 until spring 1913, I visited my grandparents in Copenhagen and attended there, besides private lessons, Wedel's private high school courses. From Fall 1913 until Easter 1914, I attended, in addition to private lessons as student of Sickenberger, "private high school courses for girls" in Munich and graduated from high school in July 1915 at the Royal Real-Gymnasium in Munich. From fall 1915 until summer 1917, I studied, at the University of Munich, theoretical and practical national economics, history of economy, civil law, philosophy and psychology. From summer 1917 until winter 1919, I studied philosophy, mathematics and civil law at the University of Freiburg i. Br.; from fall 1919 until winter 1920/21, while back in Munich, philosophy, sociology, economic history, and civil law.

References

Adler, Max. 1904. "Kausalität und Teleologie im Streite um die Wissenschaft" ["Causality and Teleology in the Dispute over Science"]. *Marx-Studien* 1: 195–433.

Adler, Max. 1913. *Marxistische Probleme. Beiträge zur Theorie der materialistischen Geschichtsauffassung und Dialektik* [*Marxist Problems: Contributions to the Theory of Materialistic Conceptions of History and Dialectics*]. Stuttgart: Dietz.

Adler, Max. 1914. "Der soziologische Sinn der Lehre von Karl Marx" ["The Sociological Meaning of Marx's Doctrine"]. Sonderabdruck aus dem *Archiv für die Geschichte des Sozialismus und der Arbeiterbewegung.* IV. Jahrgang, I. Heft. Leipzig: Hirschfeld.

Aristotle. 1984. *Metaphysics* [= *Metaphysics*]. In *The Complete Works of Aristotle, Volume Two: The Revised Oxford Translation.* Edited by Jonathan Barnes. Princeton: Princeton University Press, 1552–1728.

Aristotle. 1984. *Nicomachean Ethics* [= *NE*]. In *The Complete Works of Aristotle, Volume Two: The Revised Oxford Translation.* Edited by Jonathan Barnes. Princeton: Princeton University Press, 1729–1867.

Bergson, Henri. 1999. *An Introduction to Metaphysics.* Translated by Thomas Ernest Hulme. Indianapolis: Hackett.

Conrad-Martius, Hedwig. 1916. "Zur Ontologie und Erscheinungslehre der realen Außenwelt. Verbunden mit einer Kritik positivistischer Theorien" ["On the Ontology and Doctrine of Appearance of the Real External World"]. *Jahrbuch für Philosophie und phänomenologische Forschung* 3: 345–542.

Conrad-Martius, Hedwig. 1917. "Von der Seele. Die Unterredenden: Montanus und Psilander" ["On the Soul: The Conversants: Montanus and Psilander"]. *Summa* 1 (2): 106–136.

Conrad-Martius, Hedwig. 2024. *Metaphysical Conversations and Phenomenological Essays.* Translated by Christina M. Gschwandtner. Berlin: De Gruyter.

Fischer, Aloys. 1905. *Ueber symbolische Relationen* [*On Symbolic Relations*]. Munich: Kastner & Callwey.

Fischer, Aloys. 1914. "Ueber Nachahmung und Nachfolge. Ein Beitrag zur Phänomenologie und Psychologie des religiösen Erlebnisses" ["On Imitation and Emulation: A Contribution to the Phenomenology and Psychology of Religious Lived-Experience"]. *Archiv für Religionspsychologie* 1: 68–116.

France, Anatole. 1979. *The Gods Will Have Blood.* Translated by Frederick Davies. London: Penguin.

Geiger, Moritz. 1921. "Fragment über den Begriff des Unbewussten und die psychische Realität. Ein Beitrag zur Grundlegung des immanenten psychischen Realismus" ["A Fragment on the Concept of the Unconscious and Psychic Reality: A Contribution to the Foundation of Immanent Psychic Realism"]. *Jahrbuch für Philosophie und phänomenologische Forschung* 4: 1–137.

George, Stefan. 1974. *The Works of Stefan George.* Translated by Olga Marx and Ernst Morwitz. 2nd ed. Chapel Hill: University of North Carolina Press.

Giddings, Franklin Henry. 1896. *The Principles of Sociology. An Analysis of the Phenomena of Association and of Social Organization.* New York: MacMillan.

Goethe, Johann Wolfgang von. 2024. *Wilhelm Meister's Apprenticeship.* Edited and translated by Eric A. Blackall in cooperation with Victor Lange. Princeton: Princeton University Press.

Hegel, Georg Wilhelm Friedrich. 1975. *Lectures on the Philosophy of World History. Introduction: Reason in History.* Translated by Hugh Barr Nisbet. Cambridge: Cambridge University Press.

Hegel, Georg Wilhelm Friedrich. 1977. *Phenomenology of Spirit.* Translated by Arnold Miller. Oxford: Oxford University Press.

Hegel, Georg Wilhelm Friedrich. 1991. *Elements of the Philosophy of Right.* Translated by Hugh Barr Nisbet. Cambridge: Cambridge University Press.

Heiler, Josef. 1921. *Das Absolute. Methode und Versuch einer Sinnklärung des "transzendentalen Ideals"* [The Absolute: Methods and Attempt at a Clarification of the Meaning of the "Transcendental Ideal"]. Munich: Reinhardt.

Hering, Jean. 2021. "Remarks Concerning Essence, Ideal Quality, and Idea." Translated by Arthur Szylewicz. *Phenomenological Investigations* 1: 51–108.

Hildebrand, Dietrich von. 1922. "Sittlichkeit und ethische Werterkenntnis" ["Morality and the Knowledge of Ethical Values"]. *Jahrbuch für Philosophie und phänomenologische Forschung* 5: 462–602.

Hilferding, Rudolf. 1904. "Böhm-Bawerks Marx-Kritik" ["Böhm-Bawerk's Critique of Marx"]. *Marx-Studien* 1: 1–61.

Holzapfel, Rudolf. 1903. "Wesen und Methode der sozialen Psychologie" ["Essence and Method of Social Psychology"]. *Archiv für systematische Philosophie* IX (1): 1–57.

Husserl, Edmund. 1987. *Aufsätze und Vorträge (1911–1921).* Herausgegeben von Thomas Nenon und Hans Rainer Sepp. Vol. XXV von *Husserliana* [= *Hua* XXV]. Dordrecht: Springer.

Husserl, Edmund. 1989. *Ideas Pertaining to a Pure Phenomenology and to a Phenomenological Philosophy, Book II. Studies in the Phenomenology of Constitution.* Translated by Richard Rojcewicz and André Schuwer. Dordrecht: Kluwer.

Husserl, Edmund. 2001. *Logical Investigations.* 2 vols. Translated by Dermot Moran. New York: Routledge.

Husserl, Edmund. 2002. *Natur und Geist. Vorlesungen Sommersemester 1919* [*Nature and Spirit*]. Herausgegeben von Michael Weiler. Vol. IV von *Husserliana Materialien* [= *Hua Mat* IV]. Dordrecht: Springer.

Husserl, Edmund. 2014. *Ideas for a Pure Phenomenology and Phenomenological Philosophy, First Book. General Introduction to Pure Phenomenology.* Translated by Daniel Dahlstrom. Indianapolis: Hackett.

Ingarden, Roman. 1921. "Über die Gefahr einer Petitio principii in der Erkenntnistheorie" ["On the Danger of a Petitio Principii in Epistemology"]. In *Jahrbuch für Philosophie und phänomenologische Forschung* 4: 545–568.

Kant, Immanuel. 1998. *Critique of Pure Reason.* Translated by Paul Guyer and Allen Wood. New York: Cambridge University Press.

Karner, Josef. 1904. *Die soziale Funktion der Rechtsinstitute* [*The Social Function of Legal Institutes*]. *Marx-Studien* 1: 65–192.

Kautsky, Karl. 1916. *Ueberzeugung und Partei* [*Belief and Party*]. Leipzig: Leipziger Buchdruckerei.

Kerner, Justinus. 1845. *The Seeress of Prevorst.* Translated by Catherine Crowe. London: Moore.

Kierkegaard, Søren. 1987. "The Seducer's Diary." In *Either/Or, Part I.* Edited and translated by Howard V. Hong and Edna H. Hong. Princeton: Princeton University Press, 301–445.

Kjellén, Rudolf. 1916. *Staten som lifsform.* Stockholm: Geber.

Kjellén, Rudolf. 1917. *Der Staat als Lebensform* [*The State as a Living Organism*]. Übersetzt von Margarethe Langfeldt. Leipzig: Hirzel.

Le Bon, Gustave. 1910. *La Psychologie politique et la Défense sociale* [*Political Psychology and Social Defense*]. Paris: Flammarion.

Le Bon, Gustave. 2002. *The Crowd: A Study of the Popular Mind.* Translator unknown. New York: Dover.

Leyendecker, Herbert. 1913. *Zur Phänomenologie der Täuschungen* [*On the Phenomenology of Deceit*]. Halle: Buchhandlung des Waisenhauses.

Lipps, Theodor. 1907. "Die soziologische Grundfrage" ["The Basic Question of Sociology"]. *Archiv für Rassen- und Gesellschaftsbiologie* 4 (5): 652–674.

Mann, Thomas. 1993. *Buddenbrooks. The Decline of a Family*. Translated by John E. Woods. New York: Knopf.

Marx, Karl. 2024. *Capital. Critique of Political Economy, Volume 1*. Translated by Paul Reitter. Princeton: Princeton University Press.

Meister Eckhart. 1994. *Selected Writings*. Translated by Oliver Davies. London: Penguin.

Messer, August. 1918. *Die Philosophie der Gegenwart* [*Contemporary Philosophy*]. 2nd ed. Leipzig: Quelle & Meyer.

Meyer, Conrad Ferdinand. 1885. *Die Richterin* [*The Judge*]. Leipzig: Haeffel.

Natorp, Paul. 1912. *Allgemeine Psychologie nach kritischer Methode, Erstes Buch. Objekte und Methode der Psychologie* [*General Psychology I*]. Tübingen: Mohr (Siebeck).

Otto, Rudolf. 1924. *The Idea of the Holy*. Translated by John Harvey. London: Oxford University Press.

Pfänder, Alexander. n.d.-a. *Einführung in die Philosophie. Sachliche und historische Einleitung in die Philosophie. Vorlesungsmanuskript WS 1916/17* (126 bl.) [*Introduction to Philosophy: Substantial and Historical Introduction to Philosophy*]. Bayerische Staatsbibliothek, Pfänderiana A I 5.

Pfänder, Alexander. n.d.-b. *Grundzüge der Psychologie des Menschen. Vorlesungsmanuskript WS 1915/16* (345 bl.) [*Fundamentals of Human Psychology*]. Bayerische Staatsbibliothek, Pfänderiana C I 9.

Pfänder, Alexander. 1900. *Phänomenologie des Wollens* [*Phenomenology of Willing*]. Leipzig: Barth.

Pfänder, Alexander. 1913. "Zur Psychologie der Gesinnungen" ["On the Psychology of the Affects I"]. Sonderdruck aus *Jahrbuch für Philosophie und phänomenologische Forschung*, bd. 1. Halle: Niemeyer.

Pfänder, Alexander. 1916. "Zur Psychologie der Gesinnungen, Zweiter Artikel" ["On the Psychology of the Affects II"]. *Jahrbuch für Philosophie und phänomenologische Forschung* 3: 1–125.

Reinach, Adolf. 2012. *The Apriori Foundations of the Civil Law. Along with the Lecture "Concerning Phenomenology"*. Translated by John F. Crosby. Frankfurt: Ontos.

Rickert, Heinrich. 1913. *Vom System der Werte* [*On the System of Values*]. *Logos* 4 (3): 295–327.

Schapp, Wilhelm. 1910. *Beiträge zur Phänomenologie der Wahrnehmung* [*Contributions to the Phenomenology of Perception*]. Göttingen: Kaestner.

Scheler, Max. 1913. *Zur Phänomenologie und Theorie der Sympathiegefühle und von Liebe und Hass* [*Phenomenology and Theory of Feelings of Sympathy and of Love and Hate*]. Halle: Niemeyer.

Scheler, Max. 1917. "Vom Wesen der Philosophie" ["On the Essence of Philosophy"]. *Summa* 1 (2): 40–70.

Scheler, Max. 1973a. *Formalism in Ethics and Non-Formal Ethics of Values*. Translated by Manfred Frings and Roger Funk. Evanston: Northwestern University Press.

Scheler, Max. 1973b. "The Idols of Self-Knowledge." In *Selected Philosophical Essays*, edited by Max Scheler, translated, with an Introduction by David Lachterman. Evanston: Northwestern University Press.

Scheler, Max. 2008. *The Nature of Sympathy*. Translated by Peter Heath. New York: Routledge.

Scheler, Max. 2010. *On the Eternal in Man*. Translated by Bernard Noble. New York: Routledge.

Simmel, Georg. 1890. *Über sociale Differenzierung* [*On Social Differentiation*]. Leipzig: Duncker & Humblot.

Simmel, Georg. 2009. *Sociology. Inquiries into the Construction of Social Forms*. Translated and edited by Anthony Blasi, Anton Jacobs, and Mathew Kanjirathinkal. 2 vol. Leiden: Brill.

Simmel, Georg. 2010a. "Death and Immortality." In *The View of Life. Four Metaphysical Essays with Journal Aphorisms*, edited by Georg Simmel, translated by John Andrews and Donald Levine. Chicago: The University of Chicago Press.

Simmel, Georg. 2010b. "The Law of the Individual." In *The View of Life. Four Metaphysical Essays with Journal Aphorisms*, edited by Georg Simmel, translated by John Andrews and Donald Levine. Chicago: The University of Chicago Press.

Simmel, Georg. 2010c. "The Turn Toward Ideas." In *The View of Life. Four Metaphysical Essays with Journal Aphorisms*, edited by Georg Simmel, translated by John Andrews and Donald Levine. Chicago: The University of Chicago Press.

Smith, Adam. 1776. *An Inquiry into the Nature and Causes of the Wealth of Nations.* Vol. I. London: Strahan and Cadell.

Spengler, Oswald. 1926. *The Decline of the West. Volume One: Form and Actuality.* Translated by Charles Francis Atkinson. New York: Knopf.

Stein, Edith. 1989. *On the Problem of Empathy.* Translated by Waltraut Stein. Washington, D.C.: ICS Publications

Stein, Edith. 2000. *Philosophy of Psychology and the Humanities.* Translated by Mary Catharine Basehart and Marianne Sawicki. Washington, D.C.: ICS Publications.

Tönnies, Ferdinand. 2002. *Community and Society.* Translated by Charles Price Loomis. New York: Dover.

Walther, Gerda. n.d.-a. *Zur Problematik von Husserls reinem Ich* [On the Problematic of Husserl's Pure Ego]. Unpublished manuscript.

Walther, Gerda. n.d.-b. *Die innere Bewußtseinskonstitution des eigenen Grundwesens als Kern der Persönlichkeit* [*The Inner Constitution of Consciousness of One's Own Basic Essence as Center of Personhood*]. Bayerische Staatsbibliothek, Ana 317 A III 2.1.

Walther, Gerda. 1923. *Zur Phänomenologie der Mystik* [*Phenomenology of Mysticism*]. Halle: Niemeyer.

Weber, Max. 1913a. "Diskussionsbeiträg zu dem Vortrag von Ferdinand Schmid, Das Recht der Nationalitäten" ["Contribution to the Discussion of Ferdinand Schmid's Lecture, The Law of Nationalities"]. In *Verhandlungen des zweiten deutschen Soziologentages vom 20.–22. Oktober 1912 in Berlin* [*Proceedings of the Second Congress of German Sociologists*], edited by Alfred Weber, et. al. Tübingen: Mohr (Siebeck).

Weber, Max. 1913b. "Diskussionsbeiträg zu dem Vortrag von Paul Barth, Die Nationalität in ihrer soziologischen Bedeutung" ["Contribution to the Discussion of Paul Barth's Lecture, The Sociological Significance of Nationalities"]. In *Verhandlungen des zweiten deutschen Soziologentages vom 20.–22. Oktober 1912 in Berlin* [*Proceedings of the Second Congress of German Sociologists*], edited by Alfred Weber, et. al. Tübingen: Mohr (Siebeck).

Weber, Max. 1922. *Wirtschaft und Gesellschaft* [*Economy and Society*]. Tübingen: Mohr (Siebeck).

Weber, Max (ed.). 1946a. *Essays in Sociology.* Translated and edited by Hans Gerth and Charles Wright Mills. New York: Oxford University Press.

Weber, Max. 1946b. "The Social Psychology of the World Religions." In *Essays in Sociology*, edited by Max Weber, translated and edited by Hans Gerth and Charles Wright Mills. New York: Oxford University Press.

Weber, Max. 1981. "Some Categories of Interpretive Sociology." Translated by Edith Graber. *The Sociological Quarterly* 22 (2): 151–180.

Weber, Max. 1993. *The Sociology of Religion.* Translated by Ephriam Fischoff. Boston: Beacon Press.

Wundt, Wilhelm. 1900 – 1920. *Völkerpsychologie. Eine Untersuchung der Entwicklungsgesetze von Sprache, Mythus und Sitte* [*Social Psychology: An Investigation of the Developmental Laws of Language, Myth, and Morality*]. 10 vols. Leipzig: Engelmann.

Index of Persons

Index of Subjects

www.ingramcontent.com/pod-product-compliance
Lightning Source LLC
Jackson TN
JSHW060906100925
90677JS00015B/36